DON'T BELIEVE IT THEY'RE
OUT
TO
GET
YA!

FELLOW
DANKAHOLICS

1973

82 417

DATE DUE			
OC 4 '82	MR 11 '86	MR 11 '98	
MR 9 '83	MY 10 '8[ ]	JY 30 '98	
AP 4 '83	MY 25 '88	DE 1 '98	
JY 1 - '83	MY 25 '88		
JY 19 '83	MY 31 '88		
OC 7 '83	JE 12 '89		
MR 29 '84	DE 17 '93		
SE 27 '8[ ]	SE 12 '9[ ]		
AP 8 '8[ ]	OC 10 '9[ ]		
AP 8 '85	AP [ ]9 '9[ ]		
OC 8 '8[ ]	DE 10 '96		
AP 15 '86	FE 26 '98		

D1707178

MARIJUANA:
Your Legal Rights

MARIJUANA:
Your Legal Rights

Attorney Richard Jay Moller

Edited by Ralph Warner

A NOLO PRESS BOOK

ADDISON-WESLEY PUBLISHING COMPANY
READING, MASSACHUSETTS • MENLO PARK, CALIFORNIA
LONDON • AMSTERDAM • DON MILLS, ONTARIO • SYDNEY

Library of Congress Cataloging in Publication Data

Moller, Richard.
　　Marijuana: your legal rights.

　　Includes index.
　　1. Marijuana — Law and legislation — United States.
　　2. Criminal procedure — United States. I. Title.
　　KF3891.M2M64　　345.73′0277　　81–621
　　ISBN 0-201-04777-2　　AACR2

ISBN 0-201-04777-2 P

ABCDEFGHIJ-DO-8987654321

First printing, May 1981

With great love and respect I dedicate this book to Mom, Dad, Kathy, and Swami Muktananda for helping to make my modern American dream a nice one.

Acknowledgments

This book has greatly benefited from the help of many people. Professor Paul Hoeber taught me criminal procedure and read an early draft of the book; John Dwyer taught me to write more concisely by editing part of the first manuscript; and Kitty Jones typed the entire manuscript. I appreciate their help very much.

After Jake Warner of Nolo Press accepted the manuscript for publication, the book entered its second stage. The Nolo family suggested, among other things, that I add what are now Chapters 1, 2, and 13, as well as the Thumbnail Reviews and the Appendix. Katherine Galvin reviewed and edited the manuscript several times, Stephanie Harolde edited and typed several drafts of the book, and Linda Allison provided the wonderful art work. The Nolo family sure knows how to create books out of manuscripts.

At the final stage, Jennifer Hammett edited the book; and attorneys Steve Elias, Kenneth Jesmore, Joseph Matthews, James Mosher, and Mervin Shirin reviewed the manuscript. Many of their comments and suggestions for change and clarification were incorporated. Their generous assistance is much appreciated. I would also like to thank Brian Crockett of Addison-Wesley for all of his editorial assistance.

Most importantly, I'd like to gratefully acknowledge the major contribution of Jake Warner, whose thorough editing and felicitous phrases, sentences, and paragraphs added considerable humor, clarity, and focus to this book. If you find the book easy and enjoyable to read, Jake deserves a lot of the credit.

To Our Readers

The first thing we must do is state loud and clear that the use, possession, cultivation, and sale of marijuana is a crime. While we advocate the legalization of marijuana, we cannot and do not advocate its use. Just as one could go to jail for drinking a glass of beer in 1930, the risk of imprisonment—in a real cell behind real steel bars—for involvement with marijuana is still very real today.

Whether or not you use marijuana, we strongly believe that it is important that you understand the rules and procedures that govern enforcement of drug laws. For over and above the question of the legal status of marijuana, there is a larger issue involved in the State's efforts to stop you from smoking a joint—your constitutional right to privacy. Showing you how to assert this precious right is a prime concern of this book. Whether the issue is marijuana, laetrile, psilocybin, or even sexual activity forbidden by the "unnatural acts" statutes, we believe that the State should be required to adhere strictly to the Fourth and Fifth Amendments of the United States Constitution, which guarantee all Americans the right to be free from unreasonable government intrusions into their private lives.

By asserting and protecting your Fourth and Fifth Amendment rights, you can actually reduce your chances of arrest and conviction for drug and consensual sex "crimes." But, in order to protect your rights, it is essential that you first understand them. Giving you this understanding is where this book can be of great help to you. The advice it offers is as sound as we have been able to make it. But like well-meaning recommendations of all kinds, some of the advice we present here may not be helpful in a particular situation. So here are some qualifications. If you have access to a lawyer's advice and it is contrary to that given here, follow your lawyer's advice; the individual characteristics of your problem can be better considered by someone in possession of all the facts. Laws and procedures vary considerably from one state to the next; it's impossible to guarantee that every bit of information and advice contained here will be accurate. Please realize, too, that this book was printed in the spring of 1981. Legal rules and regulations change constantly, and you should check with a lawyer to make sure that information printed here is still current with respect to your individual situation. And finally, please pay attention to this general disclaimer: of necessity, neither the author nor the publisher of this book makes any guarantees regarding the result of any particular use to which this material may be put. Good luck!

Berkeley, California   R.J.M.
March, 1981

Contents

THE BILL OF RIGHTS

The first ten Amendments to the United States Constitution were ratified on December 15, 1791.

AMENDMENT I

Congress shall make no law respecting an establishment of religion, or prohibiting the free exercise thereof; or abridging the freedom of speech, or of the press; or the right of the people peaceably to assemble, and to petition the Government for a redress of grievances.

AMENDMENT II

A well regulated Militia, being necessary to the security of a free State, the right of the people to keep and bear Arms, shall not be infringed.

AMENDMENT III

No Soldier shall, in time of peace be quartered in any house, without the consent of the Owner, nor in time of war, but in a manner to be prescribed by law.

AMENDMENT IV

The right of the people to be secure in their persons, houses, papers, and effects, against unreasonable searches and seizures, shall not be violated, and no Warrants shall issue, but upon probable cause, supported by Oath or affirmation, and particularly describing the place to be searched, and the persons or things to be seized.

AMENDMENT V

No person shall be held to answer for a capital, or otherwise infamous crime, unless on a presentment or indictment of a Grand Jury, except in cases arising in the land or naval forces, or in the Militia, when in actual service in time of War or public danger; nor shall any person be subject for the same offence to be twice put in jeopardy of life or limb; nor shall be compelled in any criminal case to be a witness against himself, nor be deprived of life, liberty, or property, without due process of law; nor shall private property be taken for public use, without just compensation.

AMENDMENT VI

In all criminal prosecutions, the accused shall enjoy the right to a speedy and public trial, by an impartial jury of the State and district wherein the crime shall have been committed, which district shall have been previously ascertained by law, and to be informed of the nature and cause of the accusation; to be confronted with the Witnesses against him; to have compulsory process for obtaining witnesses in his favor, and to have the Assistance of Counsel for his defence.

AMENDMENT VII

In Suits at common law, where the value in controversy shall exceed twenty dollars, the right of trial by jury shall be preserved, and no fact tried by a jury, shall be otherwise re-examined in any Court of the United States, than according to the rules of the common law.

AMENDMENT VIII

Excessive bail shall not be required, nor excessive fines imposed, nor cruel and unusual punishments inflicted.

AMENDMENT IX

The enumeration in the Constitution, of certain rights, shall not be construed to deny or disparage others retained by the people.

AMENDMENT X

The powers not delegated to the United States by the Constitution, nor prohibited by it to the States, are reserved to the States respectively, or to the people.

Introduction

Are you drawn forth among a world of men
to slay the innocent? What is my offence?
Where is the evidence that doth accuse me?
What lawful quest have given their verdict up
Unto the frowning judge?

William Shakespeare
THE TRAGEDY OF RICHARD THE THIRD, Act I, Scene 4

This book simply and clearly sets forth the legal rules and regulations relating to growing, transporting, and using marijuana. It explains the laws and constitutional rights you need to know to avoid being arrested and convicted for using any substance that you enjoy and perhaps even find beneficial to your health, but which the State has decreed to be illegal. But this book does more than discuss marijuana laws—it also focuses on how you can protect and guarantee your constitutional rights to privacy in many other areas of your life. As part of this effort, it is necessary to teach you a little law. This we try to do with a minimum of legal lingo.

There is a great deal that people who know the law can do to protect their rights to privacy. For example, did you know:

- That marijuana carried in a locked suitcase in the trunk of a car is relatively safe from warrantless police searches, but that the same marijuana in a box on the back seat is not;
- That it is almost always unwise to consent to a police officer's polite or not so polite request to search;
- That fences and non-transparent greenhouses provide a landowner with considerable protection against the wandering legs and eyes of law enforcement officers;
- That in a friendly and seemingly innocent conversation with a police officer, you can compromise your constitutional rights?

1

Obviously, this sort of information is essential to you if you grow or smoke marijuana or use any other substance that a state or the federal government has declared to be illegal.

One of the principal concerns of what follows is to explain how the U.S. Supreme Court has interpreted the Fourth and Fifth Amendments of the United States Constitution. The Fourth Amendment sets forth our right to be free from unreasonable searches and seizures and the Fifth our right to remain silent when accused of a crime. We've put strong emphasis on federal constitutional law because it applies to all police officers, prosecutors, and judges throughout the country. Some states have taken positive action to guarantee you additional rights of privacy and protection from heavy-handed police practices and, when it is appropriate, we will discuss these more liberal approaches. Often, however, it will not be practical to try to explain the myriad minor differences among state laws and court rulings. Federal agencies, such as the FBI, the CIA, the DEA (Drug Enforcement Administration), and the IRS, are active in all the states and only required to follow federal constitutional law, not more liberal state laws. Therefore we prepare you to face the stricter federal rules.

Knowledge is power. By learning a little law, you can reduce your chances of being convicted for a drug crime. Your new knowledge will aid you in preventing the police from using various legal loopholes that allow them to slip around or through the requirements of the Fourth and Fifth Amendments. By understanding your legal rights, you will leave the police with no choice but to respect them, or at worst, to violate them in ways that will be so obvious that in a later court proceeding you can use the exclusionary rule to prevent the State from convicting you with the illegally seized evidence.

For example, the most important part of the Fourth Amendment is the requirement that the police obtain a specific search warrant based on "probable cause" before they can legally conduct a search. The theory behind this constitutional requirement is that the police should leave you alone unless they are reasonably certain that you possess criminal evidence, or in legal lingo, unless they have *probable cause* to search. Even though judges have too often altered the clear meaning of the Fourth Amendment by deciding that law enforcement officers do not need search warrants to conduct many types of searches, the law still requires the police to have warrants to search certain places. Knowledge of this fact is important to you because it means that by placing substances that you wish to keep private in a protected location, you force the police either to try to get a search warrant, which in many circumstances is impossible, or to violate the law. If the police do violate the Fourth Amendment by searching without a warrant or legal excuse, you can invoke the *exclusionary rule*, which requires that the judge exclude illegally seized evidence from your trial.

While the purpose of this book is to provide you with sound legal information, we do not wish to make you fearful or paranoid. It's sensible to assume that you will not be arrested and convicted for smoking a little marijuana, growing a few marijuana plants, or even using other illegal drugs, and you should continue to let your common sense guide you in these matters. Even though the police have arrested more than half a million Americans annually for the past few years for drug crimes, and marijuana was involved in 70 percent of the arrests, it is estimated that as many as forty million Americans use illegal drugs every year without being arrested.[1] Simple arithmetic shows that you have less than a 2 percent chance of being arrested if you use illegal drugs. And if you are a casual user of small quantities of marijuana, using a careful and common-sense approach to where and when you smoke, your chances of being arrested are probably considerably less than 1 percent. Still, just as it is sensible to assume that you probably will not be arrested, it is even more sensible to take practical steps to protect your privacy and constitutional rights as best you can.

Please understand that much of what follows, such as the many court-sanctioned justifications for outrageous and even brutal police invasions of your privacy, is based on the most unfair legal decisions. You will probably never be treated as badly as some of the people whose cases are discussed in this book, but unless you like to take chances, it is silly to trust that the police and judges you encounter will treat you more fairly. For every outrageous case in this book, there are hundreds of similar ones, but there are also instances where people have received better treatment. We don't focus on the more fair cases because we believe it is better to prepare for the worst and enjoy the sunshine and fresh air than it is to be overly optimistic and sing the jail house blues. We hope that some of what you read here will make you at least a little angry, because we believe that getting mad at outrageous legal rules and court decisions is healthy. We also believe in a little healthy paranoia—just enough to motivate you to learn the law and how to stay out of trouble.

While it makes great sense to do everything in your power to prevent the police from invading your privacy and seizing your marijuana, it is best to avoid viewing police officers, prosecutors, and judges as enemies. There has been a tendency among some marijuana users to think of all police officers as "pigs" and all judges as "fascists." This inclination is understandable if you reflect on the number of marijuana smokers who have suffered "cruel and unusual" punishment at the hands of the police and judges, but this sort of polarization is ultimately counterproductive, and can even result in otherwise decent people living up to your negative expectations. Treating every person who works in law enforcement as a pig is particularly silly when you stop to realize that many people who work for the police departments and courts feel as badly about these laws as you do and will often wink at minor violations.

Actually, it is our elected representatives, and not the police and most judges, who bear the major responsibility for the sorry state of American law. Why do we have absurd dietary laws (also known as *dangerous drug laws*) that prevent people from smoking a little marijuana in the first place? Why is it that although sixty million people have tried marijuana, it is still illegal? Why has our system of electing Congressional representatives and appointing judges resulted in such serious restrictions of our Fourth and Fifth Amendment rights? We can't answer all of these

questions in this short book, but we do believe that the continued existence of these laws has a lot to do with the attitude of the social class from which the majority of legislators and appellate court judges are drawn. Most of these powerful people are white, male, affluent, and middle-aged. Not surprisingly they tend to make decisions that reflect the views and attitudes of their clique. The reality, however, is that there are lots of folks in this country who are not part of this class and who have different attitudes. Perhaps it is too much to expect that our present elected representatives will change their attitudes. It would be wiser to think about changing the representatives.

We also regularly cast the U.S. Supreme Court as a villain. And it is true that all too often the Supreme Court seems intent upon making a mockery of our constitutional protections. Try to remember, however, that rules are made by a simple majority of the Court, and that some justices—unfortunately, except for the 1960s, they have usually been in the minority—have been both fair and farsighted. Also, the Supreme Court can, and does, change its collective mind as times change and as new judges are appointed. The state supreme courts, the federal and state courts of appeal, and the trial courts also have a great deal of discretion in deciding what is fair. The state supreme courts, for example, have the power to decide that their state constitutions provide more rights than does the U.S. Constitution.

Although we have tried our best to provide you with the best possible legal information, we cannot guarantee the accuracy of any specific legal rule or theory set out in this book. This disclaimer is necessary not only to protect us, but to remind you that legislators and judges can, and do, change the law overnight, and also because the very nature of our adversary system almost guarantees that honest men and women will disagree about the proper result when the law is applied to a particular situation. Although the information in the following pages will go a long way toward helping you protect your legal rights, you should check any particular points that are important to you before you rely on them.

If you are arrested and prosecuted, this book will be no substitute for a lawyer. We write primarily to help you protect your constitutional rights and stay out of trouble in the first place. We deal only in a very summary fashion with what happens if you are arrested. Indeed, our emphasis on federal constitutional rules may even prove confusing to a nonlawyer facing trial in a state court. For example, you will almost certainly need a competent lawyer to help you prove at a hearing to suppress evidence that the police violated one or more of your constitutional rights, and you will obviously need legal help if you face a jury trial. So, as soon as possible after an arrest, always seek professional assistance.

Because all of the legal cases discussed in this book are true, we have taken some pains to protect the privacy of the real people whose legal predicaments have turned out to be important in defining our law. Thus in the text we have changed all names to avoid potential embarrassment. The true case name, its legal citation, and the year of the decision can all be found in the notes. We provide you with this information to help you do your own legal research should you wish to go beyond what you find here. Law libraries are normally open to the public and librarians will usually help nonlawyers locate materials.

And finally, a brief word about gender and its relation to personal pronouns. Rather than say "he and she" and "his and her" every time both men and women could be involved in a given situation, we alternate in the use of the personal pronouns.

CHAPTER 1

A Short History of American Drug Laws: Morality or Mockery

DUKE: Laws for all faults,
But faults so countenanced, that the strong statutes
Stand like the forfeits in a barber's shop,
As much in mock as mark.
ESCALUS: Slander to the state! Away with him to prison!

William Shakespeare
MEASURE FOR MEASURE, Act V, Scene I

This book is about marijuana laws and how they affect you. But before discussing particular laws and how the judges have interpreted them to erode your constitutional right to privacy, let's take a moment for a quick review of the history of American drug laws. As you will see, public and governmental prejudices against drugs, and certain drug users, have resulted in some strange and often tortuous interpretations of the Fourth and Fifth Amendments.

In 1620, the Pilgrims landed at Plymouth Rock with thousands of gallons of beer and hard liquor to help fight the cold and the loneliness of a new land and to make friends with the Indians. Quickly, the Native Americans acquired a taste for alcohol, just as Europeans had become excitedly addicted in the previous century to the Indians' favorite intoxicant—tobacco. As always, however, the guardians of public morality were present, and as early as 1629, Massachusetts judges prohibited the sale of alcohol to the Native Americans to prevent "the excessive use or rather abuse of strong waters." At the same time, the European Americans drank to such excess in the new settlements in Virginia and Massachusetts that contemporary accounts report that "drunkeness" had become a serious and scandalous problem that wasted "precious time" and demanded an immediate solution. Nothing much was done—except to pass the laws directed at the Indians.[1]

In that same year, 1629, enterprising Europeans apparently introduced marijuana (hemp) into Massachusetts to be cultivated and used as a fiber for rope and other products. Hemp eventually became a major crop in America. In fact, in 1762, the state of Virginia began to impose penalties on those of its citizens who did not grow marijuana. George Washington, a resident of Virginia and a law-abiding citizen, proceeded to cultivate marijuana on his land.

It is perhaps surprising that there are no written reports of anyone smoking marijuana in America during this time. Spanish slave traders, however, had introduced marijuana into Brazil during the 1700s, where it was cultivated and smoked, particularly by blacks. Black American slaves may have smoked it, but they didn't keep diaries. One man who did keep a diary, however, made a most interesting notation in it. In August 1765, George Washington wrote that he "began to separate the Male from the Female hemp—rather too late."[2] This comment is probably an allusion to the fact that pollination had already occurred. Because pollination only reduces the potency of the marijuana but does nothing to affect the quality of the hemp, it is possible, though by no means certain, that our "Founding Father" was cultivating sinsemilla (seedless) marijuana to smoke it.

In 1789, the new American Congress tried to tax liquor, but gave up after Pennsylvania patriots rioted in the "Whiskey Rebellion." It was only a couple of decades before temperance reformers began to agitate for alcohol prohibition. After a couple of decades of unorganized efforts, the American Temperance Society was formed in 1827, perhaps because by then the average American drank nearly ten gallons of hard liquor each year, four times current consumption. The reformers preached that alcohol consumption not only decreased workers' efficiency and productiveness and increased the numbers of people in the poorhouses, jails, hospitals, and asylums, but that it was also a threat to the family structure. Not surprisingly, the temperance movement gained its greatest strength from evangelical Protestantism. In one bill introduced into the Tennessee legislature, the evangelists prophesied that alcohol threatened to "overwhelm and degrade society" as it was "seizing young men and dragging them away from parents, friends, and paths of virtue."[3] Some historians suggest that the temperance movement began to gain broadbased political support from moderate users of alcohol in response to the less refined drinking habits of the new immigrants, particularly the Irish and the Germans.

After several decades of fervent effort, the temperance forces persuaded the Maine legislature to outlaw alcohol in 1851. Upright Massachusetts followed

Maine's example in 1852, as did eleven other states in the same decade. The temperance movement victories were usually short-lived in the nineteenth century because most Americans believed that prohibition was "incompatible with the rights and privileges of freemen."[4] During the next decade, most states legalized alcohol again. Within thirty years, all of these thirteen states changed their minds and again legalized alcohol, although several states were persuaded to prohibit alcohol a second time.[5]

In San Francisco, the Irish were far too influential for the city officials to consider prohibiting alcohol, so prohibitory fervor was directed toward opium instead. Opium smoking was a favorite pastime of the Chinese, a powerless and not always popular minority. In 1875, the city of San Francisco outlawed opium—arresting, fining, and imprisoning many violators. During the next forty years, twenty-seven cities and states followed San Francisco's example. In 1887, the U.S. government went so far as to enact laws prohibiting the importation of opium by the Chinese—though not by Americans of European descent—and in 1890 prohibited non-American citizens from manufacturing opium. Hypocritically, while the Chinese were prohibited from importing and smoking opium, hundreds of opium-based products were being routinely sold in every drugstore, grocery store, and mail-order catalogue in the country.[6]

Although in the nineteenth century coffee was outlawed as an intoxicant in many Muslim countries, and American doctors such as Dr. T. D. Crothers warned that "often coffee drinkers, finding the drug to be unpleasant, turn to other narcotics, of which opium and alcohol are most common," the American people became quietly addicted to this diluted intoxicant without a legal murmur.[7] Coffee may be the only significant popular drug that did not give rise to restrictive drug laws. In 1980, Americans consumed more than 2.5 billion pounds of coffee.

Alcohol, opium, tobacco, and coffee had to make way for a new drug in the 1880s. It was in this decade that the western world discovered the "exhilaration and lasting euphoria"—to use Sigmund Freud's words—of cocaine. Wine, laced with cocaine, was sold with the blessings of Pope Leo XII, Thomas Edison (who believed that cigarettes were poisonous), the Czar of Russia, Jules Verne, Émile Zola, Henrik Ibsen, and the Prince of Wales. But after the initial excitement it did not take America long to enact prohibitions against the drug. Oregon outlawed the sale of cocaine in 1887, and by 1914 forty-six states had followed suit—though only six outlawed its possession.[8]

While many Americans were busy trying to outlaw the burgeoning opium and cocaine trade, their zeal carried over to America's popular homegrown drug—tobacco. From 1895 to 1909, cigarettes were banned in twelve states. Many reasons were advanced to justify the laws, some closer to the truth than others. In 1914, for example, Thomas Edison warned that cigarette smoke produced permanent "degeneration of the cells of the brain."[9] It is possible that *The New York Times* was influential in swaying public opinion. In 1884, that venerable newspaper warned:

The decadence of Spain began when the Spaniards adopted cigarettes and if this practice obtains among adult Americans, the ruin of the Republic is close at hand.[10]

The laws did little to stem the growing popularity of cigarettes, however. Cigarette sales increased from 14 million cigarettes in 1870 to 10 billion in 1911. Currently, Americans smoke 600 billion cigarettes per year, and though the "ruin of the Republic" may be close at hand, most—including, we think it's safe to say, *The New York Times*—no longer believe it is due to the consumption of tobacco.

In the western part of the United States, another drug—peyote—was more popular among the Native Americans than tobacco. And in 1899, encouraged by land speculators and Christian missionaries, Oklahoma passed the first law prohibiting peyote use—but repealed the law less than ten years later, due in part to the efforts of a Comanche Indian chief by the name of Quanah Parker. New Mexico prohibited peyote use in 1929, but did not enforce the law, and subsequently Congress rejected proposed laws which would have banned the Native American religious sacrament.[11]

The year 1914 marked the beginning of two wars in America—World War I and the U.S. government's war against narcotics. In that year, Congress passed the Harrison Narcotics Act, which severely restricted the sale of all so-called opiates—heroin, opium, and cocaine—and in the early 1920s judges decided that this law also prohibited the sale of all narcotics to addicts, even by doctor's prescription.[12]

In the early 1900s, America's intense concern about the use of drugs was at least more logically consistent than its present arbitrary prohibitions. At that time Americans recognized that alcohol was potentially as dangerous a drug as the others and also legislated against its use. Indeed, from 1907 to 1919, twenty-nine states enacted alcohol prohibition. Finally, in 1919, thirty-six American states enacted the Eighteenth Amendment, and thus made prohibition a constitutional requirement; America's first "bad trip" or drug-related nightmare began. Overnight, twenty-two million people—about 20 percent of the American population—became constitutional criminals as they consumed billions of gallons of illegal alcohol. And, in a development that was to give organized crime—and the FBI—its start, a million people became bootleggers, with as many as 500,000 setting up speakeasies.[13] As an interesting sidelight, during the 1920s New York City also had as many as 500 marijuana "tea pads" which competed with an estimated 32,000 alcohol speakeasies. A marijuana high commonly cost 25¢.[14]

Under these circumstances, effective enforcement of the Eighteenth Amendment was impossible. Still, the law was on the books and antialcohol groups, such as the Woman's Christian Temperance Union, demanded arrests and convictions. The result was increasing pressure on legislatures and, particularly, courts to ignore the Fourth Amendment protections against illegal searches and seizures. In 1921, the United States and England agreed, by treaty, to allow the routine, warrantless search of all boats within twelve miles of their coasts, and the U.S. Supreme Court began their well-established practice of riddling the Fourth Amendment with loopholes to justify warrantless searches—all in the name of "practical law enforcement." During the Roaring Twenties, the U.S. government spent $215 million to arrest more than 550,000 alcohol users, to convict more than 343,000 of them, to imprison 130,000 of them, and to collect $56 million in fines.[15] Four men and a mother of ten children were sentenced to life imprisonment for violating the Eighteenth Amendment to the Constitution too many times.[16] Those who have lived through the 1960s and 1970s will see the obvious parallels.

A nation willing to outlaw alcohol was a nation anxious to outlaw all intoxicants. Even before many of its citizens had even thought of using marijuana, between 1911 and 1915 the states of Louisiana, Maine, Massachusetts, and Vermont regulated its use. The U.S. Treasury Department prohibited the importation of marijuana for nonmedical purposes in 1915, but did not enforce its law. That same year, California and Utah passed laws prohibiting the use of marijuana, and before alcohol was again legalized in 1933, thirty-two additional states followed suit. Two important establishment fears apparently led to the marijuana legislation. The first was a racially motivated hostility toward the 500,000 Mexicans who immigrated to America between 1915 and 1930, many of whom smoked marijuana. And the second seems to be a fear that the underworld—prostitutes, pimps, and gamblers—who were "notorious" drug users—would entice good citizens, particularly young children, to become "dope fiends."[17] Stories that cocaine emboldened blacks to rape white women and to commit theft and murder helped to incite thirty-one states to outlaw possession of the nefarious substance between 1914 and 1931.[18] Other "dope fiend" stories encouraged twenty-nine states to outlaw possession of opium and heroin during these years. Congress outlawed cocaine in 1922 and the importation of heroin and opium in 1924.

The federal government's serious efforts to wipe out marijuana began about the same time that it gave up trying to prohibit alcohol—in the early 1930s. Indeed, there have been those who have suggested that much of the antimarijuana hysteria stemmed from the fear of alcohol enforcement officers that if they couldn't think up another bogeyman, they would be out of work. In 1930, Congress passed legislation which authorized the U.S. Treasury Department to establish a division capable of enforcing the nation's narcotics laws. The Federal Narcotics Bureau, led by Harry J. Anslinger, crusaded against marijuana for the next several decades. In 1932, the Bureau recommended to all states the Uniform Narcotic Drug Act for their adoption. Under this law, marijuana was classified as an optional drug that could be—albeit incorrectly—added to the list of "narcotic drugs" by any state that so desired. Many did just that, and by 1937, forty-six of the forty-eight states, plus the District of Columbia, had laws prohibiting marijuana. In that year, Congress decided to impose a $100 tax on the transfer of each ounce of marijuana to an unregistered person so that the federal police would have a lawful excuse to hunt for marijuana criminals.[19]

When these laws apparently did not sufficiently discourage the use of marijuana, Congress strengthened the penalties in 1951 and again in 1956. Two years in prison was the mandatory minimum federal sentence for possession of marijuana on a first offense, but a federal judge could give a sentence up to ten years. For a second offense, a marijuana criminal was imprisoned at least five years with a possible term of as long as twenty years.

The states followed Congress's lead. As of 1970, some state penalties were even more severe. In Missouri and Louisiana it was possible to receive a death sentence for selling marijuana to a minor on a first offense, and in Georgia for selling it to a minor on a second offense. Life imprisonment was the mandatory penalty for selling marijuana in Illinois on a second offense, and a possible penalty, depending upon the judge, for selling marijuana in Illinois, Missouri, and Utah on a first offense. One could also get a life sentence for possessing marijuana on a first offense in Texas, or on a second offense in Missouri. Alabama was more lenient, limiting the penalty for a second offense of marijuana possession to forty years in prison. For possession of a single joint in Alabama, on a first offense, the mandatory sentence was five years in prison.[20] (See the Appendix for the current marijuana penalties for all fifty states and the federal government.)

Barbiturates, amphetamines, and psychedelics have had similar histories. Once the government became aware of these drugs, controls were enacted. In the case of barbiturates and amphetamines, nonprescription use was declared illegal. This law meant that mainstream Americans could continue to legally consume sleeping pills and tranquilizers—and in fact, statistics show that the addictive drugs Valium and Librium are the favored drugs of twenty million Americans—while those Americans who prefer illegal mood-altering drugs or are unable to afford a private doctor are forced to obtain their drugs from the flourishing illegal underground. Psychedelic drugs were totally outlawed—the only exceptions being the states where court decisions have permitted Native Americans the use of their religious sacrament, peyote, and some states that have recently passed laws allowing doctors to prescribe marijuana in the treatment of certain diseases.

To summarize, it appears that many American drug laws have been directed against the minority groups who used a particular drug, rather than against the drug itself. American Indians, Irish, German, Chinese, blacks, Mexicans, and hippies have all been despised and discriminated against at one time or another by "right-thinking" Americans. Along with their "poverty," "dirtiness," and "criminal tendencies," their peculiar drug preferences have almost always come under fire. This prejudice has oftentimes led to the outlawing of the unpopular minority group's favorite drug, which transformed these particular drug users into the criminals that assimilated Americans believed they were from the beginning.

Recent Developments

Now that you understand a little of the history of drug laws in the United States, let's take a look at some of the attempts to reform them. Many persons have tried to persuade our legislators to decriminalize drug use, but they have met with little success. Some of the arguments that our legislators have rejected include the following:

- The authoritarian legislation of morality infringes on our rights to self-expression and self-determination that are guaranteed under the First Amendment of our Constitution.
- It only breeds disrespect for the law for the State to misuse it by trying to suppress the irrepressible desire of some people at certain times of their lives to use drugs.
- The investigation of victimless crime requires the police to invade our constitutional right to privacy to catch the immoral culprits.
- The State actually fosters more serious crime by outlawing vices. The syndicate bosses of organized crime gain much of their wealth and power through their violent control of the illegal market in drugs.
- Legalizing drugs would actually reduce the societal costs associated with drug abuse. Because the legal price of cocaine, marijuana, and opium would approximate tobacco, scotch whiskey, and Valium, there would be no need for drug abusers to steal to pay for overpriced illegal drugs, and there would be less reason for drug dealers to use violence to control the lucrative market in artificially expensive drugs. (The number of Americans addicted to Valium, tobacco, and alcohol, however, perhaps explains why the State does not trust its citizens to abstain freely and voluntarily from cocaine, marijuana, and heroin, or to use them in moderation.)

The State and its sometimes corrupt politicians spend time, energy, and money prosecuting cases of consensual sex and drug crime that could be spent on the more serious problems that afflict America. And society can afford to expend only a certain amount of resources on crime prevention. Therefore it can be argued that corporate and organized criminals steal their $50 to $200 billion[21] more easily because the State budgets some of its limited police funds for vice squads, rather than for additional investigation of white-collar and organized crime. Similarly, the crimes of tax evasion, hazardous working conditions, and environmental pollution too often go undetected, even though these crimes of theft, aggravated assault, and possibly manslaughter would destroy our society long before illicit drug use could.

Nevertheless, determined individuals and groups have made some progress towards the legalization of marijuana and the reform of drug laws for at least the past decade. The National Organization for the Reform of Marijuana Laws (NORML) has been a leader. Indeed, NORML has played a key role in reforming the law in all eleven states that have decriminalized the possession of a small amount of marijuana.

In addition, NORML has helped to bring important law suits challenging the constitutionality of drug laws themselves as well as the fairness and constitutionality of certain convictions and sentences. For example, NORML participated in a Virginia case before the United States Court of Appeals in which the Court, in 1979, overturned the sentencing of a black activist to forty years in prison for the sale of less than nine ounces of marijuana. The federal court ruled that a sentence of that length for that crime constituted "cruel and unusual punishment."[22] And in the same sort of case, NORML helped a twenty-year-old Missouri college student win parole after a Missouri court gave him a twelve-year prison term, later reduced to seven years, for selling $5 worth of marijuana (eleven grams) to an undercover agent.[23] The young man had already spent 16 months in prison.

NORML has also sued the government to stop the paraquat poisoning of Mexican marijuana, arguing that punishing Americans for smoking marijuana by poisoning them is unlawful and that the government should consider the environmental impact of selling this poison to Mexico. A United States Court of Appeals did direct the government to stop spraying until the environmental damage could be assessed, but then permitted the continued sale of this herbicide to Mexico.[24]

NORML has also worked to pass laws allowing doctors to prescribe marijuana for medical purposes. About half of the states now allow physicians to give government-grown marijuana to their patients who are suffering with glaucoma, cancer, or multiple sclerosis. NORML has had less success trying to stop government para-military type operations such as Operation Sinsemilla. These missions involve "strike forces" which try to wipe out the marijuana crop in areas such as northern California, Hawaii, and other areas where marijuana has become a leading cash crop.

NORML and other promarijuana advocates have also failed to convince most judges, including those in Washington, Delaware, Hawaii, Connecticut, Massachusetts, and in federal courts, of the wisdom of their main legal arguments. These include the following:

· It is cruel and unusual punishment to imprison a human being for years for possessing or selling some marijuana;[25]
· It is irrational to classify the nonaddicting drug marijuana with the more dangerous drugs such as heroin and PCP;
· It is as much an infringement on our right to privacy for the police to search citizens' bedrooms looking for evidence of marijuana as it is for them to look for evidence of birth control or obscene materials (which the U.S. Supreme Court has decided is unconstitutional for the police to do).[26]

For the latest information on the decriminalization effort, or to give your support, write to NORML, 2317 M. Street, N.W., Washington, D.C. 20037.

Although chances for judicial or legislative reform of our marijuana laws remain remote, a few judges have recognized the absurdity or the unconstitutionality of drug laws, at least in certain circumstances. Thus the California Supreme Court decided in 1964 that Native Americans could legally use peyote in their ancient religious practices:

The right to free religious expression embodies a precious heritage of our history. In a mass society, which presses at every point toward conformity, the protection of a self-expression, however unique, of the individual and the group becomes ever more important. The varying currents of the subcultures that flow into the mainstream of our national life give it depth and beauty. We preserve a greater value than an ancient tradition when we protect the rights of the Indians who honestly practiced an old religion in using peyote one night at a meeting in a desert hogan near Needles, California.[27]

Nearly all state courts that have faced the same issue have agreed with the reasoning of the California Supreme Court and allow Native Americans to use their sacrament, peyote.

Recently, the Florida Supreme Court decided that the State could forbid the members of the Ethiopian Zion Coptic Church from using marijuana in their religious ceremonies. This case drew considerable public interest after the church was "exposed" on the TV show "Sixty Minutes." But despite all of the publicity, the U.S. Supreme Court declined to review the case, so this Florida decision only controls Florida law and will probably have little effect on the law in other states. The Florida court reached its conclusion partly because the church violated local zoning laws and partly because the members smoked marijuana all day and gave it freely to children—rather than limiting its use to "adults only" religious ceremonies.[28] In other states, however, the adult members of the Ethiopian Zion Coptic Church may fare better, at least in regards to their struggle to smoke marijuana legally during daily church services. It is possible that a court in another state will approve ceremonial use of marijuana, just as some courts have respected the Native American's peyote ritual.

In the most important legal decision concerning marijuana reform to date, the Alaska Supreme Court has ruled that what Alaskans eat or smoke in the privacy of their own homes is their own business.[29] Or, to say the same thing in legal language, the Alaska Supreme Court unanimously agreed that the State did not have a compelling reason to make illegal the use of marijuana ingested in the privacy of an Alaska citizen's home.

The judges relied on the Alaska Constitution which, unlike the U.S. Constitution, has an explicit provision guaranteeing the right to privacy: "The right of the people to privacy is recognized and shall not be infringed." Chief Justice Jay Rabinowitz pointed out that marijuana is "far more innocuous in terms of physiological and social damage than alcohol or tobacco."[30]

Other judges have made intelligent observations concerning marijuana. Justice Bernard Levinson of the Hawaii Supreme Court said that "the State has failed to demonstrate sufficient justification for its intrusion into the privacy of the individual with respect to the personal use of marijuana." But he was in the minority.[31]

In Michigan, Justice Thomas G. Kavanagh stated that the marijuana law is "an impermissible intrusion on the fundamental rights to liberty and the pursuit of happiness, and is an unwarranted interference with the right to possess and use private property . . . 'Big Brother' cannot, in the name of *Public* health, dictate to anyone what he can eat or drink or smoke in the *privacy* of his own home."[32] Justice John Swainson in that same case made this comment: "Comparison of the effects of marijuana use on both the individual and society with the effects of other drug use demonstrates not only that there is no rational basis for classifying marijuana with the 'hard narcotics,' but, also, that there is not even a rational basis for treating marijuana as a more dangerous drug than alcohol."[33]

In the state of Washington, four of nine Supreme Court justices wrote in a dissenting opinion that it is cruel and unusual punishment to sentence a person to five years in prison and fine him $10,000 for possession of more than forty grams of marijuana. Unfortunately, the other five thought that the marijuana penalty was just fine—neither cruel nor unusual.[34]

The fight continues. Despite a few small victories, marijuana use and cultivation is still illegal in nearly all of the country, and there is fervent opposition from conservative religious groups to drug law reform. Of course, the best way to get America to adopt a rational drug policy is to elect state legislators and representatives to Congress who are intelligent and courageous enough to say that enough is enough, and that the American people are free citizens, fully capable of making their own informed choices as to what to eat, smoke, and drink.

CHAPTER **2**

The Birth
(and Death?)
of the Fourth and
Fifth Amendments

And yet, to say the truth,
I had as lief have the foppery of freedom
as the morality of imprisonment.

William Shakespeare
MEASURE FOR MEASURE, Act I, Scene 2

THE FOURTH AMENDMENT

The right of the people to be secure in their persons, houses, papers, and
effects, against unreasonable searches and seizures, shall not be violated,
and no Warrants shall issue, but upon probable cause, supported by Oath
or affirmation, and particularly describing the place to be searched, and
the persons or things to be seized.

Much of this book is about the Fourth Amendment—fifty-four words that
many twentieth century Americans do not recognize, but words which, in part, in-
spired the drawing of swords and the firing of muskets in the bloody struggle we
know as the American Revolution. The Fourth Amendment is still so important
today because it is the primary constitutional provision on which we must rely to
guard our privacy. When we say that the police can't enter our home or search our

land without a warrant or demand that we open the trunk of our car, what we are really saying is that to do so without our consent is a violation of the Fourth Amendment. Therefore, before we start dealing with the specifics of when and where and how the police can legally invade our privacy and the steps we can take to protect our right to be left alone, it makes sense to learn a little history. Not surprisingly, people's concern to be free from unreasonable searches and seizures goes back a long way before the first highway patrol officer demanded the right to search the first rainbow-hued old bus.

To understand why our ancestors thought that "the right of the people to be secure in their persons, houses . . ." was so important, it's necessary to look back at least to the fifteenth century. While the birth of any idea is impossible to trace, there are several events that historians agree were particularly nourishing to the ideas encompassed by the Fourth Amendment. Perhaps one of the most important of these involved the circumstances surrounding the first printed book produced by the first English printing press. The year was 1476, or exactly 300 years before the American revolutionaries began their fight against mad King George and English tyranny.

Not long after the ink dried on the first printed page, the first "offensive" book appeared. The English Royalty responded to the publication of words that they didn't like just as governments have responded to "seditious" literature since the dawn of time—with censorship. But how were the offending manuscripts to be found and suppressed? You guessed it—by the Crown exercising an unrestricted power to search, seize, and destroy. Wasn't this reaction a little extreme? Certainly the printers and authors of the day thought so, but they had no legal way to protect themselves, and thus had to rely on their own stealth. As royal officers ransacked their shops, some early printers doubtlessly began to dream about a government whose power to arbitrarily search and seize property was restricted, but in the fifteenth century this sort of dream was still a long way from realization.

By 1557, the English Crown had given the Stationer's Company the exclusive right to publish books and the power to

> search wherever it shall please them in any place . . . within our kingdom of England . . . and to seize, take, hold, burn . . . those books and things which are or shall be printed contrary to the form of any statute, act or proclamation . . .[1]

But apparently this royal writ was no more effective in suppressing dissent than government censorship is today, because we know that by 1576, the Company could enforce its monopoly only by searching every London publishing house every week. During these years, the justly infamous Court of the Star Chamber reinforced the Company's monopoly powers and increased the penalties for the crime of publishing unauthorized books. The searches and seizures continued into the next century, their use spreading into areas beyond the printed word. Smuggling had become troublesome to the Crown and, in the difficult years before King Charles lost his crown to Oliver Cromwell, the tottering monarch gave his troops the power to "enter into any vessel, house, warehouse or cellar, search in any trunk or chest and breach any bulk whatsoever . . ."[2]

Finally, in 1694, six years after the Catholic King James II was denied the throne, the English government of William and Mary took a small step forward and stopped censoring papers prior to publication. Since the Crown still encouraged the use of general (nonspecific) warrants to uncover books critical of the government after their publication, however, this step was no giant leap toward a freer society. Indeed, as late as 1762, State agents acting under the authority of a general warrant arrested forty-nine persons while looking for the author of a pamphlet critical of the government. After they finally found the author, who was a member of Parliament, they arrested him and seized his private papers. The next year he was convicted for seditious libel and expelled from Parliament. But John Wilkes fought back, along with several other printers, and won a series of court battles against the officials who arrested them. Chief Justice Pratt told the jury in one historic case that "to enter a man's house by virtue of a nameless warrant, in order to procure evidence, is worse than the Spanish Inquisition [when the Church tortured and burned so-called heretics after nominal trials] ; a law under which no Englishman would wish to live an hour" and other judges declared that these general warrants were "illegal and void."[3]

In 1766, the English Parliament also condemned the use of general search warrants, stirred in part perhaps by William Pitt's words, which although historically false, have the ring of larger truth:

The poorest man may in his cottage bid defiance to all force of the Crown.
It may be frail—its roof may shake—the wind may blow through it—the
storm may enter—the rain may enter—but the King of England can not
enter; all his force dares not cross the threshold of the ruined tenement![4]

It almost seems as if the English monarchy, frustrated by the new rules limiting their arbitrary power at home, exported the practice of indiscriminate search and seizure to the colonies. Certainly, it can be said that England never respected the privacy of its American colonists any more than it had historically respected the liberty of its own citizens. Indeed, much of the tension that led to the American Revolution arose when England began to tax foreign imports in order to prevent the colonists from trading with other countries. These taxes were so high that Americans were left with the choice of either not importing foreign goods or smuggling. For many, including the famous revolutionary, John Hancock, the choice was easy—they smuggled. The English rulers were outraged by these illegal acts and in retaliation they authorized customs officials to search the homes and warehouses of suspected smugglers on the basis of a general (nonspecific) search warrant, called a writ of assistance. Chief Justice Hutchinson of Massachusetts issued many of these warrants, which contained no information as to what was being searched for, until Bostonians expressed their displeasure by burning his home during the Stamp Act Rebellion in 1765.[5] After this act of defiance, the people of Boston continued to prevent searches by joining together in front of a targeted home or warehouse to physically resist the customs officials. Eventually, even some of King George's American judges defied their master and refused to issue the writs of assistance to the British customs officials.

By 1776, when the American revolutionaries declared their independence, the right to be free of unreasonable searches and seizures had become one of the prime issues fueling the rebellion. And when the colonists finally accepted Lord Cornwallis's surrender at Yorktown, it was generally accepted that Americans would insist on strong protections from the arbitrariness of government, even their own. Thus, in 1780, Massachusetts enacted a strong law regulating search and seizure for their new state constitution:

> Every subject has a right to be secure from all unreasonable searches and seizures of his person, his house, his papers and all his possessions. All warrants, therefore, are contrary to this right, if the cause or foundation of them be not previously supported by oath or affirmation, and if the warrant to a civil officer, to make search in suspected places, or to arrest one or more suspected persons, or to seize their property, be not accompanied with a special designation of the person or objects of search, arrest, or seizure; and no warrant ought to be issued, but in cases, and with the formalities prescribed by the laws.[6]

The same concerns that motivated Massachusetts and other states to include tough protections for individual liberties in their state constitutions were heard in Philadelphia when leaders of the former colonies met to draft the Constitution. Indeed, just two months after the Constitution was adopted in 1789, the new Congress adopted the first ten amendments which became known as the Bill of Rights. Two years later, after the ninth state had ratified this list of individual liberties, the Fourth Amendment became one of the constitutional rights of all Americans. Thus finally, in a single elegant sentence, every American was guaranteed protection from unreasonable searches and seizures. But as important as these few words have become, it would be naive to think of them as a complete shield against government tyranny. For example, the simple proclamation did not, and perhaps could not, specifically define an "unreasonable search," or make it clear exactly how and under what circumstances warrants were to be issued. And, understandably, the Amendment said nothing specifically about searches involving motor vehicles, binoculars, telephones, airplanes, or laser snoopers.

So much for the eighteenth century. How has the Fourth Amendment been interpreted and what does it mean today? The United States Supreme Court has the responsibility of interpreting the meaning of our entire Constitution, including the Fourth Amendment. In effect, this power means that every Supreme Court Justice is free to decide for himself the proper way to apply the words of the Fourth Amendment. In the almost two centuries since the Bill of Rights was adopted,

some Justices have believed that provisions against unreasonable searches and seizures should be strictly enforced. One of the most famous of these judges was Justice Oliver Wendell Holmes. In a unanimous opinion for the Supreme Court, in 1924, in a case about forced disclosure of business records, he wrote these words:

Anyone who respects the spirit as well as the letter of the Fourth Amendment would be loath to believe that Congress intended to authorize [the Federal Trade Commission] to sweep all our traditions into the fire, and to direct fishing expeditions into private papers on the possibility that they may disclose evidence of crime.[7]

In 1928, Justice Louis Brandeis explained the spirit of the Fourth Amendment in these memorable words:

The makers of our Constitution undertook to secure conditions favorable to the pursuit of happiness. They recognized the significance of man's spiritual nature, of his feelings and of his intellect. They knew that only a part of the pain, pleasure and satisfactions of life are to be found in material things. They sought to protect Americans in their beliefs, their thoughts, their emotions and their sensations. They conferred, as against the government, the right to be let alone—the most comprehensive of rights and the right most valued by civilized men.[8]

Similarly, Justice Felix Frankfurter, writing in 1950 and 1947, explained in two Fourth Amendment cases what he believed to be the proper way to interpret the Fourth Amendment:

It makes all the difference in the world whether [a judge] recognizes the central fact about the Fourth Amendment, namely, that it was a safeguard against recurrence of abuses so deeply felt by the Colonies as to be one of the potent causes of the Revolution, or [a judge] thinks of it as merely a requirement for a piece of paper.[9]

A decision may turn on whether [a judge] gives that Amendment a place second to none in the Bill of Rights, or considers it on the whole a kind of nuisance, a serious impediment in the war against crime.[10]

Unfortunately, however, many other decisions of the Supreme Court have been less farsighted. Indeed, many commentators who have examined the way the High Court has limited and restricted the Fourth Amendment have stated that it has been so systematically gutted as to be close to meaningless. But how and why has this happened? How could the Supreme Court interpret the fifty-four plain words guaranteeing that Americans shall be secure against unreasonable searches and seizures to allow police searches without a warrant?

First the why. In the 1920s, faced with the impossible task of enforcing prohibition, the U.S. government began using tricks not too different from those pioneered by the old kings of England. When the gin mill operators and rum smugglers began trooping before the Supreme Court, their lawyers claiming that the government had engaged in illegal searches and seizures, the U.S. Supreme Court simply found that the plain meaning of the Fourth Amendment was too radical. (What can you expect from the grandchildren of revolutionaries?) And from the days of Calvin Coolidge to those of Ronald Reagan, with the exception of the

1960's, most of the Supreme Court Justices have consistently interpreted the Fourth Amendment as if they considered it to be the quaint rhetoric of eighteenth-century idealists, and not to be taken seriously by people facing the practical realities of law enforcement in the twentieth century. Oh, yes, the Warren Supreme Court in the 1960s began to give meaning to the Fourth Amendment and there have been many ringing dissents by a minority of justices who have insisted that when our Constitution says that we should be secure against unreasonable and warrantless searches and seizures, it means it. Nevertheless, the sacrifice of the Fourth Amendment on the altar of practical law enforcement has been done.

But how have judges restricted the plain meaning of those fifty-four words? By legal interpretation, of course. (After all, who is better trained than lawyers to turn plain meanings into meaningless gibberish?) The Supreme Court declared that the second clause of the Amendment, which clearly specifies the requirements for a warrant, actually has nothing to do with the first part of the sentence that forbids unreasonable searches and seizures. By this convenient linguistic sleight of hand, the judges gave themselves the power to decide whether or not a particular search and seizure was reasonable solely on the basis of their own prejudices and without regard to the constitutional warrant requirements. In practice this interpretation has meant that only if judges have first decided that a particular search is unreasonable do they apply the second half of the Fourth Amendment which specifies the requirements for a warrant. And once armed with this magic rule, the judges began to decide that many types of governmental searches and seizures were so inherently reasonable that the police did not have to bother with the Fourth Amendment requirement for a search warrant. Thus, car searches, searches made at the time of an arrest, "emergency" searches, and most investigatory spying have all been held to be "reasonable searches" for which no warrant is required.

Despite a series of discouraging rulings that have allowed the police to undertake many types of "reasonable" searches without a warrant, the picture is not completely bleak and there have also been some important judicial steps in the direction of guaranteeing us more freedom. Thus after 160 years of court decisions saying that the Fourth Amendment only applied to the federal government and was not applicable to the states (read local and state police departments), the Supreme Court finally reversed itself, and, in 1961, ruled that if state or local authorities seize evidence as part of an illegal search, the State cannot use it in a criminal prosecution.[11]

What took the Supreme Court so long to give you Fourth Amendment protection against the local police? One could speculate that the judges simply preferred law and order to the civil liberties promised by the Fourth Amendment, but it's not that simple. In 1833, the U.S. Supreme Court concluded that states' rights took precedence over individual liberties and declared that all of the Bill of Rights applied only to the federal government.[12] This interpretation meant that the individual states could ignore all our constitutional protections guaranteed in the Bill of Rights. The authoritarian tendencies of all governments being what they are, many states began adopting policies as bad, or worse, than those followed in England prior to the American Revolution. It wasn't until 1927 that the U.S. Supreme Court finally began to awake to the realization that the First Amendment rights of freedom of speech, the press, and religion meant little if the states were free to pass laws abridging these fundamental human rights.[13] And, as mentioned above, it took the Supreme Court Justices another thirty years to come to the realization that the Fourth Amendment also was a dead letter unless the states as well as the federal government were forced to abide by it.

Probably the greatest controversy surrounding the guarantee of the Fourth Amendment rights has concerned what to do if an illegal search or seizure occurs. Fortunately, the U.S. Supreme Court recognized as early as 1886 that the people's right to be "secure in their persons, houses, papers, and effects" would be meaningless unless the federal government was prohibited from benefiting from the violation of this right.[14] Therefore, the High Court decided that any evidence of illegal activity seized in violation of a person's Fourth Amendment rights must be excluded from his trial, even if this action resulted in the release of an obviously guilty person. This rule of law is called the *exclusionary rule* (see Chapter 13, for how this rule works in practice). In 1914, all of the justices agreed with Justice William Day when he explained the primary reasons for the exclusionary rule:

> If letters and private documents can thus be seized [in violation of the
> Fourth Amendment] and held and used in evidence against a citizen
> accused of an offense, the protection of the Fourth Amendment, declar-
> ing his right to be secure against such searches and seizures, is of no value,
> and, so far as those [accused of a crime] are concerned, might as well be
> stricken from the Constitution. . . . [The conviction of criminals is] not to
> be aided by the sacrifice of these great principles established by years of
> endeavor and suffering which has resulted in their embodiment in the
> fundamental law of the land. . . . [To allow the use of unconstitutional
> evidence in court] would be to affirm by judicial decision a manifest
> neglect, if not an open defiance of the Constitution.[15]

Six years later, in 1920, Justice Oliver Wendell Holmes explained in a single sentence why the exclusionary rule was inherent in the Fourth Amendment and why it should not be restricted in any way: "The essence of a provision [the Fourth Amendment] forbidding the acquisition of evidence in a certain way [illegally and unconstitutionally] is that not merely evidence so acquired shall not be used before the Court, but that it *shall not be used* at all [by the State]."[16] Until the last decade, a large majority of the U.S. Supreme Court agreed with Justice Holmes that the exclusionary rule should, as much as possible, put a person whose constitutional rights have been violated back to the position in which he would have been *if* the State had respected and obeyed the Constitution. In other words, looking at our Constitution as the social contract between the American people and the government, an unconstitutional search or seizure is a breach of that contract which the State has a moral obligation to remedy. Since Warren Burger replaced Earl Warren as chief justice of the U.S. Supreme Court, however, the exclusionary rule has become a hotly debated issue.

Many judges and leading lawyers, including several justices sitting on today's Supreme Court, are simply not convinced that illegal evidence of guilt should ever be excluded from trial. They make emotional attacks on the exclusionary rule aimed at the public's fear of crime by saying that the rule sets criminals free. Of course, they fail to suggest that society has more cause to fear our country becoming totalitarian without the protection of the exclusionary rule to back up our constitutional rights. Recently, in two ominous decisions, the U.S. Supreme Court seriously restricted the exclusionary rule.[17] The practical result of one case is that if the police illegally seize your marijuana but the prosecutor has enough legal evidence to bring you to trial anyway, you will not be able to testify that you did not possess the illegally seized marijuana. If you do, the prosecutor can now call you a liar by telling the jury about the evidence seized in violation of your constitutional rights. In the other case, the High Court *required* that federal judges in some cases admit illegal evidence in the trial no matter what crimes the police deliberately committed to gather it.

Encouraged by such recent attacks on the exclusionary rule by the Supreme Court, the U.S. Court of Appeals for the southern states ignored fifty years of older Supreme Court cases in the summer of 1980 by directing all federal judges in the southern states to admit illegally seized evidence at trial so long as the police acted unconstitutionally in "good faith" (whatever that is).[18] The southern prosecutors and federal judges have just begun to exploit this latest loophole. The Supreme Court has not yet ruled on this loophole, but it is difficult to be optimistic about the present Supreme Court, four of whose members were appointed by Nixon. When and if the Supreme Court dismantles our constitutional rights by approving a "good faith" exception to the exclusionary rule, it will be left to the state Supreme Courts, the Congress, or the state legislatures to give back meaning and life to the Fourth and Fifth Amendments of our Constitution by reaffirming the exclusionary rule.

These restrictions of the exclusionary rule must be taken seriously because, as noted, several members of the Supreme Court want to abolish it altogether. Although the U. S. Supreme Court has long recognized that the exclusionary rule was designed to prevent judges from being made accomplices of governmental lawbreakers, some justices of the Burger Court argue that the only purpose of the exclusionary rule is to deter police misconduct.[19] On the basis of this "straw man," they then claim that there are other ways to deter illegal police actions and that there is no way to deter "good-faith," but illegal, police actions. In case of overzealous, unlawful police behavior, for example, they say that the officers themselves should be punished, but the illegal evidence should not be excluded from court, nor should the guilty be released. They go on to argue that releasing criminals to uphold a constitutional principle is not worth the price to society.

In our view this argument is nonsense. The "punishing the police" alternative have never worked in America and short of the police engaging in conduct so outrageous that it resembles Gestapo tactics, it is not likely to work in the future. Further evidence that only the exclusionary rule can protect your Fourth Amendment rights is found in recent American history. Prior to 1961, when the state courts were not constitutionally required to apply the exclusionary rule, the police routinely and flagrantly violated, if not ignored, the Fourth and Fifth Amendments. (For example, from 1931 to 1962 the Los Angeles County Municipal Court handled more than 500,000 serious cases, but issued only 538 search warrants.)[20] As long as illegal evidence could be used in court, and the police had no fear of sanctions, they searched and seized pretty much as they liked. Reform of local police practices only came when illegally seized evidence was barred from the courtroom.

Of course, the justices who want to emasculate the Fourth Amendment have reasons why they want to limit our rights to privacy. These reasons may have little to do with the Constitution, but if you doubt how real they are, read the words of Justices Lewis Powell, Warren Burger, and Harry Blackmun quoted from a case decided May 27, 1980:

> The public has a compelling interest in detecting [and convicting] those who would traffic in deadly drugs for personal profit. Few problems affecting the health and welfare of our population, particularly our young, cause greater concern than the escalating use of controlled substances. Much of the drug traffic is highly organized and conducted by sophisticated criminal syndicates. The profits are enormous. And many drugs, including heroin, may be easily concealed. As a result, the obstacles to detection of illegal conduct may be unmatched in any other area of law enforcement [and therefore the police should be able to act with few restraints.]
>
> The jurisprudence [legal philosophy] of the Fourth Amendment demands consideration of the public's interest in effective law enforcement as well as each person's constitutionally secured right to be free from unreasonable searches and seizures. In applying a test of "reasonableness," courts need not ignore the considerable expertise that law enforcement officials have gained from their special training and experience. The careful and commendable police work that led to the criminal conviction at issue in this case satisfies the requirements of the Fourth Amendment [because there are virtually no more requirements.] [21]

THE FIFTH AMENDMENT RIGHT TO REMAIN SILENT

"No person . . . shall be compelled in any criminal case to be a witness against himself."

The other constitutional right that will be emphasized in the following pages is the right to remain silent. As with so many of our basic rights, there are many who would like to restrict or even abolish this right. The fact that many unpopular groups from the Communist Party to the Mafia have found refuge in this protection lends superficial credence to this view. Thus it becomes particularly important for us to pause for a moment to understand why the Fifth Amendment is one of our most important protections against tyranny.

There is no simple way to determine what someone is thinking or whether a person is guilty of a crime. In early England, truth was arrived at in various ways. One way was trial by combat which forced a suspect to fight a highly trained soldier to the death. If the suspect survived against these odds, he was freed. Trial by fire required officials to burn a suspect's arm and see if the wound healed properly. If it did not, the infected person was pronounced guilty. Trial by drowning required officials to throw a suspect into a pond to see if he would sink to the bottom. If the suspect was lucky, he would be rescued before he drowned. If he floated on the surface of the water, he was pronounced guilty.

In 1215, the Catholic Church instituted the Inquisition to make certain that the British and other European peoples believed in the true religion.[22] Apparently, the Church had decided that this method was a more reliable way to ascertain the truth. The search for heretics fueled the Inquisition's fires until 1641. Suspected nonbelieving heretics were required to take an oath swearing to speak the truth in response to all the inquisitor's questions. If the suspects lied after taking the oath, the religious judges declared them guilty of perjury and often heresy as well. If they refused to take the oath or to answer all questions, the inquisitors simply pronounced them guilty of whatever crimes they were suspected of committing. When necessary, the Church used torture to persuade suspected heretics to take the oath and admit their guilt. If the suspects admitted their guilt and recanted, however, the inquisitors usually spared their lives and allowed them to reaffirm their allegiance to the Catholic Church. But there was a rub—if the suspects did not confess to their crimes against the true religion, imprisonment, torture, or death by fire awaited them. Not surprisingly, few people refused to take the oath.

The seemingly effective methods of the Inquisition impressed the English Crown. The Inquisition's oath method appeared to be more efficient and reliable than trial by combat, fire, or drowning. This discovery was comforting to a State that saw political deviance to be at least as threatening as heresy was to the Church. The Star Chamber and other prosecuting bodies of the English State soon began to require of suspected criminals the same sort of oath demanded by the Inquisitors. This inquisitional style of justice claimed many victims, including Sir Thomas More, who was executed for refusing to incriminate himself. John Silburne, another victim, was tortured and imprisoned for much of his life for claiming the right to remain silent in the face of the true accusation that he wrote many books criticizing the English government and court system. Finally, about 1568, some of the leading English lawyers and judges began to reject the inquisitional truth-telling oath by declaring that "No man is bound to betray or accuse himself," (Chief Justice James Dyer, 1568)[23] and "No man . . . shall be examined upon secret thoughts of his heart, or of his secret opinion" (Chief Justices Edward Coke and

John Popham, 1607).[24] By the 1700s, the right to remain silent in the face of accusations, whether religious, political, or criminal, was established in England.

In America, the struggle to elevate the right to remain silent to a principle of justice lagged behind the English effort. The judges who conducted the Salem witchcraft trials in 1692 forced about fifty people to testify to being devil's helpers, sometimes after hours of torture. These judges went so far as to condemn to death and execute nineteen principled persons who refused to confess or bear witness against themselves. In addition, they jailed another 200 people on suspicion of cavorting with the devil. Though other injustices caused by requiring an accused to condemn himself by his own testimony plagued the colonies, probably the majority of American judges during the 1700s refused to punish or torture those persons who claimed a right to remain silent. Certainly by the time the American colonists declared their independence from England, the right to remain silent in face of one's accusers was well established. The eight states that added a bill of rights to their state constitutions included the hard-earned principle that no one can be "compelled to give evidence against himself."[25] When the Bill of Rights to the U.S. Constitution passed, the principle was likewise included, although in a slightly changed form: "No person . . . shall be compelled in any criminal case to be a witness against himself."

Unfortunately, however, progress toward respecting people's essential right not to incriminate themselves has been a spotty thing. Generally speaking, the U.S. Supreme Court has interpreted the Fifth Amendment in much the same way as the Fourth Amendment—that is, all too often it has twisted its words and ignored its spirit. For example, not until 1936 did the U.S. Supreme Court decide that this federal constitutional right prevented state government from forcing suspects to confess by physically abusing or torturing them.[26] And it was not until 1964 that the Supreme Court decided that the states—as well as the federal government—must respect your Fifth Amendment right to remain silent.[27] Up until this late date, the police, prosecutors, and judges in some states could ignore the Fifth Amendment and force you to testify against yourself even though federal police, prosecutors, and judges had to respect your Fifth Amendment right to remain silent. Finally, in 1966, the U.S. Supreme Court required the police to tell you of your right to remain silent after your arrest.[28]

Even today there are exceptions to the general rule that you don't have to testify against yourself. For example, the U.S. Supreme Court has never prohibited the State from forcing you to confess to the grand jury upon threat of imprisonment for the period of time you remain silent while the grand jury remains in session. This rule goes back to 1896, when a bare majority of five (out of nine) justices decided that the State could force a witness to speak before a grand jury as long as it promised the witness immunity from prosecution concerning any matter about which he was forced to testify.

Justice Stephen Field was appalled by this decision and expressed himself passionately, as follows:

No phrases or words of any provision, securing such rights or privileges to the citizen, in the Constitution are to be qualified, limited or frittered away. All are to be construed liberally that they may have the widest and most ample effect . . . [The right to remain silent springs] from that sentiment of *personal self-respect, liberty, independence, and dignity* which has inhabited the breasts of English-speaking peoples for centuries . . . In scarcely anything has that sentiment been more manifest than in the abhorrence felt at the legal compulsion upon witnesses to make confessions which must cover the witness with lasting shame and leave him degraded both in his own eyes and those of others . . . [The right to remain silent was the] result of the long struggle between the opposing forces of the spirit of individual liberty on the one hand and the collective power of the State on the other . . . The essential and inherent cruelty of compelling a man to expose his own guilt is obvious to everyone, and needs no illustration . . .[29]

From the time of this decision, the State had the power to force Americans to confess their "crimes" and implicate their friends, but at least the persons who submitted to this humiliation to avoid jail could not be convicted for the events about which the grand jury forced them to testify. In 1972, however, five justices of the U.S. Supreme Court, led by Chief Justice Warren Burger, further tortured the words of the Fifth Amendment. These five judges decided that you should not get complete immunity from prosecution after a grand jury forces you to talk, but only "use immunity."[30] Use immunity means that the grand jury can force you to testify by promising only that your compelled testimony will not be used by the State at your trial. But here's the catch: If both you and your friends confess to avoid spending time in jail for the crime of remaining silent, the State can now convict all of you — not of course by using your own forced testimony against you, but by using your testimony against your friends, and their testimony against you. (See Chapter 12 for a more complete discussion.)

CHAPTER 3

Surveillance: Your Garden is Only as Private as You Make It

He hath a garden circummured with brick,
Whose western side is with a vineyard backed;
And to that vineyard is a planched gate,
That makes his opening with this bigger key.
This other doth command a little door
Which from the vineyard to the garden leads.
There have I made my promise
Upon the heavy middle of the night
To call upon him.

William Shakespeare
MEASURE FOR MEASURE, Act IV, Scene 1

So you've decided to move to the country, to tend your garden. You want to buy a little land of your own in the wide-open spaces and can't wait for that clear air, pure water, and the opportunity to grow your own food. And why not toss in a few marijuana seeds among the flowers and vegetables?

Well, you may not want to plant this particular type of God's seeds, because doing so can be dangerous. Sad to say, even if you are growing marijuana on your own land for your own use, BIG BROTHER may be watching you—and watching legally!

Until 1967 the Supreme Court did not consider governmental surveillance, eavesdropping, and spying to be the type of searches from which the Fourth Amendment was intended to protect us. Even now, the High Court has decided that the government is free to look onto your property without a search warrant as long as the State's agents do not invade your "reasonable expectation of privacy." Unfortunately, judges determine what your reasonable expectation of privacy is and, consequently, you can expect very little. As this chapter shows, most judges still consider many kinds of surveillance without a search warrant to be reasonable, lawful, and acceptable, either because they believe that it is not really a search at all or because they believe that if it is a search, it does not invade your reasonable expectation of privacy. Of course, it goes without saying that to arrive at this conclusion and deny your right to privacy, the judges have to ignore the spirit of our Constitution (see Chapter 2). Practically speaking, as the law now stands, the police can survey your land from airplanes and helicoptors, walk around your land trying to get a peek at what's going on within your home, and often use binoculars or telescopes to aid their vision—all without a search warrant. Indeed, the State can even use marijuana stolen by thieves who trespass on your land to convict you. Are you feeling "reasonably" angry and helpless? Well, don't despair—there are some things that you can do to protect yourself.

Judges will grant you at least some privacy if you actively work to create and protect it. To assert your right to privacy you must act in a manner that makes it *perfectly clear* to everyone that you strongly, and *reasonably*, expect the State to respect it. For example, to keep people off your land, you must fence it in and post 'keep out' signs. To prevent the examination of your greenhouse or sunporch with binoculars, you must build with glazed glass or non-transparent plastic. And generally speaking, the more private and enclosed you make your garden or field, the more likely it is that a judge will condemn warrantless State surveillance. So, although, in the last analysis, a windowless closet in the interior of your home may be the only true haven from our technological wonderland, this chapter suggests that, with a knowledge of your legal and constitutional rights, there are several more practical—and less paranoid—steps you can take to protect yourself.

THUMBNAIL REVIEW
What the Police Can Do "Legally"

· The police can examine your property from the outside at any time of night or day, with or without flashlights or binoculars, though sometimes they are restricted from using telescopes from long distances.

· The police can legally look into your home or greenhouse without a search warrant from any place they have a legal right to be—such as the sidewalk, your neighbor's yard, or the top of a building across the street and down the block.

• The police can legally enter and search any part of your land that is open to the public. This rule of law means that if you allow Girl Scout cookie sellers to come to your front door or garbage collectors to go through your backyard, the police may be able to do the same without a search warrant.

• The police can legally trespass on any open land or private road that does not specifically warn the public to keep out.

• The police can legally examine your land from planes and helicopters with the latest technological equipment. To conduct this kind of search, the police do not need a reason for suspecting you of growing marijuana. Judges have ruled that such random searching is perfectly legal.

• The police can legally use marijuana stolen from you by private individuals to convict you, because the State is legally innocent of any wrongdoing.

What You Can Do to Protect Yourself

• Your best protection is to act in a way that demonstrates to the world that you strongly and reasonably expect privacy. Here are some of the precautions you can take to exhibit this expectation, though some of them may be more trouble than they are worth, given your circumstances. If you are in doubt, it makes sense to be extra cautious.

• Never grow marijuana in window boxes, gardens, or porches which are visible to people from beyond your property.

• You can shutter your windows or use glazed glass for the windows of your home or greenhouse which would otherwise be easy to see into.

• You can fence your land, lock your gate, or post 'no trespassing' signs. These precautions will probably keep out Girl Scout cookie sellers, as well as trespassers and the police.

• If you don't want the public (and the police) on your property, you can place your garbage can and mailbox outside your locked front gate.

• It is illegal for you to grow your marijuana in the woods or on any other private, public, or government land. And of course, if you do grow your marijuana on any property but your own, you have no reasonable expectation of privacy and no legal protection against trespassers. At the same time, if the marijuana is not on your own property, it is less likely to be traced to you if the police do discover it.

PROTECTING YOUR PRIVACY

Though you may be tired of hearing it, it's worth repeating that it's the judge who determines what your *reasonable expectations of privacy* are, not you. Despite this fact, you are not powerless—far from it. You determine the facts that come before the judge. And if there is one judicial rule that shines through all the legal technicalities and gobbledygook, it's this one—if you consistently act as if you want and expect your privacy, you are more likely to get it. Unfortunately, to prove to many judges that you expect your home to be private, you may have to turn it into something close to a fortress. This fortress mentality is encouraged by an exception to the Fourth Amendment which allows the authorities to spy into your home or greenhouse from any place they have a legal right to be.

Since the disadvantages of boarded windows are obvious, many people find that keeping drapes closed and using clouded glass for the windows of their home or greenhouse is sufficient to prevent the police from looking in. To keep most police from accidentally and legally trespassing on your land, you must announce to them your desire for privacy by building a fence or posting signs around your land. Unfortunately, this precaution may not work against thieves who, if they trespass on your land and steal your marijuana, can turn the evidence over to the police, who can then use it to convict you.

It is obviously difficult to protect yourself from the routine aerial surveillance techniques of many police departments. Some people solve this problem by planting small gardens in completely enclosed greenhouses, while others hide small outdoor gardens far from their homes. But in any of these situations, the general rule remains—the more carefully you protect your privacy, the more likely that, to catch you growing, smoking, or selling marijuana, the police will have to invade what even the judges consider to be your reasonable constitutional expectations of privacy.

POWERS OF THE POLICE

The Police Can Legally Look into Your Home or Greenhouse

Police can usually use binoculars and telescopes to look into your home, greenhouse, or land as long as they do their looking from an area in which they have a legal right to be. Whatever marijuana the police can spot in this way can legally be seized and used to convict you. Recently, some judges have restricted warrantless binocular or telescope intrusions into your home, but most judges continue to approve them. Again, since the police can legally make random searches without specific authorization or focused suspicion, it's up to you to protect your privacy. Otherwise, you cannot reasonably expect the State to respect it.

A second-story lesson

Two students at Washington State University learned a lesson the hard way after they foolishly placed marijuana plants in their second-story apartment window. A roaming detective sitting in his car, parked across the street from the students' apartment, spotted the suspicious looking plants. He then confirmed his suspicion using binoculars. The police arrested the students, but at the suppression of evidence hearing before trial (see Chapter 13 for a thorough discussion of this procedure), the judge decided that the detective's search was illegal because the students had a right to expect that the police would not look into their windows with binoculars. The Washington State Supreme Court, however, decided that the search was legal because the students had failed to keep their marijuana behind closed curtains. Their naiveté in placing their marijuana where it could be seen with binoculars convinced the judges that the students had no reasonable expectation of privacy. Consequently, the marijuana could be, and was, used to convict the students.[1]

The FBI catches their man

In a similar case, John Holbrook learned that robbers and Peeping Toms are not the only people who creep about at night looking through windows. A well-trained FBI agent, careful not to trespass on Holbrook's land, set up a four-foot ladder alongside a railroad track not far from Holbrook's Pennsylvania home. Then, using binoculars to peer through Holbrook's windows, he was able to spot football betting cards. Later the police arrested Holbrook, but at the suppression hearing, the judge rules that the government spying was illegal. The Pennsylvania Superior Court reversed the ruling, saying that the spying was legal because the FBI man did not trespass on Holbrook's land and because Holbrook did not pull the window shades. These facts meant, according to the judges, that the FBI man did not intrude upon Holbrook's reasonable expectation of privacy.[2] If you need further proof that your idea of a reasonable expectation of privacy is not the same as most judges', you need only to read on. Unfortunately, in addition to being unreasonable, the reasonable expectation of privacy standard is applied so vaguely and inconsistently that it is often difficult to predict how any particular judge will rule. If you doubt this hypothesis, try to guess the outcome of the following two cases.

An FBI Telescope examines an Hawaiian scene

FBI agents spied upon Peter Kay's Hawaiian apartment with a high-powered telescope from a quarter of a mile away, and later with high-powered binoculars from a building opposite Kay's apartment. The agents' observations of Kay's apartment convinced a judge to authorize a wiretap on his phone.

Judge Samuel King of the U.S. District Court of Hawaii condemned the FBI's use of a telescope in these words:

> To permit governmental intrusions of the sort at issue in this case to re-
> main uncontrolled would violate the basic foundations of privacy, security
> and decency which distinguishes free societies from controlled societies.[3]

Nevertheless he allowed the evidence to be admitted. How did Judge King arrive at this decision? He first concluded that focusing with a *telescope* on Kay's home from a quarter of a mile away violated Kay's reasonable expectation of privacy, and therefore the judge suppressed the evidence resulting from this search. But he did not suppress the evidence based on the *binocular* search of Kay on his porch. Because he determined that the FBI agents did not absolutely need binoculars to see Kay on his porch, he contended that it did not matter that the agents wanted to improve their view.

Did Judge King condemn the binocular search *into* Kay's home? He didn't directly answer this question because he had already concluded that the agent's "unaided" observations of Kay on his porch gave the FBI probable cause to wiretap his phone. Thus the judge concluded that despite the illegal telescope search and the questionable binocular search into Kay's home, the U.S. government could convict him with the tape recordings of his telephone conversations (see Chapter 4 for the wiretapping discussion).

And then we have the following California case.

The L.A. Playboy Building search

A Los Angeles police officer, positioning himself on a hilltop 200 to 300 yards away from the Playboy Building on Sunset Strip in Hollywood, looked into its windows with high-powered binoculars. Despite what you may have guessed, he wasn't looking at the "bunnies." Instead, he testified that through the uncurtained windows on the eighth floor, he was able to see that the suspects were dealing in pornography. On the basis of this evidence, the police obtained a search warrant, searched the office, and seized the "smut."

This bust led, finally, to three judges on a California Court of Appeal, who had to decide the big question: Did working on the eighth floor of a building, without curtaining the windows, mean that the occupants had no reasonable expectation of privacy? In "reasonable" California, two of the three judges decided that this binocular search violated the defendants' reasonable expectation of privacy. It is fair to say, however, that many, if not a substantial majority, of the judges in other parts of the country would have agreed with the third judge, who dissented as follows:

> It was incumbent on [the pornographers] to preserve their privacy from visual observation by merely drawing the drapes. Absent such an obvious and simple action, I cannot find their expectation of privacy either justifiable or reasonable.[4]

> **SELF-HELP NOTE:**   To have to resort to closed curtains, closets, or clouded-glass greenhouses that make precise identification of objects on the other side impossible—even with the best binoculars or telescopes—may be odious, but they are all effective ways to make it very clear that you expect your privacy to be respected.

The police can easily and legally look into the area around a city or suburban home

Most court decisions have concluded that you have no reasonable expectation of privacy *inside* your home unless you take steps to shutter out the world. While it's hard to accept closing out the sun as a prerequisite to establishing one's privacy, at least it is fairly easy to close the curtains. But what about outside of your house? As should be obvious from the above examples, judges have decided that you have very little reasonable expectation of privacy in your backyard or on your porch. The general rule seems to be that if the authorities can see it, they can grab it.

The police discover three backyard gardens

Ronna Dwyer believed that her well-fenced backyard was private when she planted a few marijuana plants in her sunny California garden. But when her neighbor, Mrs. Wilson, invited police to her second-story window to look at the marijuana plants in Dwyer's backyard, her expectation of privacy vanished. When the case came to court, the California Supreme Court decided that the warrantless search was legal.[5] In another California case, the Vitales placed a few marijuana plants on their porch for the obvious reason that marijuana likes sun. A suspicious police officer thought he recognized the plants from the street. To make certain, he went to a neighbor's backyard with his binoculars. After determining that the plants were of the cannabis variety, Officer Boyle obtained a search warrant and searched the Vitale's home. He found the marijuana plants which were now inside and arrested the family. Again, California judges ruled that the search, seizure, and arrests were legal.[6]

Not even a six-foot fence covered with vines and bushes completely surrounding a small backyard garden is enough to convince most judges that a gardener has a reasonable expectation of privacy. Marion Wylie grew a little marijuana in such a well-protected garden in the back of her Washington, D.C. home. Officers Bruno and Brucker, responding to a tip, asked Wylie's next-door neighbor for permission to take pictures from his back porch. To make their "plain view" observations, it was necessary for one of the officers to stand on a box and for the other to lean around the home. A federal judge approved of the warrantless search which provided the basis for a search warrant authorizing the seizure of the marijuana.[7]

> **SELF-HELP NOTE:** High fences are, of course, considerable protection against unwanted eyes, but they provide no guarantees. In addition to unavoidable problems of holes and cracks, there is the even more troublesome fact that fences don't have "lids."

The police can legally enter any part of your land that is open to the public or the "cookie seller" loophole

Even if you are fortunate enough to own a home that is totally secluded and private, judges have still decided that you have *no* reasonable expectation of privacy in the area around your home *unless* you somehow prevent *all* members of the public from entering your land. If you allow a member of the public to walk to your front or back door, then the police can legally do the same, while keeping a look out for any marijuana in "plain view." In other words, if delivery people come to your back door, if mail carriers come to your front door, if hunters cross your country property, or if the public uses your private road, then the police can legally do the same in most situations.

Two west coast cases

One day, David Crockett and a friend were smoking marijuana in their car which was parked in front of Crockett's home in a secluded and heavily wooded area of Oregon. The public road was 150 to 200 feet away. When two police officers walked up the long driveway to investigate suspected drug activities, they came across the two friends. Three Oregon judges reversed the decision of the trial judge who had ruled that the police violated Crockett's reasonable expectation of privacy. These appellate judges decided that the police had as much right to walk up the driveway without a warrant as "brush salesmen, newspaper boys, postmen, and Girl Scout cookie sellers." Since Crockett did not actively exclude these folks from entering his land, the Oregon Court of Appeals found that he had no reasonable expectation of privacy and thus no Fourth Amendment protection.[8]

Judges not only dream up loopholes such as the "cookie seller" loophole, but they also have a tendency to stretch them beyond the original justification. For example, the California Supreme Court, which is usually quite fair, decided to stretch the cookie seller loophole by a "scant twenty feet" in a case involving Dwight Blakeboro. Blakeboro lived in a cottage in back of a garage and grew three little marijuana plants in a keg which he kept partially hidden under a fig tree behind the garage. The plants were impossible to see from his back door. You would think, therefore, that a Girl Scout, her mind happily dwelling on anticipated cookie profits, wouldn't be able to see the plants in "plain view," and that therefore they were private. But the California Supreme Court decided that the police were legally justified in searching the entire backyard when they came to Blakeboro's back door to investigate a marijuana rumor. Here is how the judges destroyed Blakeboro's reasonable expectation of privacy and affirmed his conviction.

> Although [the marijuana plants] were in a rear yard that was fenced to an undisclosed extent, they were located a scant 20 feet from [Blakeboro's] door to which presumably delivery men and others came."

Justice Mathew Tobriner strongly dissented:

> [The marijuana plants] were not on a portion of the property open to the general public nor to [such persons] as mailmen, milkmen, trash collectors and the like . . . No evidence in this case shows that the marijuana plants could be seen until the officer left the area open to the public and approached to a point approximately one foot from the plants. Consequently, the evidence must be excluded.[9]

SELF-HELP NOTE: While your enthusiasm for erecting fortresses may not be overwhelming, the truth is that the best way to preserve your Fourth Amendment protection from warrantless searches and seizures may be to fence your land and lock your gates. It is a sorry commentary on our society that judges leave you practically no alternative but to place your garbage can and mailbox on the street, to lock your gate, and perhaps rig a bell for guests to ring from the street. If you decide that these precautions border on the insane, or are simply too expensive, you can try to keep away all cookie sellers and delivery people (and thus the police) by hanging a 'no solicitors' sign.

Country land poses special problems or the "lost in the woods" loophole

In many parts of the United States, people have traditionally felt free to cross over open, unfenced land with little concern as to whether or not they were technically trespassing. Unfortunately, this freedom to wander is becoming little more than a memory in many rural areas. And one reason why the 'no trespassing' signs are multiplying like fruit flies in a peach orchard is that judges have ruled that people who don't post them have little or no protection against random searches.

Unless land is fenced or posted at frequent intervals, how are the police supposed to know when they are trespassing, judges have reasoned. Indeed, some judges have gone so far as to note how easy it is to become "lost in the woods" as further justification, even when the police know that they are trespassing. So even when you do string barbed wire fence and post signs, some judges will still find a way to declare that you have no reasonable expectation of privacy in your own woods.

East coast, west coast—marijuana in the woods

The judges of a California Court of Appeal justified the warrantless search of a marijuana patch located in the woods by saying that the police "didn't know whether they were on public or private land; the area was not 'posted' against trespassers and there were no fences." In fact, Peter Dalton, the landowner, met the police on the path to the patch and told them they were trespassing. The police ignored him and continued on their way. Dalton was convicted.[10]

All of the justices of the New Hampshire Supreme Court agreed that George Harmeling and his wife—who "were of the hippie cult"—had no reasonable expectation of privacy in a patch of marijuana surrounded on three sides by thick woods and on the fourth side by an overgrown field. Why? Even though the patch was on Harmelings' land, it was a quarter of a mile from their home. Apparently, for these New Hampshire judges, in order to escape the "lost in the woods" loophole, which justifies the police trespassing on your woodlands, you must grow your marijuana close enough to your home so that the police can use the "cookie seller" loophole instead![11]

Another George—George Jones—learned that the judges of Pennsylvania have also found a number of ways to detour around the Fourth Amendment. Jones cultivated his garden on his mother's land, in a field not visible from any public road. The land was posted with 'no trespassing' signs and a barbed wire fence sharply defined its boundaries. In spite of Jones's obvious efforts to preserve his privacy, the police came on the land to investigate an anonymous tip that was not legally sufficient to justify a search warrant (see Chapter 5 for search warrant requirements). The police found a "tent, various gardening implements, approximately 200 live marijuana plants, and a five or ten pound can of Miracle Grow fertilizer." Five of the seven judges of the Pennsylvania Superior Court agreed that the warrantless search was legal because Jones had no reasonable expectation of privacy in his own "open field."[12]

While most court decisions have been on the order of those just discussed, there are others which have protected your constitutional right to privacy even in the absence of fences and signs. For example, a California Court of Appeal decided that a warrantless land search for a marijuana patch was illegal because the growers had shown a "reasonable expectation of privacy as to their marijuana garden," hidden as it was "in an isolated narrow ravine . . . . The garden was protected by trees and a four-foot wire fence covered with brush and branches." Because the "officers unreasonably invaded [the growers'] reasonable expectation of privacy in their garden," the search and arrest were illegal. The judges also stated that the lack of a "locked gate" at the entrance to the marijuana growers' road, and the absence of "boundary fences or 'no trespass' signs" along the growers' property, did not "foreclose an objective expectation of privacy."[13]

> SELF-HELP NOTE: Many landowners who live in the country are grouping together to maintain common fences with locked gates at the entrance to their land. Often there will be a combination lock on the gate, with the combination known only to the landowners and close friends. In some circumstances, such precautions will help protect your constitutional right to privacy by giving notice to the world that you strongly expect privacy. Unfortunately, in other circumstances, the law may put you in another no-win situation. Depending upon where you live in America, 'no trespassing' signs, fences, and locked gates may attract more police attention than they will ever discourage.

To fence or not to fence

Arthur Weber bought 200 acres of rural land along the Oregon Coast near Coos Bay. He posted 'no trespassing' signs around his entire property and built a gate across the main driveway. Unlike the previous owner, Weber refused to allow local fishermen and hunters to cross his land to reach a thin strip of federal property along the ocean.

Several months later, the U.S. Customs Bureau happened to open an office in Coos Bay. Because Weber had taken precautions to protect his privacy, Customs Officer Larry Cole became suspicious. He ran a background check on Weber and learned of some unspecified suspicious circumstance. So, Cole hitched two rides in a Coast Guard helicopter, first taking telephoto pictures of Weber's property and then checking out the scene with binoculars. The officer hid "seismic sensors" at the entrance to Weber's property to monitor all passing vehicles, and for several weeks police officers used "a variety of vision-enhancing devices," including binoculars, to keep the ranch under "nearly constant surveillance." The story is a long one with a predictable ending: the judges ruled that the airplane searches were legal for reasons explained in the next section and six men were convicted for conspiracy to import 17,000 pounds of marijuana.[14] The moral of the story is that it may be better to do without signs and fences in a community where taking such precautions would be considered suspicious activity by the police.

The police can legally survey your land from planes, helicopters, and satellites

Even if you live in the country, far from the main roads, and take the trouble to fence your land and post signs, law enforcement authorities still have ways to invade your privacy. Many local law enforcement agencies send trained officers with telescopic equipment aloft in airplanes and helicopters to check on your activities. Thus terraces, porches, backyards and open land that cannot be easily searched from the ground are inspected from above.

How can it be legal for "Big Brother" in the sky to engage in such random surveillance of citizens? Surely the Fourth Amendment must offer Americans some protection from this sort of invasion of privacy? Very little. Judges, by resort to verbal sophistry, justify routine, warrantless aerial surveillance by classifying it as "mere plain view observations." Thus the judges do not consider that sheriffs' deputies, who are trained to recognize marijuana and are authorized to fly just over private land with their binoculars in sharp focus, are engaging in searches. Since there is no real search going on, the Fourth Amendment obviously doesn't apply. Neat, huh?

From the jungles of Hawaii to the foothills of the Sierra Nevada

Here are a couple of real cases by way of example. James Sheehan moved to the island of Hawaii in search of privacy. Although Sheehan may have believed that he had found his private paradise, the judges of the Hawaii Supreme Court made it clear that he was still stuck in twentieth-century America. They ruled that he had no reasonable expectation of privacy. Chief Justice William Richardson gave the following description of the scene:

> The events leading to [Sheehan's] arrest began on July 17, 1974, when police were conducting a general surveillance via helicopter of the Captain Cook, Kona, area looking for criminal activity. In this sparsely populated and relatively remote area of the Island of Hawaii, [Sheehan] leased about four acres of land on which his residence was located. His property was adjacent to a forest reserve just below a high ridge and was surrounded by abandoned coffee farms, wild guava growth and numerous macadamia nut, mango and avocado trees. His land could not be seen from the nearest public road, nor from neighboring property, and to get to the house one had to pass through a locked gate and travel up an unimproved road. As the police helicopter flew over Mr. [Sheehan's] land, Officer George [Harris] , using binoculars, ob-

served a patch of marijuana about 9 x 12 feet containing three rows, each with approximately four plants estimated to be between 8 and 10 feet tall. This patch was about 15 feet south of the [Sheehan] house. Although there was conflicting testimony, the court below found that the helicopter maintained an elevation of around 300 feet throughout the surveillance.

After landing, Officer [Harris] and other police officers proceeded to property adjoining [Sheehan's] land. From this neighboring land Officer [Harris] was unable to see the marijuana patch he had previously observed and climbed a 15-foot avocado tree in order to gain a better view. While still unable to see the marijuana patch, he did observe other marijuana plants.

Based upon Officer [Harris's] information, a search warrant was issued and was executed on July 18th. No one was at the [Sheehan] residence at the time . . . A search of the land and house yielded approximately 31 marijuana plants. The plants were scattered throughout the property with no more than five or six together in any one area. The marijuana patch which had been seen from the air contained only two plants and about ten freshly cut stumps. . .

[Sheehan] was finally arrested at Hookena Beach in his Chevrolet van. The van was subsequently searched and 41 marijuana plants weighing approximately 52 pounds were discovered.

[Sheehan] moved to suppress all evidence seized on the basis that the initial helicopter observation violated his rights under the Fourth Amendment to the United States Constitution and Article I, Section 5, of the Hawaii State Constitution.[15]

The judges all agreed that Sheehan had no Fourth Amendment expectation that the police would not fly over his land, particularly since "other planes and helicopters occasionally flew overhead." They explained that the police in the helicopter were not really searching, because "a search implies a prying into hidden places for that which is concealed and it is not a search to observe that which is open to view." So, the next time the planes buzz low over your home or land, you can rest easy in the knowledge that the officers looking down at your marijuana with their binoculars are not really searching.

The California courts provide two more examples. Peter Faust moved to the beautiful foothills of the Sierra Nevada where the summer sun is bright and warm and people are relatively scarce. Had he found a private refuge at last? Nope, afraid not. In response to an informer's tip about a marijuana patch, the Sheriff of Nevada County, California, sent deputy police officers in an airplane to see for themselves. To get a good look at Faust's marijuana patch, which contained about 400 plants, 15 to 20 feet high, the deputy police officers used powerful binoculars. To get even better looks, the plane made three passes over Faust's land, each one lower than the one before, until the plane hovered only 300 feet over Faust's garden. The judges decided that this airplane search was legal because "one who establishes a three-quarter acre tract exhibits no reasonable expectation of immunity from over-flight."[16] Another California court approved an aerial search by a helicopter, 500 feet in the air, from which police examined hundreds of backyards through "20-power gyro-stabilized binoculars" until they found the contraband for which they were looking.[17]

Low-flying planes are not the only method used by police to discover small marijuana gardens. Probably the most effective way for police to discover marijuana patches is to take infrared photographs from high-flying planes. These photographs can reveal small marijuana patches hidden in the brush or forest. American satellites, with their space-age technology, are also equipped to distinguish plant types. Recently, these satellites have been tracking smuggling boats bringing Colombian and Mexican marijuana into the country. For years, these satellites have been monitoring the size of the corn and wheat crops in Russia, China, and America, the poppy crop in Turkey and Thailand, the coca crop in Peru and Columbia, and the marijuana crop everywhere. While there is no evidence that satellite information is used as part of domestic criminal prosecutions, it is certainly possible that the federal government does inform local authorities when they locate large marijuana fields.

The police can use stolen marijuana to convict you

If you do grow a few plants on your own property, whether on your land, in a plastic-covered greenhouse or a closet, it is usually illegal for the police to seize them without a search warrant. But the police can arrest *you* if your marijuana comes to them by way of thieves and trespassers. In areas of the country where marijuana rip-offs are common, this legal rule has created a real problem. The law works like this. If marijuana thieves tell the police where their ill-gotten booty came from, the police can use this information to procure a warrant to search your property. It does not matter whether your marijuana was in your garage, your greenhouse, or your garden. When a private citizen, without encouragement or assistance from the police, trespasses on your land or breaks into your buildings, the State can use the stolen evidence to convict you. Why? The State is "completely innocent" of the wrongdoing. The fact that someone had to commit a crime in order to obtain evidence of your marijuana is ignored, and a conviction usually ensues. The thieves are seldom prosecuted. This policy leaves otherwise law-abiding citizens with little protection from thieves who are practically encouraged to steal from people whose only crime is to grow a few pot plants. Hence it is not difficult to understand why, in marijuana-growing areas of the country, many people have reluctantly purchased guns.

The good neighbors of Mississippi and California

A Mississippi man told the police that his neighbor, Eugene Whalen, was growing a field of marijuana. Since Whalen's thousand plants were not visible from the informer's yard, the police told him that they needed more information in order to obtain a search warrant. Apparently encouraged by this statement, the thieving neighbor entered Whalen's property, pulled up some of his plants, and turned them over to the police.[18]

In a similar case, a Berkeley, California woman called the police to report her neighbor's marijuana activities, and the police said only that they would contact her later. Before hearing from the police, the woman sneaked into Edward Crocker's garage, stole some of his marijuana, and called the police about her "find."[19] Though in both cases a judge would have considered the marijuana to be illegally seized if the police had taken it themselves, or suggested that the neighbors steal it, both the California and Mississippi judges determined that, in these cases, the trespassers went onto their neighbors' land and stole the marijuana without police encouragement. As a result, the police were free in both cases to use the stolen marijuana to establish probable cause and obtain search warrants. Because the State was "completely innocent" of the thefts that provided the bases for the search warrants, the search warrants legitimated the searches and subsequent arrests. Naturally, the California and Mississippi prosecutors did not bring charges against the neighbors for theft.

Steps You Can Take
The more secret your garden, the more privacy you can expect

As you have seen, most judges do not consider outdoor gardens to be private. Thus, the police can often legally invite themselves onto any land that is open to the public; and they can sometimes trespass on your land, or view it from afar with sophisticated equipment. But in cases where the police choose a particularly outrageous spying technique, such as flying planes or helicopters so low over your land that they skim the treetops, if not your head, many judges will rule that your privacy was illegally invaded.

In one case, a California Court of Appeal decided that a helicopter search, which turned up two marijuana plants, was illegal because Gregory Shaw had "a reasonable expectation of privacy to be free from noisy police observation by a helicopter from the air at 20 to 25 feet and that such an invasion was an unreasonable governmental intrusion into the serenity and privacy of his backyard."[20]

> *Question:* Would Gregory Shaw have had a reasonable expectation of privacy to be free from quiet observation by a spy plane laden with advanced photographic and telescopic equipment from the air at 500 to 1000 feet?
>
> *Answer:* Probably not.

Law always lags behind technology. In the area of searches and seizures, the unwillingness of judges to come to terms with the reality of the 1980s is particularly apparent. Thus if a policeman climbs over your fence and trips over a 'no trespassing' sign, many judges will decide that he made an illegal search. The same is true if he flys a plane a few feet over your pasture and spots marijuana with the naked eye. But if the same officer flys an ultramodern helicopter 500 feet over your backyard and uses equipment sensitive enough to spot a tic on Rover's nose, you have no protection when he spots the pot of marijuana Rover is sleeping next to.

In the face of such "brave new world" techniques, privacy is fast becoming a mythical concept, fences and signs notwithstanding. To achieve something close to complete legal protection, you have to build totally enclosed greenhouses with special glass or plastic that lets the sunshine in while blocking out the harmful vision of your friendly, neighborhood helicopter cop. Remember, this book is not telling you to take this precaution. It's just that other ways of hiding your marijuana are legally more risky.

The Florida plastic-covered hothouse

Clyde Holtermann grew his marijuana in his backyard, in a quickly constructed hothouse which he covered with plastic. Holtermann lived in a part of rural Florida where the hothouse was not "plainly visible to the public." Apparently, it was a good distance from his front and back doors, his neighbors, and the public road. As Officer D'Orazio was scooping ice cream at his ice cream parlor, an informer apparently told him that Holtermann preferred marijuana to ice cream. When Officer D'Orazio closed shop that night, he immediately went to Officer Russell's home for assistance. At 11:30 PM that night, the two off-duty police officers arrived at Holtermann's home without a search warrant. (It is doubtful that they could have obtained a valid warrant even if they had tried. See Chapter 5 for requirements for obtaining warrants.) They walked through Holtermann's side yard and into his backyard, where they spotted the plastic-covered hothouse. Officer Russell shined his flashlight through a hole in the plastic, revealing a quantity of slumbering marijuana. The Florida judges of a court of appeal agreed that under these particular circumstances, Holtermann did have a "reasonable expectation of privacy," because the hothouse was within the area immediately around his home.[21]

The legal pros and cons of tending a garden on someone else's land

Some gardeners, concerned about their lack of legal protection on their own land, cultivate marijuana on government land or on wilderness land owned by lumber companies or other absentee owners. As this approach involves trespassing, it is doubly illegal. Illegal is not always the same as impractical, however, and under many circumstances growing marijuana in somebody else's woods does make it more difficult for the police to prove ownership. It is ironic that since the police can so easily circumvent your Fourth Amendment privacy protection, it is often more risky to grow even small amounts of marijuana on your land than it is to trespass and grow it elsewhere.

The main advantage to growing marijuana off your land is that it is more difficult for the State to prove that it is yours unless you are caught watering, cultivating, or harvesting it. Of course, dedicated officers could stake out a marijuana patch on public land, but if the patch is small, they may not bother.

One of the disadvantages of growing marijuana on someone else's land is that it is likely to make it easier to steal. And some people who live in the country fear marijuana thieves more than the police. A legal disadvantage, in addition to committing the crime of trespassing, is that you have *no* Fourth Amendment protection against illegal searches and seizures of your garden if you cultivate it on someone else's land. Nearly all judges agree that you have *no* reasonable expectation of privacy on land on which you are trespassing, even though you may have decided to trespass only because most judges also believe you have little reason to expect privacy on your own open land (see Chapter 8 for a full explanation of the "You Can't Complain" Loophole).

SELF-HELP NOTE: Sensible steps, such as locking the doors to your greenhouse, your home, and your garage and installing burglar alarms, will deter many thieves. Unfortunately, some thieves will not be stopped by these measures and some property owners may be tempted to take more threatening or violent steps to scare thieves away. This approach is usually not wise. Aside from the moral issues involved, the legal status of a person who uses violence against a trespasser is always questionable, especially when the violence is used to defend property as opposed to human life. A detailed discussion of when and where self-defense is justifiable is clearly outside the scope of this book. Suffice it to say that if you are tempted to use violence or dangerous traps to defend your property—don't!

And now, after preparing you for the worst, here is a reminder that it's not always this bad—some judges take a more enlightened view of the Constitution and laws that protect our freedom and privacy. Whether or not you are faced with an "enlightened" or a "tortured" view can depend to a large degree on where you live.

THE BEST YOU CAN EXPECT FROM A JUDGE

· A few judges will condemn warrantless searches conducted with binoculars, telescopes, or laser beams, particularly into your home.

· Some judges will rule that the police can walk only to your front door without a warrant, even if you post no signs and build no fences.

· A handful of judges will condemn all airplane searches of your land unless the police have "focused suspicion" that suggests that you—rather than your neighbors—are growing a forbidden plant.

· Some judges, particularly in California, will not allow the State to use illegal evidence, even if it is taken by private security guards or by thieves.

CHAPTER **4**

Entrapment and Wiretapping

But they have a good cover; they show well outward.
The Prince and Court Claudio, walking in a thick-pleached
alley in mine orchard, were thus much overheard by a man of
mine.

William Shakespeare
MUCH ADO ABOUT NOTHING, Act I, Scene 2

Without a trusting environment, it's hard to be open and friendly; and unless we
live among open and friendly people, life can quickly degenerate into a lonely
proposition. Unfortunately, public authorities, in the name of law enforcement, are
doing much to destroy this essential trust with their use of undercover agents and
electronic eavesdropping techniques. To unleash these freedom-threatening tactics,
which have long been favorites of police states, against citizens who choose to use
marijuana or engage in some other behavior that society defines as a vice is degrading to the government, expensive for taxpayers, and impotent to curb people's
fondness for the forbidden.

This chapter may depress you, but do not let it scare you or make you paranoid
and distrustful of other people. The purpose of the information set out here is to
make you aware that the State possesses various methods of operation ("dirty
tricks"), to explain their legal consequences, and to suggest suitable steps that you
can take to protect your freedom. Although it is unlikely that the State will use
these methods against you unless you are a heavy marijuana dealer or grower, it is
wise to be safe and understand your rights.

THUMBNAIL REVIEW
What the Police Can Do "Legally"

• Undercover police officers in most states can encourage and entice you to commit a crime and the State can convict you if you fall into the trap, as long as a judge decides that you were predisposed to commit the crime.

• Undercover police can stage an entire drug transaction using their own drugs or even phony drugs. They can promise you money and drugs to get you involved and if you are tricked into accepting a role in this sort of staged setup, the State can convict you for violating the law.

• Undercover police can legally threaten known marijuana users or sellers with prosecution and imprisonment and then promise them freedom in return for informing on others.

• Undercover police can secretly tape record their conversations with you or, by use of a tiny transmitter, can broadcast your conversation to other secret agents to tape-record.

• Police can eavesdrop on and tape record all your conversations that they can overhear in such public places as restaurants and telephone booths. They can even record what they can hear through a thin-walled motel room if they have access to the next room.

• The police can place a "pen register" on your phone. This device will record every phone number you dial. Officers can also legally search the phone company's records of your completed phone calls.

• The police in most states can use all of the above investigatory methods without obtaining a search warrant, without probable cause to suspect you of wrongdoing, and without any court supervision.

• By meeting several relatively loose requirements, the police can obtain a special warrant from a judge to tap your phone.

• The police can break into your home, car, or social club to plant a bug, an eavesdropping microphone, or other listening device without meeting any requirements in addition to those required for wiretapping your phone.

What You Can Do to Protect Yourself

• You can avoid talking about your marijuana with anyone except good and trusted friends.

• You can avoid marijuana talk in public places where unwelcome ears can overhear.

• You can avoid using the telephone for conversations involving marijuana.

• *Above all, you can avoid unnecessary paranoia.* The police are unlikely to try to subvert your best friends or bug your home and wiretap your phone unless you are involved with marijuana in a big way.

ENTRAPMENT

Avoiding Police Setups

Most police departments have undercover narcotics officers. Although many of these officers don't take marijuana too seriously and are primarily concerned with more dangerous drugs, most will happily arrest you for marijuana possession or sale should they get the chance. Fortunately, though, most undercover narcotics work is so haphazard and random that usually only the foolishly naive or careless are caught in the traps. By restricting marijuana talk or dealings to good and trusted friends, face to face, in private places, almost all police setups can be avoided. It's especially wise to be extra careful, to trust your intuition, and to refuse to talk drugs if you find yourself in a situation that seems even a little weird or odd.

An interview with a former undercover narcotics agent

Meet Joe, an undercover narcotics officer who worked in San Francisco in the 1970s. Joe explained that sometimes he drove around town in an old Mustang provided by the police department picking up hitchhikers. He was a friendly looking, bearded, long-haired man, about twenty-three and many of the grateful riders would light up a joint to share with their obliging host. At this point, Joe would flash his badge and take the marijuana smokers to the station. Then it was time for the "deal." If the hitchhikers refused to tell Joe who sold them the marijuana they would be prosecuted. But after being threatened with legal proceedings and jail time, many were willing to disclose their source of supply in exchange for a chance to "walk out of the station." Thus casual acquaintances and sometimes even good friends were betrayed. Occasionally the arrested marijuana smoker would provide a dealer's name and telephone number. Joe described how easy it was for him to call a suspected dealer on the phone and introduce himself for the first time:

"Hey, Bob. This is Joe. Remember me?"

"Joe? I'm not sure."

"You must remember. We met last summer at the park."

"Oh, yeah? I think I remember you now."

"Sure. I'm the guy with the van and Annie, my German shepherd."

"Oh, sure. How are you?"

"Great. Listen, I'm going up north and need some marijuana. Do you know anyone who can help me?"

If Bob supplied the marijuana or if Bob introduced Joe as an old friend to Linda and Linda supplied Joe—either way, Joe made a bust.

IMPORTANT: Most cities still have vice squads and the undercover officers still work in much the same way—arresting every careless drug user they randomly come across in the hope that he will inform on his supplier rather than risk jail.

The U.S. Supreme Court has decided that you have no constitutional right to expect that government agents will not encourage you to commit a crime, or that secret agents will not befriend you and gain your trust for the sole purpose of setting you up for a bust. The U.S. Supreme Court has placed one important restriction on federal undercover agents and informers, as a matter of basic fairness. While federal agents can encourage with impunity so-called *predisposed* people to become criminals, federal judges will not convict the completely innocent victims of a setup. In legal lingo, this situation is called *entrapment*. But because the U.S. Supreme Court has said that while entrapment is unfair it is not constitutionally forbidden, state supreme courts have been free to develop their own rules. Some state courts have declared that there is no such thing as entrapment. In those states, the police can use any means of persuasion to trick or entice you into committing a crime, while other state courts have required that officers follow stricter rules when it comes to luring people into criminal acts.

IMPORTANT: One of the most common mistakes that nonlawyers make is to assume that the rules prohibiting entrapment are broad. They usually are not. A great deal of the behavior of narcotics officers that you might think is entrapment does not qualify as such under the narrow judicial rules now followed by the federal government.

Most state supreme courts follow the U.S. Supreme Court's view of entrapment that the police can entrap only the innocent, not the predisposed. When federal prosecutions are involved, and in prosecutions in all of the states that follow the federal rule, judges and juries usually consider counterculture types to be predisposed to the use of marijuana and therefore guilty regardless of what the undercover officer did to encourage marijuana use. In states such as California, Alaska, Michigan, and Iowa, where court rulings afford the individual more protection, judges determine whether or not undercover officers illegally entrapped you by looking at the conduct of the agents rather than your so-called predisposition. These states generally forbid undercover agents to set up anyone by the use of a technique that is so forceful and persuasive that the person can be viewed as giving in to the enticements of the officer. But remember, it is only in a small minority of states that the law of entrapment protects you from outrageous setups by state police. The federal police can set you up in any state.

Lawyers agree that in practice it is extremely difficult to prove that a law enforcement officer unlawfully entrapped you. Both juries and judges tend to be skeptical about an entrapment defense, in part because they are often self-righteous about their own ability to refuse the most enticing invitation to commit a crime. An entrapment defense typically succeeds *only* if the undercover officers were guilty of fairly outrageous behavior.

> **IMPORTANT:** Sometimes you will have a choice between a judge or a jury and sometimes it is better to have a judge rather than a jury decide whether or not you were entrapped. This situation is a good example of one in which you should hire a local lawyer who is thoroughly familiar with both state law and local procedure (see Chapter 13). If you conduct a defense based on entrapment, you will almost always face a struggle with the police, who seldom admit to entrapping their victims and are likely to tell a story which conflicts with your version of what happened. Another great problem with an entrapment defense is that you have to admit your crime to the judge or jury before claiming that you were entrapped. Obviously, after the judge or jury knows you are guilty, you face an uphill job of convincing them that you were entrapped.

Charles the pool player

In the so-called leading case concerning entrapment, Chief Justice Warren Burger wrote the opinion for the U.S. Supreme Court justifying the following scheme. Jules Olsson, a police informer, went to the Pud Bar in St. Louis, looking for action. He broached the idea of drug dealing to Charles Hammett, a pool-playing friend who was hanging out at the bar. Hammett was interested but couldn't find a source among any of his friends. So the informer simply arranged for Hammett to buy drugs from a federal DEA agent and then sell them to a second agent. The majority of the High Court approved of this setup even though it did not uncover "ongoing drug traffic," but only tempted short-sighted Hammett to commit a crime. They justified imprisoning Hammett, stating that he was "predisposed" to selling drugs, and shrugged off the fact that the State had provided the suppliers and the buyers. Justices William Brennan, Thurgood Marshall, and Potter Stewart disagreed to no avail: "The Government is doing nothing less than buying contraband from itself through an intermediary and jailing the intermediary."[1]

Before regaling you with more examples of what some judges believe is not entrapment, the following two cases are examples of what a high court finally decided was entrapment—but only after other judges and juries decided that it was not.

An informer hooks a former heroin addict

In a famous case, a jury, a trial judge, and three judges of a U.S. court of appeals all agreed that a government informer named Kazanzakas did not entrap Billy Stewart. The setup occurred in 1951, as follows: Both men were being treated for heroin addiction when informer Kazanzakas repeatedly begged Stewart to find him some heroin to alleviate feigned withdrawal pains. Stewart finally succumbed to the pleadings of his new "friend" and bought the informer some heroin. Undercover agents busted Stewart and he received a ten-year prison sentence, while Kazanzakas was released without serving any time because of his agreement to work as an informer for the Federal Bureau of Narcotics.

Nine U.S. Supreme Court justices, however, unanimously reversed the decision, when they agreed that Stewart *was* a victim of entrapment. Chief Justice Earl Warren stated that there was "no evidence that [Stewart] himself was in the [narcotics] trade." He emphasized that the evil of entrapment is that "the Government plays on the weaknesses of an innocent party and beguiles him into committing crimes which he otherwise would not have attempted. Law enforcement does not require methods such as this."[2]

Big brother turns on a teenage boy

In 1973, a North Carolina jury, trial judge, and three judges of the state court of appeals all agreed that Frederick St. Pierre should serve at least three years in prison for possession of LSD. The North Carolina Supreme Court unanimously reversed his conviction because St. Pierre had been entrapped. That all seven Supreme Court judges were shocked by the same evidence that twelve jurors and four judges found acceptable tends to show that the American criminal justice system can sometimes be about as reliable as a crapshoot. The North Carolina judges summarized the evidence in the following way:

> The uncontradicted State's evidence in [this] case discloses that a twenty-eight-year-old police officer posing as an army sergeant ingratiated himself into the confidence and affection of the sixteen- or seventeen-year-old [boy] for the purpose of using him to find and buy drugs. He accomplished his purpose by seeking [St. Pierre's] companionship, continually calling [his] home, and allowing [him] to drive his automobile. During this time he assured [St. Pierre's] troubled parents that he would "look after their son." After establishing the relationship of a "big brother" with [St. Pierre], the police officer "got him to make more than one drug buy . . ." The State's uncontradicted evidence shows that the criminal design and intent to [possess LSD] originated in the mind of [the officer] and that he, by fraud and persuasion, induced [St. Pierre] to commit the criminal act.
>
> We do not wish to leave any impression that we oppose the necessary undercover activities of law enforcement officers. We are too well aware of the destructive effect of the drug traffic upon the health and moral fiber of this country to place an unnecessary limitation upon those who seek to enforce our drug laws. The methods of the drug trafficker are so clandestine and insidious that it becomes necessary for the State to use undercover agents, who may rightfully furnish to the plyers of this trade opportunity to commit the crime in order that they may be appre-

hended. It is only when a person is induced by the officer to commit a crime which he did not contemplate that we must draw a line . . . *There was not a scintilla of evidence to show any predisposition on the part of [St. Pierre] to possess LSD.* We therefore hold that [Frederick St. Pierre] was a victim of entrapment . . ."[3]

The "I have a deal you can't refuse" approach

Have you ever wondered how drug enforcement officials operate? Many of them are professionals, having taken courses and seminars on what conduct judges have typically condemned as entrapment and what conduct they have condoned. The agents learn their lessons well, as the following cases demonstrate. Observe how the undercover agents randomly chose their targets, and remember that the State has been known to use informers or undercover police to entrap drug users, even when their involvement with drugs is only casual. Some of the examples set out here involve drugs other than marijuana, but the legal principles of entrapment are the same regardless of the drugs involved. And remember—although it is probably true that many American police departments do not make enforcement of marijuana laws a top priority, many undercover officers are happy to make arrests for marijuana possession and sale when they can.

A case of mistaken southern hospitality

Two Georgia ladies trusted a couple of guys who had befriended them. Timothy Breen trusted his two lady friends, even when they brought along two guys he didn't know. The guys asked Breen for some marijuana. Breen had none of his own, but because he was good-natured, he made several phone calls to other friends. He finally got hold of some marijuana, bought it with the money the two men had given him, and gave it to the women's new friends. He made nothing on the deal. The women were just as surprised as Breen when their new boyfriends identified themselves as undercover agents and arrested Breen.[4]

Question: Did this deception qualify as entrapment?

Answer: The Georgia judges convicted him. Three judges dissented.

Agent "Haystack" of Wyoming

Government agents are not required to have evidence that you are predisposed to sell marijuana before they offer a deal you can't refuse. In fact, most judges will not believe that you were unlawfully entrapped by the police, no matter what the circumstances. You might think, for example, that a clear case of entrapment would be one in which an informer forced you at gunpoint to become involved with drugs. But remember that you must convince a judge or a jury that the informer in fact threatened you with a gun. Gary Jesmore, for instance, testified that "Haystack," an informer who disguised himself with a "Mohican" haircut,

threatened him with a gun before he agreed to sell Haystack some hashish. Another witness verified the story, and Haystack, a felon convicted of armed robbery, admitted to carrying a gun. Haystack, however, denied using his gun.

Question: Did this evidence show entrapment?

Answer: No. A jury convicted Jesmore for the sale of hashish. The Wyoming Supreme Court approved. Two justices disagreed.

"Susie the spy" of Missouri

Susan Gray, a narcotics agent, admitted that she had called Glendon Huck about thirty-five to forty times over a period of a month and a half, asking him to sell her some drugs. Huck consistently refused until Susie called him and told him she was "very sick," "throwing up," "breaking into a rash," and that she needed cocaine. Huck said he knew someone who might be able to help her. He drove to Kansas

City and picked up about a gram of cocaine, worth $60, for Susie. Two weeks later she called and said that she was sick again, but this time Huck told her to go to a health center. When she pleaded with him, saying "she was hurting," gullible Glendon gave in and went back to Kansas City to pick up another $60 worth of cocaine for Susie. At trial, Huck honestly admitted to using "marijuana, hashish and a little cocaine."[6]

> *Question:* Did Susie entrap Glendon?
>
> *Answer:* No. The judges decided that anyone who used narcotics must have a "predisposition" to sell them, and that anyone who had a predisposition to sell narcotics could never be entrapped by a secret agent, regardless of how often or how piteously she begged. The judges sentenced Huck to fifteen years in prison for being unable to say "No" to Susie and for admitting that he used drugs.

A Wisconsin high school reunion

Some people get paid for doing nothing more than hanging out with old friends. One undercover officer was in a bar waiting for a dealer when he met a high school friend from the old neighborhood whom he had not seen in five years. When the officer said he wanted some marijuana, Phillip Hennessy obligingly offered to find him some.[7]

> *Question:* Was Hennessy a hardened marijuana pusher or a nice guy who fell into the agent's trap?
>
> *Answer:* Though the judges did not answer this question, they gave Hennessy an indeterminate sentence of up to five years in prison for selling his old friend $10 worth of marijuana.

Even intimate friends can be legally used to set people up

The following two cases are exceptional, but they are true. They are included to enlighten you about how difficult it is to prove "entrapment." Although there have been legal cases with similar facts where the defense of "entrapment" was established and upheld by the court, such instances are rare.

A Michigan under the covers operation

Irma Phelan had known Dewitt Rather for more than ten years and she trusted him. They had once been engaged. Years earlier they had each married, but they were now both getting divorced. They were sleeping together and discussing marriage when Rather asked Irma if she knew anyone who sold drugs. Like many people, she did know someone. Rather, an undercover agent, then asked her to get some drugs so that he could sell them to a friend of his (another undercover agent).[8]

Question: Did the Michigan judges convict Phelan for the sale of these drugs or did Rather entrap her?

Answer: One judge disagreed, but the majority approved her conviction. There was no entrapment.

A Hawaii in-house deal

Undercover police are usually well-paid, well-trained, and well-supplied with the best dope in order to enhance their chances of making arrests. For six months, Kerry Day, a paid informer working in Hawaii, asked Paul Entine to buy him some drugs. At the same time, he offered to sell Paul hashish and offered him a chance to smuggle cocaine from South America. How did Entine meet Day? Day responded to a newspaper ad for a room to rent and Entine rented him a room in his home. Entine continually refused the drug deals, but the informer persisted, even after he had moved out of Entine's house. Later, when visiting, Day would sometimes spend the night at the Entine's home. As thanks, Day gave Entine and his wife some hashish and marijuana and took them to dinner. One night, after countless, unsuccessful phone calls to Entine, the informer concocted a story about a friend who really needed some drugs. Entine finally sold Day some hashish oil which a real friend of his needed to sell.[9]

Question: Did his long-time "friend" entrap Entine?"

Answer: No. Entine was convicted and imprisoned. One judge dissented.

WIRETAPPING

POWERS OF THE POLICE

Undercover police can use hidden microphones, tape recorders, or cameras

You must not only be careful not to buy marijuana from or sell it to police officers, but you must also be cautious not to speak to them.[10] They can legally tape-record your conversations. You may believe that this invasion is an illegal search and seizure which should require a finding of probable cause, a search warrant, or at least some suspicion that you are involved with marijuana (see Chapter 5 for the search warrant discussion), but unfortunately, there are no such requirements. Your conversations are not protected. Even if you speak with undercover officers in the privacy of your own home, the agents can legally be wired with a tape recorder or with a microphone that will broadcast your speech to the police outside.

Also, if you are unlucky enough to speak with an undercover police officer over the telephone, she may legally tape record your conversation without having probable cause or a search warrant. Why? Because judges have ruled that you have no reason to expect that the secret agent will not repeat your conversation to someone else, you have no reason to expect that she will not record your conversation for all to hear. Also, warrants or court orders are not required for the secret police to watch you via hidden cameras or unmarked police cars. They have unbridled discretion to investigate anyone whom they suspect of illegal activity, whether it's political, sexual, or drug-related.

Obviously, the fact that you don't believe that the activity should be illegal has no bearing on the question.

> **NOTE OF SANITY:**   It is worth repeating that to offer you the most complete protection from police abuse and legal loopholes, this book includes extreme cases. It is always important that you filter this information through the fine sieve of your own common sense. After reading these cases, you may feel certain that the police are following you about, tapping your phone, or trying to entice you to talk into a hidden microphone. Most probably they are not. This book is simply explaining what legal powers the police have and providing examples of both the most frequent and the most exceptional cases.

Eavesdropping in public is legal

Undercover officers are also free to legally record your conversations if they take place at a location open to the public. This rule of law means that it is legal for an officer to record your words from the phone booth next to the one in which you are speaking or the restaurant booth next to the one in which you are sitting and talking. The only sure way to protect yourself from such eavesdropping is never to speak freely and openly when a stranger might be able to overhear.

Even when you are in your own apartment or motel room, it is legal for the police to record what they can hear through the walls. The assistant manager of a Ramada Inn in Ohio, for example, called the local police to report that the occupant of Room 120, Jason Dangerfield,

> was exciting concern because of an excessive number of incoming calls to Room 120, together with outgoing long distance calls; because of a parade of poorly dressed and bearded young people going to and from [the] room; and because of [their] sizable food and bar bills.

Chief Powell and Officer Delorey arrived at the motel and asked the assistant manager to admit them to the room next to the suspect's room. Chief Powell "lay down (sic) on the floor with his ear near the locked door on the common wall" and overheard a conversation about marijuana. Officer Delorey heard someone say that the marijuana was very good quality, "running from gold to deep red." Because the police believed that Dangerfield and his friends were about to leave, they went out into the hallway. From there, Officer Delorey could see some marijuana on the bed in Room 120 through the partially opened door. Because of the so-called emergency, the police burst in without warrants, searched the entire room, and arrested everyone (see Chapter 7 for more on warrantless search emergencies). The Ohio judges justified the eavesdropping by blaming the potheads for being careless and speaking too loudly: "The officers were in a room open to anyone who might care to rent. They were under no duty to warn [the marijuana criminals] to speak softly."[11]

Telephone wiretaps are legal in some circumstances

The ugly truth is that Americans can never be sure that the State is not legally listening to and tape-recording their most intimate conversations. More pernicious than searches and seizures authorized under the Fourth Amendment, wiretapping is a prolonged, secret search which indiscriminately seizes everything you say. Wiretaps usually intercept telephone conversations, though microphone eavesdrops are also used to record all conversation within a particular area. Wiretapping is a particularly obnoxious invasion of privacy because, unlike other searches and seizures, wiretaps are often long-term and are always secret. Ask yourself if you haven't said lots of perfectly legal things on the telephone that you would be extremely upset to know were being recorded.

If the Fourth Amendment requirements were more strictly applied, most wiretapping would be unconstitutional. According to Congress and the Supreme Court, however, serious crimes like marijuana use justify wiretaps. Even though actual taps may be rare, millions of Americans cannot be certain whether they are speaking privately on the telephone or whether they are speaking to the police as well. In 1978 (the most recent year for which there are available figures), for example, the majority of legal wiretaps were placed to investigate gambling and drug offenses. According to government sources, the police installed wiretaps in 249 single-family homes, 112 apartments, 125 business locations and 23 out-of-the-way places, such as a public pay telephone, a car, and a social club.[12]

Since wiretaps are very expensive, averaging more than $10,000 each, the police will probably not bother to tap your phone unless they suspect that you are a big dealer. The highest cost for a single wiretap in 1978 was $332,770. Perhaps the high costs explain why the federal police obtained only 6347 warrants for wiretaps from 1968 to 1977 and the state police obtained approximately the same number during those ten years. These court-authorized wiretaps were hardly a minor intrusion, however, because they allowed the police to overhear the conversations of more than 500,000 Americans. What's worse is that although judges later found that many of the wiretaps failed to meet the legal requirements discussed in the next section, their decisions protected only the people whose phones were officially wiretapped or who spoke on the phone. The privacy of thousands of Americans who were the subject of phone conversations on illegally tapped phones was not protected by the law. The judges will not allow you to object to the illegality of a wiretap on your friend's phone if the law-breaking police only learn about your vices from your wife or close friend. This rule of law is explained by the "you can't complain" loophole in Chapter 8.

NOTE: There is a requirement that your phone cannot be wiretapped for more than thirty days. This rule is usually little more than a formality, however, as judges seldom refuse thirty-day extensions, unless you have said absolutely nothing suspicious on the phone for the first thirty days. And once a wiretap is legally authorized for one "serious" crime such as marijuana activity, evidence of any other crime can be used to justify the extension of the wiretap.

There are some requirements for wiretapping that are supposed to safeguard your privacy, but because many judges ignore them, many police officers ignore them also. For example, your telephone conversations are not supposed to be automatically tape-recorded. That is, the police are expected to listen actively to your conversations and be ready to turn off the tape recorder and hang up the phone when it becomes obvious that the conversation does not concern marijuana or other criminal activities.

Police officers, however, have little reason to pay attention to this rule, since judges have approved, among other intrusions, automatic recording, the tape-recording of obviously innocent phone calls of a babysitter to her high school friends, and the complete tape recording of 1595 phone calls over sixty days when less than 150 of them had any relationship to criminal activity.[13]

Also, the police are supposed to notify you after wire-tapping your phone. Unfortunately, however, they have little incentive to give you this notice, because nothing happens to them, or to the tape recording, if they fail to do so. Moreover, there is absolutely no requirement for the police to notify the persons with whom you spoke on the phone about the fact that their conversation was recorded unless they were named in the search warrant. Even if the police legally wiretap your phone, you cannot expect them to notify you until they are ready to arrest you.

The police can legally get a list of the people you telephone

Also unprotected by the Supreme Court's interpretation of the Fourth Amendment are the identities of the people whom you call on the telephone. The police can legally check the phone company's accounts of your completed phone calls, or they may place a pen register on your phone that records every phone number you dial. Probable cause and search warrants are unnecessary because the U.S. Supreme Court has conveniently determined that you do not reasonably expect the numbers you dial to be private.[14] This assumption makes little sense. The only reason the police want the phone numbers is to help establish probable cause that you are discussing criminal activity on the phone. Calling known marijuana dealers, for example, along with other suspect activity, may be sufficient to demonstrate probable cause that you are involved with marijuana.

The police often need to obtain probable cause to believe that you are involved with marijuana, especially when they suspect that you possess or cultivate it, but can't prove the fact. One reason that a probable cause showing is important is that it is an important legal prerequisite for obtaining legal permission to wiretap your telephone. Wiretapping is supposed to be a method of last resort, justified only when normal searches and investigatory techniques would fail or would be too dangerous. Once probable cause is established by use of phone company records and other circumstantial evidence, however, many judges are ready to assume that most criminals, including marijuana offenders, are dangerous enough to justify a wiretap.

It is nearly impossible to prove that someone illegally wiretapped a phone

There is no way of knowing how often the police illegally wiretap phones. If the police ever search your home or arrest you on the basis of "reliable" information from an "unnamed informant," you can never be certain that the police did not simply wiretap your telephone. If you are ever arrested and suspect that your phone has been wiretapped, you will have the burden of convincing a judge that the police may have tapped your phone. Only if the judge believes you, will he order the prosecutor to examine the official wiretapping records for evidence of a tap on your phone. In the unlikely chance that such records exist, you must then prove that the wiretap was illegal so that the judge will suppress the evidence. Even if the wiretapping evidence is excluded from court, however, the prosecutor may still be able to prosecute you by showing that the police discovered sufficient evidence to convict you independently of the illegal wiretap.

If wiretapping records do not exist, it may be impossible to determine whether the police, a private detective, or your imagination is responsible for the unusual noises in your phone. For the police to wiretap your phone, they only have to tell the telephone company, with whom they always have a good relationship, to connect your line with the police wiretapping office. The telephone company claims that they make this connection only if there is a warrant.

Aside from telephone operators, private persons can no longer legally monitor your phone conversations. To discover an illegal wiretap and to determine who initiated it, however, is very difficult. Nevertheless, if you can prove that someone has illegally wiretapped your phone, you can sue them.

The police can legally place eavesdropping bugs in your home whether or not you have a telephone

Some people have simply resolved never to speak about marijuana on the telephone. Unfortunately, the police can record your private conversations in your home whether or not you use a telephone. Once the police get a warrant to record your private conversations, it is just as legal for them to bug your home as to wiretap your phone. A "bug" is an eavesdropping microphone that intercepts all oral communications within a confined area, such as a room or a car. What this legal rule means is that if the police want to search your home in addition to recording your every conversation, they obtain a wiretapping warrant. With such a warrant they can decide whether or not to break into your home to plant a "bug" rather than to tap your phone without entry into your home.

The U.S. Supreme Court approves the FBI bugger technique

The U.S. Supreme Court recently approved this bugging practice in a case where FBI agents broke into Lawrence Dolar's office late one night. They had received an authorization for a wiretap, but not for a secret entry. Yet for three hours, the FBI agents inspected Dolar's office until they finally decided to hide the bug in the ceiling. The agents never officially reported anything they discovered during this search because they were not supposed to be searching, just planting the bug. Three weeks later they broke into Dolar's office again, without a special search warrant, this time to remove the bug. The majority of the Supreme Court Justices believed that the police can be trusted to break into your home to plant a microphone only when a wiretap is impractical. They showed no concern that the buggers might unlawfully search your home in the process and did not appear to believe that requiring a judge at least to consider whether there was a need for the police to enter homes secretly would help to protect your privacy.[15]

And now, after preparing you for the worst, here is a reminder that it's not always this bad—some state court judges take a more enlightened view of the Constitution and laws that protect our freedom and privacy.

THE BEST YOU CAN EXPECT FROM A JUDGE

· In some states, judges will condemn all dirty tricks, including staged setups and the use of good friends as secret agents to entrap you.

· A handful of judges, most particularly in California, will condemn the secret recording, without a warrant, of your conversations in any situation.

· Many state courts will condemn the use of electronic equipment to record your conversation without a warrant.

· High courts in a few states condemn the warrantless installation of a pen register on your phone.

· Some state courts will require the police to make an extremely convincing showing that they have no alternative but to wiretap your phone.

· The judges in a few states do not allow the police to break into your home to plant a bug without special authorization in addition to the wiretapping approval.

CHAPTER 5

Search Warrants, Informers, and the Fourth Amendment

The warrant's for yourself: take heed to't.

William Shakespeare
MEASURE FOR MEASURE, Act V, Scene I

If you have never been particularly interested in learning how the police obtain and execute a search warrant, perhaps this introduction can spark your interest. This chapter is one of the most theoretical in the book, but take heart, it's also one of the shortest. Moreover, the material set out here can be important. Once you know what kind of information the police and their informers need to obtain a valid search warrant, you will better understand how to protect yourself and will be in a better position to understand the specific legal loopholes that the police use to justify the warrantless searches which are discussed in Chapters 6 through 10. Again, in this chapter you will see how judges reduce the Fourth Amendment to a quagmire of loopholes, making it extremely difficult for the average citizen to safeguard her privacy. After comparing the literal language of the Fourth Amendment, phrase by phrase, with the courts' interpretation of these same words, perhaps you will agree that judges have allowed their personal politics to lead them to some bizarre results.

While reading this material, you should keep in mind an important rule that transcends all others. If the police ever do confront you with a search warrant, you have no choice but to cooperate, unless you are enthusiastic about being charged with the crime of "obstructing justice" and being handcuffed to the nearest telephone pole. But what if you are certain that the police have not followed the proper procedures in getting the warrant in the first place? Even so, you must cooperate. You cannot determine whether the police followed the Fourth Amendment requirements when obtaining a search warrant for you, your home, or your car until after the police have conducted the search. Only then can your lawyer, the prosecutor, and the judge review the warrant. Until a judge decides otherwise, it is presumed that a search warrant is valid.

THUMBNAIL REVIEW
What the Police Can Do "Legally"

· The police can and commonly do avoid the hassle of obtaining a search warrant by using one of the many legal loopholes that justify warrantless searches (see Chapters 6 through 10).

· To obtain a search warrant, the police must show that there is "probable cause" that a crime has been committed and that evidence of that crime is in the particular place to be searched. Theoretically, probable cause must be based on *facts* that would convince a reasonable person that a crime probably has been committed or that there was evidence of a crime in a designated place. Unfortunately, however, judges are lax in their determination of what constitutes "probable cause" and often issue warrants based upon unsupported conclusions or irrelevant details.

· The police can meet the requirements for a search warrant by relying on informers' statements without having to document their truth.

· The police can meet the requirement that a search warrant must name the particular items to be searched for by using the general description of "any narcotic drug anywhere on the suspect's premises."

· The police can execute the search warrant at any time of day, and often at any time of night. They can even break down your door in some instances, supposedly to guard against the potential destruction of evidence (such as marijuana) or the chance that you will use violence.

What You Can Do to Protect Yourself

· You can avoid giving informers or the police any reason to suspect you of drug-related activities.

· You should not resist a search, but you should never consent to a warrant-less search (see Chapter 6).

· You should see a lawyer after the police search you, your home, or your car to see if you have grounds to challenge the legality of the warrant (see Chapter 13).

WARRANTS AND THE FOURTH AMENDMENT

As you know, some people believe that the Fourth Amendment of the United States Constitution is fundamental to the concept of a free society. In this spirit, try reading it again:

> The right of the people to be secure in their persons, houses, papers, and effects, against unreasonable searches and seizures, shall not be violated, and no Warrants shall issue, but upon probable cause, supported by Oath or affirmation, and particularly describing the place to be searched, and the persons or things to be seized.

As discussed in Chapter 2, the U.S. Supreme Court has interpreted the Fourth Amendment to mean that warrants are required *only* for searches that would be "unreasonable" if done without a warrant. Since the judges think that a great many searches are reasonable without search warrants, the police do not have to obtain a search warrant in many situations, and usually do not bother. Though statistics are difficult to find, it is clear that the police obtain more search warrants today than they once did. In 1966, for example, the San Francisco Police Department obtained only seventeen search warrants, even though in the same year 29,000 serious crimes were reported.[1] In the early 1970s, the police used search warrants in approximately 10 percent of their drug-related searches and seizures.[2] Today, police departments may obtain search warrants for 20 percent or even 30 percent of their searches. Still, even today, police most often find it easier to use legal loopholes to justify their searches than to obtain warrants.

As to the requirements of warrants, themselves, a careful reading of the Fourth Amendment should convince you that in order to protect all Americans from the tendency of governments to become totalitarian, the authors of the Bill of Rights intended that search warrants be issued only on a finding of probable cause. The words clearly state that a finding of probable cause must be based on sworn testimony ("Oath or affirmation"), and that each warrant describe "particularly" or specifically "the place to be searched, and the persons or things to be seized." Yet the Fourth Amendment is not interpreted to carry out its clear meaning. By a logic that is so convoluted that it hardly qualifies to be characterized as such, the U.S. Supreme Court has managed to relax the requirements of the Fourth Amendment sufficiently to allow the police to conduct searches and seizures pretty much as they please. Thus today the Fourth Amendment no longer protects what the founders of our republic stated to be our inherent freedoms, but instead it has been twisted into a shield for police snooping.

WHAT THE POLICE MUST PROVE TO OBTAIN A SEARCH WARRANT

Assuming that the police have sufficient information to meet the search warrant requirements of the Fourth Amendment (as interpreted by judges), it is still something of a hassle for them to obtain a warrant. First they must write out, in the form of an affidavit, all of the facts which justify their request to search. Then they must write out the search warrant itself. In the warrant they are required to explain whom, what, and where they want to search, and what they expect to find. Finally they must take the affidavit and warrant to a magistrate or judge for approval. Not only do many police officers dislike such paper work, but they also do not like to ask a judge for permission to search, especially if they have to awaken his honor in the middle of the night to do so. Many police honestly feel that asking them to explain themselves in writing before they search is nothing less than shouting at them: "We don't trust you." They lose sight of the fact that the American revolutionaries enacted the Fourth Amendment not because they distrusted any particular police officer, but because they did not trust every police officer's employer—the State—to respect the individual's right to freedom and privacy.

The drafters of the Fourth Amendment intended that either a magistrate or a judge should determine whether or not a search warrant complies with the Fourth Amendment. This procedure is supposed to allow an objective and dispassionate third person to review a police officer's conclusions. It is thought to be necessary because an officer is too likely to be caught up in the excitement of the chase. While sound in theory, the system has fallen far short of expectations. An overriding problem is that many magistrates identify with the police and are often no more objective or dispassionate about enforcing the Fourth Amendment than are the most exuberant police officers.

Even though some magistrates may not prevent an illegal search of your home, the requirement that there be a search warrant is still advantageous. The exclusionary rule should protect you from being convicted with evidence that was discovered with an invalid search warrant (see Chapter 2). Thus, because the formal search warrant requirements are backed by the exclusionary rule, your constitutional right to be free from warrantless and unreasonable searches is more likely to be protected than if no warrant were required.

Because of the hassles involved in obtaining a search warrant, most police take full advantage of the legal loopholes that justify searching without one. These exceptions include:

• *Consent searches.* Subtle and not so subtle intimidation and even trickery are used to persuade you to consent to warrantless searches (see Chapter 6).

• *Searches accompanying an arrest.* If the police arrest you, they can also legally search the area around you without a warrant (see Chapter 7).

• *Car searches.* The Fourth Amendment warrant requirement almost never applies when the police stop and search your car on the street (see Chapter 8).

• *Emergency searches.* Judges will also waive the warrant requirements if the police can convince them that there was an emergency or that they thought they were in danger (see Chapter 7). As you will see, some judges are often lax in requiring that the police back up claims of an "emergency" or an "imagined danger."

The more professional police departments, however, are obtaining search warrants more frequently. There are several reasons for this change. If a warrant is issued, judges presume, and usually conclude, that the warrant is valid. And conversely, in some states, such as California and New York, judges have become stricter about excluding evidence from trial when the police did not have a warrant. Also, many large city police departments, as well as the FBI, DEA and IRS, now employ lawyers to handle the entire procedure of obtaining search warrants, thus removing the burden of paper work from enforcement personnel. A final and perhaps most important reason for the trend toward the greater use of warrants is that the judges of the U.S. Supreme Court have so relaxed the Fourth Amendment requirements for obtaining warrants that, in many situations, getting one is pretty much a formality.

The Concept of Probable Cause

Informers can supply necessary cause for warrants

The first clause in the Fourth Amendment requires that in order for a search warrant to be issued, the police must show probable cause. In legal lingo, probable cause means that there are sufficient facts to convince a reasonable person that contraband (or other evidence of a crime) can "probably" be found in a certain place. Suspicion or rumors that you cultivate or possess marijuana are not sufficient to establish probable cause. Theoretically, someone must personally see you growing or carrying marijuana, or hear you say that you have marijuana or are growing it, for probable cause to be established.

Logically, the facts demonstrating probable cause must be true for probable cause really to exist. But judges do not accept this logic and therefore do not require that the police prove that the information is true before issuing a warrant. Instead, they require only that the police show that their information establishing probable cause is reliable. Well, okay so far, but what kind of information do the judges consider reliable? Unfortunately, this step is where the system breaks down. For example, they often consider information from convicted criminals given to the police in return for money or reduced charges or sentences to be reliable. They make this assumption even though the informers have an obvious conflict of interest and often a strong incentive to lie.

In parts of the country where many people keep some marijuana in the house, an informer can take a wild guess that someone has some marijuana and often be correct. There are no foolproof safeguards to prevent the informer from saying he saw marijuana when in fact he only heard rumors, had vague suspicions, or simply

wanted to get someone. In fact, the U.S. Supreme Court has decided in several cases that an informer does not even have to relate facts directly connecting the accused person with marijuana for a judge to issue a warrant. All the informer needs to know are enough details to make it appear that he knows what he is talking about. For instance, a detailed description of the interior of your house may be enough to support the assertion that the informer knows there is marijuana there. The U.S. Supreme Court established this precedent in a case where probable cause for an arrest warrant was established by an affidavit describing the clothes and the "real fast walk" of James Dickens, who was expected to arrive in Denver, Colorado, on a particular train, carrying drugs.[3] Of course, getting off a train and "walking real fast" does not give anyone probable cause to believe that Dickens was a drug runner, but nevertheless, the Supreme Court approved the warrant because the informer gave an accurate description of innocent details. The reasoning in this case has gone a long way towards elevating vague suspicion and rumor to the equivalent of "probable cause."

> NOTE: Several state supreme courts have established stricter requirements for obtaining a warrant—that is, they require a more detailed showing of probable cause. So if you are ever a victim of a search, don't presume it's legal until the judges in your state rule on the matter.

If the police have facts that give them probable cause to believe that you have marijuana on a given day, however, these same facts will not necessarily support the same conclusion a month later, or even the next day. Some facts change faster than others. For instance, New Jersey judges decided that there was still probable cause to believe that the Burgers had marijuana eighteen days after the police observed them packaging large quantities of " 'green vegetable matter' into small plastic bags," and observed "heavy visitor traffic" at their house.[4] The Maine Supreme Court, however, found that a delay of thirty-one days was too long for there to be probable cause to believe that Malcolm Warren still had marijuana "in light of the nature of marijuana as a substance which can be easily concealed and moved about."[5]

The story of an imaginative informer

In a rural area of New Mexico, the sheriff suspected many people (especially younger ones living outside of town in the hills) of growing marijuana. The sheriff sent out Stan, a paid informer, to gather information. So far, Tom, a local hill dweller who grows a little marijuana, had been smart enough to avoid the informers, and his signs and fences discouraged them from dropping by to introduce themselves. Finally, Stan gave up trying to catch Tom redhanded and went to the county sheriff's station and falsely stated that "several people have told me that Tom grows marijuana in his greenhouse and always has some in his house. I haven't gone to his home yet because there are fences and 'keep out' signs around it and he has a dog the size of a small elephant—but he must grow dope since he only works part-time and, yet, has bought land, building materials, and a four-wheel-drive truck. I've also seen Tom smoke marijuana."

A sheriff's officer wrote this information in an affidavit, affirmed that Stan was reliable, and then requested a search warrant authorizing the search of Tom's home, sheds, greenhouse, and truck for marijuana.

> *Question:* Would a conscientious judge issue a search warrant based on this affidavit?
>
> *Answer:* No. A conscientious judge would not issue a warrant based on these rumors and vague suspicions, but not every judge is conscientious.

Furthermore, if Stan had said that he personally knew that Tom had marijuana in his home and his greenhouse and then described the interior of Tom's home, many judges, relying on past Supreme Court cases, would approve of a search warrant based on this type of evidence, even though it is all too easily fabricated. (Note: As this story indicates, greenhouses may not completely protect your privacy.)

Probable cause must be based on "Oath or Affirmation"

The next phrase in the Fourth Amendment requires that the particular facts necessary to establish probable cause must be established by *oath or affirmation*. This requirement was designed to make certain that law enforcement officers or informers are telling the truth before a judge issues a search warrant. Obviously, if the person who sets out the facts that lead to the issuance of a warrant is lying, the whole process is meaningless. Unfortunately, judges don't seem to understand this fact and have allowed many statements of doubtful reliability to satisfy this requirement, including rumors and secondhand information. Some judges commonly find that the oath or affirmation requirement of the Fourth Amendment is satisfied so long as the officer or informer swears in court or in an affidavit that her statements are true, without any additional requirement that there be some reason to believe that the information given is factual. And frequently an informer will tell the police "particular facts" and the officer will then swear in court or in an affidavit that he is truthfully relating what the informer told him. The officer cannot, and is not required to, swear to the truth of the information received. Instead, she is only required to show that the informer is normally "reliable" for her statements to be accepted by a judge. Reliability need not be shown if the informer is a police officer, however, since police are presumed to be honest. Finally, the reliability of most marijuana informers is established if the informer has previously supplied the police with "good" information.

> NOTE: It's important to remember that many judges are conscientious and do attempt to protect the privacy of the people who come before them, just as many police officers will not resort to tricks or lies to fabricate a reason to conduct a search. Unfortunately, however, when it comes to "criminal" conduct such as using marijuana, you can't sensibly trust the police or the judges to respect your rights. Therefore, self-protection is absolutely mandatory.

A case of a real smelling sleuth

United States Drug Enforcement agents obtained a warrant based on information supplied by a San Diego train station employee who said that he smelled "what he believed to be the aroma of marijuana emanating from [Bobby Pelzel's] luggage." The judges decided that the informer was reliable because he had previously discovered nearly a ton of marijuana in the same manner, and so was undoubtedly "an experienced smeller of marijuana, with a proven ability to detect that odor even through the walls of suitcases." Even though the seventy-seven pounds of marijuana was wrapped "in red paper, covered with plastic and placed in garbage bags covered with talcum powder," and even though the informer had been wrong in about fifteen out of thirty cases, the judges said: "It cannot be disputed that marijuana has a distinctive pungent odor."[6] Who can argue with that logic?

It bears repeating that judges routinely consider informers to be reliable even though they have been accused or convicted of crimes and have been promised money or a greatly reduced sentence in return for information leading to the conviction of others. Judges seem to believe that convicting people of marijuana crimes justifies the use of information provided by people with obvious conflicts of interest. In some circumstances, even if your lawyer can prove to the judge that an informer lied, a search warrant issued on the basis of those lies may still be found to be valid if your lawyer cannot show that the police should have known of the lies.

Often the problem is even more difficult than proving that a known informer lied. For instance, no matter how expert your lawyer is, she will have an impossible time trying to show that the police should have known about the lies of an unidentified informer. And because in so many situations the police need not divulge the informer's identity, there are even cases where they have invented phantom informers. Obviously this extreme type of deception makes it unlikely that your lawyer can prove that an informer lied, and lawyers are then forced to try to convince the judge that the police lied about there even being an informer. And if this possibility doesn't give the police enough leeway, there is an additional rule that says that even if your lawyer can convince the judge that the police lied, the search warrant may still be valid if there was enough true information in the affidavit and search warrant to establish probable cause. Naturally, this loophole gives little incentive to the police to be honest.

> **NOTE ON POLICE SETUPS**: It is certainly true that the police have occasionally planted marijuana on innocent people, but this trick is probably not common. As society's attitude toward marijuana use mellows out, police are making marijuana arrests less of a priority. According to several police officers, they have heard of the police planting marijuana only in situations where growers or dealers were flaunting their status and the police had found it impossible to catch them using legal methods. The real tragedy is that the law is loose enough to allow the police and their informers to set you up.

Search Warrants Must Specifically Describe the Place to be Searched and the Persons or Things to be Seized

The third phrase in the second clause of the Fourth Amendment requires that the search warrant particularly describe "the place to be searched, and the persons or things to be seized." Unfortunately, judicial decisions have rendered this requirement almost meaningless with respect to marijuana and other illegal drugs. Judges have ruled that the search warrant need not specify whether your marijuana is hanging from the rafters or packed in bags or buried under the floor. In one instance, the warrant that authorized the search of Francis Levine's Colorado home did not even specify marijuana. The undercover officer said that he had observed cocaine, hashish, and LSD in the house; and the magistrate issued the warrant for "any and all narcotics or dangerous drugs."[7] When the police conducted their search, they found only marijuana, which suggests that this warrant was based solely on vague rumors and that it did not "particularly" describe the "things to be seized" with any accuracy. The Colorado Supreme Court ruled otherwise, however, and Levine was convicted.

Similarly, judges have ruled that the place to be searched need only be set out with enough specificity to enable the police to find the right house, so as to prevent them from conducting neighborhood searches. Judges have even ruled that it is not necessary for the warrant to specify a particular room in a house or even to distinguish between the house, garage, or shed. One court, for example, approved a search of a house and yard for marijuana when the search warrant specified the residence by street number only.[8] Some judges do require the description of the premises to be a little more specific, but the important thing to know is that you can't count on it.

The Police Are Supposed to Execute a Search Warrant in a "Reasonable" Manner

The law in many states requires that the police use the search warrant within approximately ten days after the magistrate has issued it. In almost half of the states, the law also requires that the police begin the search during the day, which under federal law means between the hours of 7:00 AM and 10:00 PM unless there is good reason for a nighttime intrusion. In fourteen states, however, the law allows the police with a warrant to break into your home in the dead of night without good cause simply to make sure that you do not destroy your marijuana. In the other states, the law is unclear.[9]

Before entering your home forcibly, the police are supposed to "knock and announce" the fact that they have a warrant and want to enter. In circumstances that suggest possible trouble or an emergency, however, the police are allowed to break in without knocking (see Chapter 7) or to knock and pretend that they are a friend or next-door neighbor.

The Los Angeles police one-up Hollywood

To gain entrance into a home protected by a locked iron gate, the Los Angeles police in one case, staged an elaborate play. Before going to Michael Tulcin's home, the police set off firecrackers to simulate gunfire. Then the police knocked on Tulcin's gate. When he answered it, they asked him to step outside to check his parked car for possible damage from the "gunfire." When he opened the gate, the police grabbed it, announced that they had a search warrant and ran into his home.[10]

Another true Los Angeles police story

Sometimes the police want to get you to take contraband out of your house. The police can use this trick, for example, when they don't have a search warrant and don't want to bother getting one. After the police hid themselves outside the homes of Lorrie Rodriguez and Ignacio Garber, for instance, an officer called the suspected drug dealers, claiming to be a friend. He said: "The police are coming; get rid of the stuff." When Rodriguez and Garber ran from their homes carrying paper bags, the police surprised them. Flustered, they threw their bags of drugs on the ground. The police picked up the evidence and arrested them. Thus there was no need to bother with a search warrant.[11]

EXAMPLE: The Story of Sasha and Rose

The police searched Sasha and Rose's home with a search warrant at nine o'clock one evening. A "reliable" informer had described the interior of the home and had told the police that he knew that there were marijuana plants there. The search warrant authorized the police to search for marijuana *and* all other narcotic drugs. After knocking and announcing that they had a search warrant, the police immediately used a pass key to unlock the door. Thus they entered the home without giving Sasha or Rose time to open the door.

> *Question:* Is the nighttime execution of the search warrant legal?
> *Answer:* Yes, even in those states that require "good cause" for a nighttime search, nine o'clock in the evening is *not* considered to be the nighttime.
> *Question:* Is the general description in the search warrant authorizing the seizure of "all other narcotic drugs" valid?
> *Answer:* Probably yes, even though the informer did not mention the possibility of other drugs. Somehow, the judges consider alleged marijuana users to be regular drug addicts.
> *Question:* Is the quick police entry legal?
> *Answer:* Probably yes. If the police testify to hearing noises that suggested that Sasha or Rose might be trying to destroy evidence, a judge would probably approve the fast entry.

What You Can Do to Protect Yourself From a Search With an Illegal Warrant

Because of the general looseness of search warrant requirements, and because informers and even the police can easily stretch the truth or lie to obtain a warrant, the fact that a search warrant has been issued doesn't afford you a lot of protection. At the time that the police show up with a search warrant, there is clearly nothing you can do but allow them to search, after verbally *making it clear that you are complying with the warrant and not independently consenting to the search.* Never try to physically resist or impede the search. After the search is carried out you should see a lawyer. Even though the warrant is presumed to be valid, a lawyer experienced in the field may find some significant defect in the way it was issued or with some other aspect of the search. Therefore, to repeat, it is critical that you consult an expert lawyer who specializes in criminal law if the police search your property with a search warrant and arrest you. If you cannot afford such a lawyer, then consult a public defender or court-appointed counsel—most of whom are competent to advise you (see Chapter 13).

And now, after preparing you for the worst, here is a reminder that it's not always this bad—some judges take a more enlightened view of the Constitution and laws that protect our freedom and privacy.

THE BEST YOU CAN EXPECT FROM A JUDGE

• Some judges are more skeptical than others about police stories that try to justify warrantless searches.

• Some judges are more strict than others about what kind of facts constitute probable cause.

• Some judges are more suspicious than others about the reliability of informers, particularly unnamed informers.

• Some judges are more solicitous than others about the required "particularity" of a search warrant.

• Some judges are more stubborn than others about requiring the police to execute search warrants during the day and only after knocking at your door.

CHAPTER 6

Warrantless Consent Searches: Learn to Say No

You consenting to't,
Would bark your honour from that trunk you bear,
And leave you naked.

William Shakespeare
MEASURE FOR MEASURE, Act III, Scene I

Americans have a tradition of hospitality. In the old days, doors were rarely locked, and even now, when most Americans have learned to be a bit more cautious, we still welcome all sorts of people into our homes. Even when a law enforcement officer or other public employee appears at our doorstep, your first thought may be to invite them in, or at least to stand aside if they invite themselves in. When you act hospitably, however, you may be voluntarily giving up your Fourth Amendment rights.

It would be quite silly to invite a police officer into the kitchen when there was a joint in the ashtray, wouldn't it? But that hasn't stopped thousands of people from doing it. Remember that though one pig built his house of brick and actually kept the big bad wolf out, there were two who trusted to vague hopes and half measures, and became supper.

Outlined in this chapter are three essential rules to remember in order to avoid giving your consent to warrantless searches. First, you must know your rights. With a little attention to the next few pages, that hurdle should be easily leaped. Second, you must not hesitate to assert your rights, even if it requires you to be inhospitable and impolite. And third, you must be ready to spot police tricks aimed at getting you to give your consent without realizing it. As you will see, the police have developed a number of devious schemes to trick you into "consenting" to searches. You may even be shocked by seeing the police turn citizens' ignorance, indecision or fear about exercising their right to object to warrantless searches into a "free and voluntary consent." It's not always a pretty picture.

THUMBNAIL REVIEW
What the Police Can Do "Legally"

· The police can legally ask you to consent to a search of your self or your property without telling you of your right to refuse.

· In many situations, the police can legally act as if they have your tacit consent and simply walk past you into your home if you make no move to stop them.

· Sometimes, the police can legally ask you to consent to a search even though their request is little more than a thinly-veiled threat.

· In some circumstances the police can legally secure your consent after pointing a gun at you and illegally arresting and handcuffing you.

· Oftentimes, the police can legally get your consent to a search by saying that they will obtain a search warrant if you refuse consent, when in fact they have no legal grounds to get a search warrant. In other words, they can legally lie to you.

· The police can continue to ask you to consent after you refuse.

· The police can try to persuade you to sign a written consent form so that it will be easy for them to prove your voluntary consent.

· The police can search your car or home if they get the consent of certain members of your family, friends, or housemates. (Consent cannot be legally given by your landlord, landlady, or next-door neighbor unless it appears that you have abandoned the house.)

What You Can Do to Protect Yourself

· Refuse to consent to all requests from law enforcement officials to enter your home or land, or to search you, your vehicle, or your personal property, unless they produce a search warrant. If you voluntarily consent, any police search is automatically legal.

· If the police try to invite themselves onto your land or into your home, invite them out again—politely but firmly.

· Continue to refuse to consent to warrantless searches, regardless of how many times they ask.

• Tell any of your friends who are on or about your property or who use your car to refuse to consent to a warrantless search.

• Even if the police scare you, do not consent.

• Even if the police threaten you with arrest, refuse consent.

• Even if the police ask to search your home, land, or property when there is no marijuana present, refuse consent. But never physically resist the police, whether or not they have a search warrant.

• *BUT,* if the police find a couple of joints and promise not to arrest you in exchange for the right to search, and if you have no more marijuana or you think that you can trust them, you may want to consent to the search.

NOTE: If the police physically harm you or threaten to hurt you, consent. Nearly all judges will realize that your "consent" was involuntary under these circumstances (if you can prove them). And, of course, your physical safety is also an important consideration.

SEARCHES: YOUR CONSTITUTIONAL RIGHTS

Assert your right to be free from warrantless and unreasonable searches

Even if you have nothing to hide, it is important for you to assert your constitutional right to be free from warrantless searches. Unless you become accustomed to asserting your rights when you have nothing to fear, it will be more difficult for you to stand up for your rights when you do have a stash. Furthermore, why should you allow the police to invade your privacy without requiring them to follow the Constitution? It is a matter of basic common sense that if you allow officers of the State (whether they happen to serve King George, the FBI, or the local sanitation district) to do as they please, they will, and in so doing will become a greater threat to your constitutional rights. When you have nothing to fear you have an ideal opportunity to stand up for your rights. Even if your stubbornness annoys the police and they search your property anyway, there is nothing to find, hence, nothing to lose.

More practically, it is always wise to be on the safe side, as you always run the risk that the police will find a little marijuana that you had lost under the seat of the car or had forgotten under your bed. And, once the police begin to search, the sad truth is that it is not unheard of for them to "lose" and find their own marijuana in your house. So why take the risk?

IMPORTANT: The material in this chapter is some of the most important in this book. Why? The police encourage consensual searches, knowing that the easiest way to get around the Fourth Amendment is to convince you to consent "voluntarily" to a search. In fact, the police are so good at this ploy, that a great many searches resulting in conviction are by consent, not search warrant.

You may say now that you would never consent to a police search without a warrant, but it is amazing how many people have consented, at least according to the police and the judges. Unfortunately what you think of as consent and what the judges have decided is consent, are likely to be different—very different.

If you are ever arrested, the determination of whether you consented to a search is decided before trial at a "suppression hearing" (as are other challenges to a search). A judge will hear evidence as to how the police conducted the search, and if he finds that the police search of your home, car, or personal effects was illegal, he should "suppress" any evidence the search uncovered. Or, to put it another way, evidence discovered as part of an illegal search can't be used against you.

If the police made their search after obtaining a search warrant, then you or your lawyer must prove that the warrant was invalid or was served improperly (see Chapter 5). In contrast, if the police searched without a warrant, then the prosecutor must, in legal lingo, *carry his burden of proof* to convince the judge that the police had reason to use one of the legal loopholes explained in Chapters 7 through 10, or that you freely and voluntarily consented. How does the judge decide whether or not you freely and voluntarily consented to the search? He simply listens to the police officer's story, to your story, and to any other witnesses. Commonly, a citizen will claim that he did not consent or was pressured into giving consent, while the police will claim that consent was voluntarily given. Guess who the judges are more likely to believe? While differences in opinion as to whether consent was voluntary may frequently be honest, all too often the police simply invent your "consent" to cover their own sloppy or impetuous warrantless searches. Therefore, it is important for you to make it perfectly clear to the police that you are asserting your right to refuse to consent to warrantless and unreasonable searches. Of course, it is always helpful to have witnesses whenever possible.

POWERS OF THE POLICE

The police can obtain your consent to a warrantless search without informing you of your rights

The police may legally ask you to consent to a search without telling you that you have the right to say no. Supposedly, the fact that the police ask for your consent implicitly tells you that you have a right to refuse. Unfortunately, this legal logic has little relation to reality. The police, after all, are authority figures, and for many people their requests are commands.

For example, the police may come to your home or stop your car as part of an investigation. If you are like most people, your first reaction will be to cooperate with their requests, or at least to play it cool to avoid provoking them. But the police know this and they can play it cool, too. They may well engage you in small talk until eventually they ask: "Do you mind if we look around a little?" acting as if it were a routine check. To this request, many persons are afraid to say no. They think that a refusal may be taken to indicate guilt or may put them in some other form of jeopardy. So they say okay, hoping that the friendly officers won't search thoroughly enough to find any illegal materials.

> IMPORTANT: A police request to search your person, home, car, or land is not an order. The Fourth Amendment of the United States Constitution implicitly gives you the right to refuse. It is neither illegal nor impolite to say no—it is usually wise.

The "I have no choice, do I?" situation

When the Oregon police pulled over Vernon Holmes and asked him for permission to search his car, he assumed that he had no choice but to agree. The judge's opinion described the scene in this way:

> [Holmes] testified that he replied to the first [police] request to search the car by saying, Would it do any good to say 'no?' and when asked a second time he replied, "Well, if I say no, won't you just take me down to the station and do it there?" Again, the officer asked, 'Do I have your permission to search the car?' and [Holmes] testified he said, 'I guess so.'

A police officer testified that Holmes had immediately given the police permission to search. If Holmes had known of his right to say no, he might not have been convicted of possession of marijuana and sentenced to three years imprisonment.[1]

The police can obtain your "voluntary" consent to a warrantless search through intimidation

You probably assume that it is illegal for the police to scare you into consenting to a search without a warrant. After all, what good is it for you to have a right to be protected from unreasonable searches in theory if in practice you are afraid to exercise it? Unfortunately, there has been much abuse in this area and the truth is that the police commonly do or say things that make citizens go along with a search because they are afraid to refuse consent.

Does this state of affairs mean that the police can legally beat you or otherwise physically force you to go along with a search? No, absolutely not. Unfortunately, it does mean that judges have found consent to be voluntary when lesser, but still serious, types of intimidation have occurred. In some cases, the fact that the police have pointed a gun at a person's face, questioned him for an hour, handcuffed him, or even illegally arrested him, has not been considered sufficient intimidation to prevent the judge from ruling that the person's consent to be searched was voluntary. To repeat: Intimidating conduct on the part of the police must normally be quite heavy-handed before you can be certain that all judges will decide that your consent was coerced and involuntary.

Gun barrel consent

Here is an extreme case that, while not typical, does illustrate how far some judges will go to find a voluntary consent to a search. After hearing a police bulletin over the radio, two Pennsylvania police cars pulled over Theodore Solomon and Paul Roderick. In the words of the judges: "The troopers then emerged from their patrol cars armed with a .30 caliber carbine and a .12 gauge pump shotgun, and instructed the occupants of the van to get out and 'spread-eagle' against the van." The judge later determined that the initial stop of the van and the shotgun arrest were illegal and that there was no probable cause to search the van. The police, however, had convinced Solomon and Roderick to sign a paper consenting to the police search of their van which was loaded with 225 pounds of marijuana. Despite the guns and the illegal arrests, the judge decided that the defendants' "hard-boiled bravado" showed that their written consent was voluntary. Therefore, the warrantless search was legal.[2]

Judges disagree about a woman's consent

Nica Dowinsky was more fortunate, apparently because she had not shown "hard-boiled bravado." Although the trial court judge convicted her for possession of marijuana after concluding that she had voluntarily consented to the Maryland police searching her suitcase, an appellate judge decided otherwise and reversed the conviction. Her story goes like this: Before she gave her "consent" to search, the police had illegally arrested and detained her for two hours without advising her of her constitutional rights or providing her with a lawyer. Moreover, they had "twice beaten" her male companion in her presence "for passively resisting arrest in connection with a minor charge" and roughly searched him.[3] Although many judges may find "consent" to be involuntary under similar circumstances, particularly if a woman is involved, some judges may not. Again, your only real protection is to refuse to consent to a search under any circumstances.

The police can legally use false pretenses to get you to consent to a warrantless search

Here is a particularly obnoxious form of legal intimidation. Many judges have decided that if you refuse to consent to a police search, the police can legally threaten to hold you while they try to obtain a search warrant. If you continue to refuse consent, they can, and probably will, carry out their threat to detain you. And not only is this sort of threat legal, but judges have ruled that it does not constitute intimidation even in a situation where the police have no legal grounds to obtain a search warrant. Think about it. This rule of law means that even if you consent to a search after the police illegally threaten to detain you, your consent may still be called voluntary.

From a legal standpoint, even if you are sure that the police will be able to get a warrant, it is better not to consent. Why? Even if a judge does authorize a warrant, your lawyer will be able to challenge its legality in court (see Chapter 13) and, if successful, the judge will suppress or exclude the evidence illegally seized under the authority of a defective search warrant. But if you consent to a search to avoid having the police detain you while they attempt to get a warrant, there is little or nothing your lawyer can do, except to try to show that the police forced you to consent involuntarily, which as you know isn't easy.

The police call Marshall's bluff

When the Florida police told Martin Marshall that they would obtain a search warrant if he refused to consent, Marshall brazenly responded, "Go ahead and search. I have nothing to hide." Marshall did have something to hide—somewhat more than five grams of marijuana. He was convicted and sentenced to five years probation. Marshall gave up his legal right to have his lawyer challenge the legality of a search warrant by consenting to the warrantless search. If Marshall had refused to consent, the police might have left him alone or illegally searched him. Either way, he might have avoided being convicted. If Marshall had refused consent, he could have been convicted only if the police had obtained a valid search warrant based on probable cause.[4]

Protecting Yourself From a Warrantless Search

Don't consent to even a limited warrantless search

It is extremely unwise to consent to any sort of search even if the police tell you that they only want to take a "quick look." This precaution remains true even though you have hidden something so well that the police would have difficulty finding it.

Some people seem to think that by refusing to consent to a search, they are admitting guilt. Not so. By refusing to consent to a warrantless search you are simply asserting your Fourth Amendment right to be free from unreasonable searches and seizures. It is true that refusing consent may make the police suspicious and it is even possible that they will go ahead and search anyway, but such a search without a warrant and without your consent will probably be illegal and the State cannot convict you with illegally seized evidence. To repeat, if you "voluntarily" consent, *any police search is automatically legal.* If you do not consent, you not only protect your rights, but practically speaking, you have a much better chance of avoiding a valid arrest for possession of marijuana.

A little "consent" is a dangerous thing

Louis Jung thought he could bluff the New Mexico police by consenting to a search limited to the trunk of his car. Since his marijuana was carefully packaged in foot-lockers in the trunk and in suitcases on the rack of his car, he thought that he was

safe. But after the police looked into the trunk, they asked him if they could look into the three locked footlockers. Jung replied that he would rather the officers didn't look, because the lockers did not belong to him. Thereupon, the officers told him that they smelled marijuana and said that he would be detained until they could obtain a search warrant. Though the police could probably have obtained a search warrant under these circumstances, Jung again foolishly consented, making the entire search of his car and footlockers legal.[5] Had Jung refused consent to any search from the very first request, chances are better that he would not have been convicted.

> **WARNING:**   Even if you have hidden your personal belongings in a place where the police do not ask to search, it is still unwise to consent to a search. If you don't follow this advice and do consent to a search of any part of your house, car, or land, it is possible that your consent will be interpreted—or misinterpreted—as applying to other areas. For example, your consent to a search of one room in your house may be interpreted to allow the search of the entire house, or your consent to a search of the land just behind your barn may be interpreted to mean two miles behind the barn. In doubtful situations, the police like to obtain your consent in writing, but this is not a requirement. An oral consent is valid.

EXAMPLE: The "What Are You Trying to Hide" Con

Here is a little story that unfortunately has occurred time and time again.

"Are you Susan and Stephanie? We'd like to look around."

"What's the matter, officer?"

"Nothing's wrong. We just want to look around. That's okay, isn't it?"

"What are you looking for?"

"You've been arrested before, haven't you?"

"Yes, but we've finished our drug education program and we're off probation."

"Listen, we don't want any trouble. We're just doing our job. You don't have anything to hide, do you? We only want your permission to check out your place."

"Is this legal, officer? What if we don't give you permission?"

"If you don't let us look around now, we'll just go and get a search warrant. It'll go worse on you then."

"We don't have a choice, do we?"

"You have a choice—of being cooperative or not. Either we check out your place now or later. So far, you act like you have something to hide. Now, don't get me wrong. I'm not accusing you of anything. Sign this paper and we'll just forget about your reluctance to cooperate."

"We have to sign something?"

"Just a formality. This form says that you give your voluntary consent to a search of your home."

"But we're not guilty of anything. Go ahead and look for yourself."

"Here, sign this."

The police conducted their search and found an ounce and a half of marijuana in the bread box. They arrested both women.

Question: Would the warrantless search of Susan and Stephanie's home be legal if they both signed the consent form?

Answer: You bet.

Question: Would it be legal if only one of them signed?

Answer: One signature is more than enough.

Question: Would the search be legal if both Susan and Stephanie refused to sign the consent form?

Answer: Probably yes, since one of the women verbally consented.

Question: Would the police have been able to conduct a legal search if both women refused?

Answer: No, not without a warrant, which they probably couldn't get.

A happier outcome was possible in eleven states

If Stephanie and Susan had lived in one of the eleven states that assess only a fine for the crime of possessing less than an ounce or so of marijuana (see Appendix), then some police officers may have treated them differently. The police officers could have simply given both Susan and Stephanie a ticket if they both were willing to claim ownership of half the marijuana, which would have been three-quarters of an ounce each. If you are quite certain that your state has a "one-ounce law" and you believe that you can trust the police officers who have just searched your home, then you might want to take the risk of admitting partial ownership. Sometimes it is easier to strike a fair deal with the police immediately in order to save yourself a court hassle. It is important to realize, however, that police officers in all states would have the choice of arresting both Susan and Stephanie for possession of the one and a half ounces of marijuana unless one of the women admitted sole ownership. But because a lawyer would have a good chance of getting both women a simple fine for possession of less than one ounce, it would be silly for either woman to claim sole ownership of the marijuana in order to protect the other. (See the "Silence is Golden" discussion in Chapter 11.)

> **NOTE:**   Suppose now that Susan and Stephanie signed the form or simply stood aside and allowed the search. Could they later claim that they had been "intimidated" into giving consent? Of course, and they should. Would the claim that they had been coerced succeed at a hearing to suppress evidence? It depends on several things, including whether or not the police honestly testified to what was said, the attitude of the particular judge hearing the case (judges have quite a bit of discretion in this type of case), and also the case law of the particular state where the case was heard. On balance, Susan and Stephanie would have an uphill battle and the odds would be against them.

Always assert your right to be free from warrantless searches

As this book has emphasized, the Bill of Rights—including the Fourth Amendment—was adopted to protect your freedom and privacy. Whenever the police confront you, simply act like the bona fide member of society that you are, and do not let them scare you. If the police tell you that they have a search warrant, politely ask to see it. But whether or not they show you the warrant, it is illegal and also dangerous for you to use force to try to keep them from "carrying out their duties." If the police insist, let them proceed as they will, reminding them that you are not voluntarily consenting to be searched. The law says that evidence seized under the authority of an invalid search warrant, or after the police claim to have a search warrant that doesn't exist, cannot be admitted against you at trial. You really have no other choice but to submit to police authority, since you will never know whether or not the warrant is valid until after you are arrested and the case goes to court. Even then, judges, prosecutors, and defense lawyers commonly disagree about the validity of particular search warrants. But remember, if you consent to a search *before* the police tell you that they have a search warrant, the State can convict you with any evidence the police find, even if the search warrant they had was invalid.

> **IMPORTANT:** If the police search your house over your objections, there is always the chance that they will later falsely claim that you consented. How do you deal with this prevarication? The best way is to have a witness. Never be shy about yelling for a neighbor or a housemate if you are feeling intimidated. If there are no witnesses around and you have time to think ahead, it is wise to lock the door and hide the key. If the police enter anyway, the fact that they had to break the lock to do so will be some evidence of your unwillingness to consent.

EXAMPLE: Harry—a Man Who Knew His Rights

Harry was driving home in his pickup from the Do Drop Inn late one Friday night when a police car with flashing lights pulled him over.

"Please get out of the truck," the police officer requested.

"What's the problem, officer?"

"You know the problem. You just left a bar and you weaved across the median strip. It looks to us like you're drunk."

Fortunately for Harry, and for everyone else on the road, he passed the preliminary drunkenness tests. He walked a straight line and stood on one foot without falling, and thus under state law he was neither too drunk nor too stoned to drive. (Different states and counties have quite different ways to test for drunkenness. Under the laws of most states, the police can administer breath, urine, and blood tests, but they often don't if the suspect passes the agility tests.)

"We'd like to let you go home, but we need to check your pickup for drugs and alcohol."

As Harry remained silent, one of the officers approached the truck.

"But I'm not drunk. You can't search my truck."

"You just said that it was okay when we asked if we could search your pickup."

"I did not. And you didn't ask me about consenting to a search. You told me you were going to search and I didn't say anything because I'm helpless to stop you from doing what you want."

"Why don't you want us to search your truck, hippy?" the other officer interjected. "Are you hiding drugs?"

"I may have long hair, but unless I'm badly mistaken, it is not something that disqualifies a person from being a United States citizen. I have constitutional rights and I expect you to respect them. You only want to search my truck because I have long hair."

The first officer flashed his flashlight through the truck, but didn't see anything. Then he looked in the glove compartment, supposedly for Harry's registration.

"What's in this locked iron box?" the other officer asked, tapping a box bolted to the frame of the pickup behind the window to the cab.

"My tools."

"Open it."

"No."

"Give me your keys."

"I don't have the keys for my tool box."

"Let's break it open."

"No, Jim. It's too much of a hassle. Next time, kid, drive on your own side of the road. Here's the ticket. You can pay it by mail."

Question: Did Harry voluntarily consent to a search before he spoke up?

Answer: Probably not, but a court decision would depend on further facts, which would probably be determined largely on the basis of police testimony. If the police lie, it would have a lot to do with the attitude of the judge.

Question: Would Harry have voluntarily consented to a search if he had opened his tool box when the officer said "Open it"?

Answer: Probably not if the police are honest. Harry could argue that he wasn't consenting, merely following orders. If the police had testified that they said "*Would* you open it?" instead of "Open it," however, it probably would not have mattered that Harry had earlier refused to consent to their search. Remember, it is legally possible to change your mind and stupidly give consent after you have first withheld it.

Question: If the police broke the lock, could they still have shown that Harry voluntarily consented?

Answer: Probably not. While it is human nature to shade the truth some, and police often do it to make themselves look good, they generally avoid blatant lies. And in this situation, it would be folly to lie, as any sensible judge would consider a broken lock strong evidence that Harry did not consent.

If the police promise you a good deal, you may want to consent

There is one circumstance that should give you pause to reconsider your promise to assert your right to be free from unconstitutional warrantless searches. This situation can *only* occur when you are caught with a small amount of marijuana and you don't have more in your possession. Some police officers remember being young and fancy-free at one time and do not arrest folks for a little marijuana, particularly if they act respectfully toward the officer. As marijuana use becomes less controversial, this attitude is more common. In many ways, it is similar to what many police officers have been doing for years with people who have had too much to drink. If the drunk looks respectable and isn't violent, they put him in a cab and send him home; but if the drunk is uncooperative and sasses the officer, it's into the drunk tank.

Thus if the police confiscate a few joints and promise not to arrest you if you consent to a search, and if you think that you can trust them and you have no more marijuana, then go ahead and consent. Obviously, you have nothing to lose by consenting and as you will see in the next chapters (7-10), once the police find marijuana, there are other ways to justify their warrantless searches, even if you do not consent.

Warn your friends not to consent to warrantless searches

It is in your interest to share the information in this chapter with your friends and family, particularly those persons who are staying in your house or who borrow your car. People who live in group or communal houses should be particularly careful. Why? Nearly anyone's consent to a search of your home or car will make the search legal if the police are reasonable in asking that person for permission. Because judges consider it reasonable for the police to ask most roommates, houseguests, and older children for permission to search your house, they will usually approve the warrantless search if permission is given. Unless your room is individually locked or clearly separate from the rest of the house, you have little protection against the foolish consent of a fellow householder.

Judges normally rule, however, that it is unreasonable for the police to ask your landlady, landlord, neighbor, or young child for permission, and will not approve searches based on this sort of consent. The police can ask virtually anyone driving your car for permission to search it. If your friends consent under such circumstances, the police search is legal and whatever the police find can be used to convict you as the owner of the house or car.

The story of Billie Joe and Elmer

The police in Independence, Missouri went to Elmer Tivnan's home at the request of the U.S. Secret Service, supposedly to question him about a counterfeiting operation. In the words of Judge Warren Jones of the federal court:

> The officers rang the doorbell and Billy Joe [Conaway] answered. The officers identified themselves and [Conaway] opened the inside door a few feet and stepped back. The officers opened the unlocked screen door and entered the house. They smelled a strong odor of marijuana and saw an open shoe box containing marijuana on a table. As Officer [Howard] was asking [Conaway] about [Tivnan's] whereabouts, a noise came from the basement. Officer [Stillman] went to investigate. In the basement he discovered [Tivnan] and found in plain view a large quantity of marijuana in eleven plastic bags and two pillow cases. There was also a quantity of marijuana in a clothes dryer. [Tivnan] and [Conaway] were arrested, [and convicted].[6]

Because Conaway "had been staying in the house for several weeks and had the run of the house," the U.S. Court of Appeals decided that he had authority to consent to the police entering Tivnan's home. These judges also decided that Conaway had freely and voluntarily consented to the police entering Tivnan's home filled with marijuana and marijuana smoke when he "opened the *inside* door a few feet and stepped back." They reasoned that what was probably Conaway's scared and spontaneous reaction to finding police officers at the door was actually an "implied invitation" for the police to enter. In other words, the judges thought it was reasonable for the police to believe that they had permission to enter. Once in the house, of course, the police were justified in seizing the marijuana in plain view in the front room and in the basement when they took "a quick and cursory view of the residence" (see Chapter 7).

Before inviting the police into your home, take care to hide your personal belongings

There may be times when you want to invite the police into your home. One of the most common reasons is returning to your home and finding that it has been burglarized. Indeed, your feelings of outrage and violation may cause you to phone the police immediately. But be careful. No matter how distraught you are, you had better take care to hide your marijuana before the police arrive if you do not wish to be victimized again—this time by the law. Because the police have a sworn duty to uphold all the State's drug laws they may well arrest you if they see a couple of joints on the kitchen table or even a roach or two in the ash tray next to your roommate's bed. Thus if you are not careful you may find that the only "criminal" the police ever catch is you.

A burglary becomes a bust

Police officers won't really arrest you for a little marijuana found in your home when you report a burglary, you say? Well, perhaps many won't but that knowledge won't help you much if you are one of the unlucky ones. In 1979, the newspapers reported that Deborah Halvonik, the wife of Paul Halvonik, who was a judge of the California Court of Appeal, carelessly invited the Oakland police into her home to investigate a burglary. The police investigation did not help find the burglar, but one of the police officers saw marijuana plants in the Halvoniks' home. The police excitedly did further investigation—not of the serious crime, but of the marijuana crime. After the police had kept the Halvoniks' home under surveillance with binoculars they returned with a search warrant authorizing the search and seizure of the marijuana plants. Both Halvoniks pleaded guilty to possession of marijuana and Paul Halvonik, an able judge, was forced to resign from the judiciary.

And now, after preparing you for the worst, here is a reminder that it's not always that bad—some judges take a more enlightened view of the Constitution and laws that protect our privacy and freedom.

THE BEST YOU CAN EXPECT FROM A JUDGE

• A few judges will look twice at the "voluntariness" of your consent if the police have not told you of your right to refuse.

• Some judges will look closely at the "voluntariness" of your consent if the police have used their implied authority and threatening manner in an obvious way.

• A few judges will hesitate to find that you had consented after the police have forcefully arrested you.

• Some judges will disapprove of a search if the police obtained your consent to it by threatening to arrest you illegally or by lying to you about their ability to get a search warrant.

• A few judges will condemn the warrantless search of your personal belongings on the basis of the consent of friends, housemates, or even family.

CHAPTER **7**

Warrantless Searches: Your Home is Hardly a Castle

MISTRESS OVERDONE: But shall all our houses of resort in the suburbs be pulled down?

POMPEY: To the ground, mistress.

MISTRESS OVERDONE: Why, here's a change indeed in the commonwealth! What shall become of me?

William Shakespeare
MEASURE FOR MEASURE, Act I, Scene 2

Our homes are as varied as we are. They are truly a reflection and extension of our personalities. And whether we live in a tent, a Pontiac stationwagon, an apartment, or a suburban house, for most of us home is the one place where we want to be assured of privacy—a place of refuge from a busy world.

But in reality, whether or not we can enjoy our legal right to privacy and security in our homes depends upon the State's willingness to respect and protect it. The extent to which the State *ought* to respect our privacy in our homes is a major concern of this chapter. Nearly all historians agree that the founders of our nation intended the Fourth Amendment to protect Americans against arbitrary searches of their homes authorized by general warrants, or by no warrants at all. Regretably, the U.S. Supreme Court has interpreted the Fourth Amendment in

93

such a way that the average American has very little expectation of privacy in the home. In fact, the Supreme Court has made a mockery of the idea that "your home is your castle" by weakening search warrant requirements, as well as by inventing numerous exceptions to the requirement that the police obtain a warrant at all.

It might be funny, if it weren't so sad, that the only way to force the police to respect your constitutional rights and to treat your home as your castle is to build something which, in fact, resembles an ancient castle—high stone walls, moat, drawbridge and all. Assuming that you can't afford or don't want this kind of protection, you will simply have to submit to a warrantless search of your home if the police "break in." As mentioned throughout this book, you should never physically try to prevent the police from illegally entering or searching your home. If you do, you can be certain that they will respond with vigorous force and will probably arrest you for assault and battery on a police officer or for "obstructing justice." And even if it turns out later that the police should not have been there in the first place, your arrest for obstructing an officer will stand. The better way to proceed is to make it clear that you are not consenting to the search, and then to leave the rest to a court hearing. You, or more likely your lawyer, will have an opportunity to convince a judge that the police were not faced with an emergency sufficient to justify a warrantless search of your home.

THUMBNAIL REVIEW
What the Police Can Do "Legally"

· The police can often find a legal pretext whenever they want to enter and search your home and everything in it without a search warrant. These excuses frequently include:

· Breaking into and searching your home without a search warrant if they have "probable cause" to believe that you have marijuana that you are about to destroy.

· Breaking into and searching your home without a warrant, claiming that they smelled marijuana or opium coming from your home.

· Breaking into your home to arrest you without a warrant if they have reason to believe that you are committing *or* have committed a crime and that you are about to escape.

· Breaking into your home if you run or even walk away from them into your home when they have reason to stop you.

· Getting you to "consent" to a search (see Chapter 6).

• The police are supposed to knock and announce their purpose before breaking into your home unless they have reason to believe that you may destroy evidence, escape, or defend yourself. Judges tend to be quite receptive to police explanations of these so-called emergency circumstances.

• Under some circumstances, the police can secretly enter and search your home without a warrant by pretending to be a friend.

• The police can enter your home with an arrest warrant if they have reason to believe that the person to be arrested is inside.

• After the police arrest you in your home, they can search the area immediately around you and make a "plain view nonsearch" of your home.

• After the police arrest you in your home, they may search your bedroom and closet while gathering your clothes—if you are not properly dressed—or if you request clothes.

• After the police arrest you in your home they may in some circumstances search your entire home for other suspects.

• If the police find your marijuana during an illegal search of your friend's home, they can use the illegal evidence to convict you.

What You Can Do to Protect Yourself

• Your best protection is to place your marijuana in a locked container in an out-of-the-way place in your home.

• Make your home as secure as possible.

• Shut your windows and avoid disturbing your neighbors when you are smoking marijuana.

• Never run into your home and towards your marijuana at the sight of the police.

• Avoid giving the police an excuse to arrest you (that is, pay your traffic tickets and respond to official letters requiring something of you).

• If the police knock at your door, answer it as quickly as possible. If the police have an arrest warrant, go outside and shut the door behind you. If the police don't have an arrest warrant, you will probably want to stay in the house.

• If the police come to arrest you with an arrest warrant, everyone else in your home should stay calm. They may want to follow you outside so that the police have no reason to enter the house to look for suspects; or they may want to make sure no marijuana is in open view or hidden in the same room in which they are.

• If you are arrested, inform the police that you will go as you are and don't need or want additional clothing.

• Choose your friends with a little care. Don't keep your marijuana at a friend's home.

MARIJUANA IN YOUR HOME

Most of you will have little choice but to keep your most personal belongings in your homes. How, then, can you attain the maximum amount of privacy within your living space? The best way to accomplish this is simple: *Keep your marijuana in a locked box or safe or trunk or suitcase, and store the locked case in an out-of-the-way place.* This precaution is wise because, as you will see, the police can commonly find a legal excuse to justify searching without a warrant nearly every unlocked place in your home.

But if the police surprise you at your home with your marijuana in an unlocked place, this chapter suggests other ways to protect your home from a warrantless search.

After reading what follows, some readers may conclude that keeping their marijuana locked up all the time is more trouble than it's worth, and that even though the law allows the police lots of excuses to justify a search if they want to search badly enough, they are themselves unlikely to be searched. You will have to judge this possibility for yourself. Some people can doubtlessly smoke marijuana at Fifth Avenue and Forty-Second Street in New York City for a week and never get arrested, while others draw the blue-jacketed police like peanut butter and grape soda attract yellow jackets on a summer afternoon. It is the task of this book to explain the law and yours to decide how to put the knowledge to use.

POWERS OF THE POLICE

The Police Can Claim that You Might Destroy or Remove Evidence To Justify a Warrantless Search

If the police have probable cause to believe that marijuana is in your house *and* that someone is about to destroy or abscond with it, judges have decided that it is legal for them to search your home immediately without a search warrant. Obviously this ruling tends to encourage the police to exaggerate their fears that evidence is about to be destroyed. And unfortunately, judges generally do not second-guess the police but instead tend to believe whatever justification the police have thought up. As long as there was anyone in the house, most judges willingly believe an officer's story that a warrantless search was necessary to prevent the destruction or removal of the marijuana, even though the police could have delayed a search for several hours while they applied for a search warrant.

A Flimsy Emergency

In one federal case, the police searched Joseph Tompkins's apartment without a search warrant after staking out his place for more than twenty-four hours in response to a landlord's tip. Two of the three judges of the U.S. Court of Appeals believed that there had been an emergency. Judge Donald Lay disagreed, since the police had admitted as much: "The officers at the scene testified that as long as they were not discovered, there was no reason for concern that the drugs in the apartment would be destroyed [by Tompkins] before they could get a warrant." Judge Lay also recognized that if "indications of an impending departure" could justify an emergency search, "the Fourth Amendment's search warrant requirement [would become] a *facade.*"[1] Yet precisely this flimsy excuse was enough for the majority of this court to approve the warrantless search.

An "Automatic Emergency"

In a similar case, the highest New York State court used the possibility of destruction of evidence or escape to justify both a warrantless search of John Corrigan's dresser drawer and his warrantless arrest in his home for selling three joints to an informer. A majority of the judges believed that in this situation there was an automatic emergency because marijuana can easily be destroyed. In addition, these judges said it was necessary for the police to arrest the marijuana dealers immediately because they were "apparent members of the drug culture" who might disappear. In a dissenting opinion Judge Sol Wachtler, joined by two other judges, stated the obvious truth of the matter: "[There was] virtually nothing to support a reasonable belief that the defendants or the marijuana were likely to vanish."[2]

> NOTE: Remember that each of the above examples describes individual situations and the decisions of individual judges in determining whether a warrantless search was legal. Of course, another set of judges might have made a different ruling. Remember that the case examples in this book are meant to describe how little protection the Fourth Amendment really provides, especially when those being searched are engaged in "unpopular" or "antisocial" activities.

The Police Can "Freeze" a Home without a Warrant

A device that police can use when they want to ensure the legality of searching your home is to "freeze" it or "secure" the premises. This technique doesn't involve a massive stack of ice cubes; it simply means that the police prevent anyone from entering, leaving, or moving around inside the home. Police freeze a house to ensure that nothing is destroyed while they attempt to obtain a warrant. But doesn't freezing a home in and of itself constitute a "seizure" and thus violate your constitutional rights if done without a warrant? Read on.

A Big Deal

In one case, a U.S. Court of Appeals believed that the police were justified in freezing Stephen Milanovich's home without a warrant because of the risk that the police could not prevent Milanovich and his friends from removing or destroying 348 pounds of marijuana. What kind of danger was enough to convince three federal judges that the police "needed" to break into Milanovich's home without a warrant, arrest him and his friends, and freeze his home? The police had watched the house for two hours and had arrested two people leaving with a few pounds of marijuana. But couldn't the police have as easily continued to watch the house for a few more hours while they obtained a search warrant, instead of breaking in? Probably, but this court still found the break-in, arrests, and freeze order to be legal.[3]

The Police Can Search a Home If They Smell Marijuana

One favorite excuse used by police to justify breaking into a home without a warrant can be called the "smelly speculation" loophole. It works like this. The police walk around your house sniffing at open windows or even at cracks under the doors. If they smell an illegal drug, judges have ruled that they have "probable cause" to believe that you are right then committing a crime in your home. There is therefore an "emergency" justification to break into your home immediately before you consume all the evidence.

Many people have remarked that some police officers have an uncanny ability to smell marijuana through walls and at considerable distances. Defense attorneys have suggested more than once that drug enforcement officers engage in "creative smelling." And while there have been cases where judges have invalidated searches because they have refused to believe that a particular agent could smell a particular joint, many other judges have believed super-sniffer officers.

Two Smelly Stories with Different Endings

In one case, the police went to Frank Bird's house to check out a possible narcotics suspect. When Bird answered the door, the police broke in and arrested everyone. The majority of the California Supreme Court decided that the police were justified in breaking into Bird's home without a warrant because they "detected the odor of burning marijuana emanating from within." This smelly speculation was enough to justify the arrest of Bird and everyone else inside.[4]

In another case, however, a judge refused to believe a police officer's story that he broke into Gary Perlstein's home because "air rushed out of the apartment" smelling of marijuana when Perlstein opened his door. Apparently, Perlstein's lawyer convinced the judge that the officer was inventing an aroma to justify his otherwise illegal search. Although the officer did find marijuana, he found no evidence to introduce at trial that Perlstein or anyone else had been smoking it.[5]

Police Agents and Informers Can Enter Your Home without a Warrant

It is perfectly legal for undercover police and paid informers to enter your house at your invitation since you cannot "reasonably" expect that people are not secret agents. These undercover officers can arrest you, and the informers can inform on you, if you offer them a joint or if they see any illegal drugs on your premises.

The police are not allowed, however, to impersonate someone in order to get an invitation into your home when their intention is to search it without a warrant. Therefore, a policeman cannot legally dress up as an Avon lady, a meter reader, a telephone repairman, or a campfire girl in order to trick you into letting him into your house. How the police dress on their own time is up to them, but if they get into your house as a result of this type of deception, any search they make is illegal.[6]

The Police Can Search a Home Claiming "Hot Pursuit"

Judges have decided that if the police are in hot pursuit of a suspect, they may enter her home without a warrant. Sounds almost reasonable doesn't it? Now consider this—judges have gone on to rule that even if the law enforcement agency engineered the situation that led to the "hot pursuit," it is still okay. It's starting to sound a little less reasonable, isn't it?

A Southern California Setup

In a case out of Los Angeles, informers went to the home of Marcela Fitzpatrick and Philip Gold to buy drugs, while Drug Enforcement Administration (DEA) agents hid outside. After examining the substance and agreeing on a price, the informers left the house supposedly to get money from their truck, but in reality to signal to the DEA agents. When one of the informers took off his jacket, the agents "converged on the house," yelling to Fitzpatrick and Gold to stay on the porch. Then they "ran on to the porch of the house, knocked at the front door, announced their identities, and forced entry after the suspects ran into their home." The agents had no search warrant. (One agent testified in court that after knocking he and the others had waited about fifteen seconds before breaking into the home. Even though this rather self-serving testimony was difficult to dispute, the trial judge thought that the circumstances showed that the agent had lied about waiting before breaking in.)

In any case, upon entrance, the feds arrested two men in the house. At the bathroom door, which was locked, one of the agents heard the sound of running water. In the words of the judges, "the agents announced their presence and, after waiting about thirty seconds, forced the bathroom door. [Marcela Fitzpatrick] emerged from the bathroom with a smile on her face." Apparently she had flushed most of the drug stash. Nevertheless, the agents discovered some of the contraband on the kitchen floor "in plain view." The judges believed that this warrantless entry and search were legal because the DEA agents had successfully created a "hot pursuit emergency" to prevent the destruction of evidence. The fact that the "set-up" had been planned many days before didn't influence this ruling. The dealers were convicted.[7]

> **SELF-HELP NOTE:** What can you do if the police suddenly pay you a surprise visit in your home? To repeat, the wisest course is politely to ask the police to leave, but to neither resist nor flee if they don't. If you are

outside your home when the police show up, you also run a greater risk by running than by greeting the police outside and politely asserting your rights. If you run into your home, the police may legally run in after you without knocking and can legally search your home, to some extent, in the process of catching you. Therefore, if you are most concerned about protecting your home from a possible warrantless search, don't run into it.

EXAMPLE: Sandy Provokes the Sheriff

Here is one example of how one man got into trouble—and with a little luck, got himself out again.

Sandy lived on a hillside in Kentucky. For some reason that was never made clear, the local sheriff had a deputy watch Sandy's home from a good vantage point down the ridge. The deputy, using high-powered binoculars, saw Sandy light something the shape and size of a cigarette and pass it to several friends who had joined him on the back porch. Later in the day, the agent claimed to have crawled closer to the house so that he could "positively identify the substance being smoked as marijuana." The sheriff's office had quickly prepared for a raid that evening, but decided to wait for the next group of friends to drop over.

Sandy, however, began preparing to leave for the evening and a decision was hurriedly made to "move in." The first Sandy knew about all of this was when he was on his way out to his car, which was parked in his front yard. Suddenly he heard a noise and looked up to see a truck full of men plow into his gate. His first thought was to run into his house to get his gun. Fortunately, once inside the house he took a quick look at the men swarming through his yard and saw that they were police. So, instead of reaching for the gun, he threw the remaining little bit of marijuana in the box on the mantle into the garbage. At this point, the officers burst in, placed Sandy under arrest, handcuffed him, and "froze" his home. Then, without bothering to obtain a search warrant, they proceeded to search. They found no loose marijuana, but found a locked trunk under Sandy's bed. Excited, an officer broke the lock and found almost a pound of sinsemilla flower tops—Sandy's personal stash for the year. Down to the station and into a jail cell for the night went Sandy, who didn't say a word to the police. Sandy's lawyer arranged for bail the next day, and Sandy was home for lunch.

Question: Would a judge rule that the binocular search was legal?

Answer: Probably yes. In making that search, the police did not violate Sandy's "reasonable" expectation of privacy because the police did not trespass on his land.

Question: Would a judge rule that the police did not need a search warrant or an arrest warrant to raid Sandy's home?

Answer: Probably yes. In similar circumstances, many judges have ruled that there was an emergency because marijuana disappears easily. Also as Sandy ran into his home, a judge would be likely to rule that the sheriff's men could follow him using the "hot pursuit" exception to the search warrant requirements.

Question: Would a judge decide that the police legally searched Sandy's house for marijuana in plain view and legally froze Sandy's home to prevent his friends from entering to take marijuana?

Answer: Yes, these actions would almost certainly be approved on the theory that the police were in hot pursuit and Sandy might destroy the evidence if they waited to get a warrant. Sandy was lucky that none of his marijuana was in "plain view."

Question: Would a judge rule that the police legally broke into Sandy's locked trunk without a search warrant?

Answer: No. The trunk wasn't open (as proved by the broken lock) and wasn't in plain view. Following recently established case law, the judge would rule that a search warrant was necessary to break into the trunk (see Chapter 8). Since the officers had no warrant, the search wasn't legal. Furthermore, the police may not have been able to obtain a search warrant because the sight of Sandy smoking did not necessarily give the police "probable cause" to believe that he had more marijuana in his home.

NOTE ON SANDY'S LUCK: Sandy felt a great sense of relief when the judge ruled that the trunk search was illegal and dismissed the case. Friends remarked about his good luck. But how lucky was he really? In addition to losing a pound of marijuana and spending a night in jail, he had to lay out $2,000 for a lawyer. Some luck!

An Arrest at Your Home Can Legitimize a Warrantless Search

If you are arrested in your home, there are several legal justifications for a police search. Knowing this fact, the police often want to make an arrest in a home.

Once the police are legally inside your home to arrest you for any crime, even if it is failure to pay your traffic tickets, they can seize without a warrant any contraband in "plain view." They can also search the area within your leaping distance, which usually includes the entire room in which they arrest you; and they can often search your closet and bedroom if you need or ask for clothes. Thus if the police have probable cause to arrest you and they want to check out your home for marijuana, you can expect a knock at your door. Although it is illegal for the police to deliberately wait until their "suspect" is at home so that they can search the premises without a search warrant while they are making the arrest, officers commonly do it. The police know that judges seldom invalidate searches on the theory that the police unlawfully waited around just so they could arrest you at your home.

In 1980, the U.S. Supreme Court decided that the police must follow the Fourth Amendment before making a routine arrest at your home. The High Court said that if there is no emergency justifying a break-in, the police must obtain an arrest warrant before arresting you at home.[8] This new interpretation of the law makes illegal the former police practice of arresting you at home without an arrest warrant. It does not, however, prevent the police from arresting you at home with an arrest warrant and then searching for marijuana. Therefore despite the new rule the police have the same incentives to wait to arrest you until you are at home in order to look for evidence of other crimes.

Here, now, are some of the various legal justifications for warrantless searches that accompany legal arrests in your home.

"Plain View" Searches. As long as the police are legally inside your home to arrest you or to investigate a burglary at your request (see Chapter 6), they can legally seize without a search warrant any contraband in "plain view." Remember, the judges do not consider a plain view search to be a "real" search. Therefore you should always be careful about leaving marijuana, half-smoked joints, and other drugs lying about. It's worth repeating that the safest place for your marijuana is a locked container in an obscure nook of your home.

The "Leaping" Loophole Search. Wherever the police arrest you, they may search an area within your "grabbing" distance. As you might imagine, judges tend to interpret this area to be quite wide, hence the name "leaping" loophole. After your arrest, the police can conduct a thorough search of your leaping area for weapons, evidence of crime, and, of course, marijuana. Theoretically, judges invented the leaping loophole to allow the police to prevent you from grabbing a gun and shooting an officer or from grabbing your marijuana and eating it. Unfortunately, however, the police commonly use this loophole to conduct warrantless searches for reasons unrelated to protecting themselves. One of the most unfortunate uses of the "leaping" loophole is when the police deliberately wait to arrest you at your home to justify a search of at least the room in which they arrest you for evidence of crime or vice. As unbelievable as it may sound, some judges have even allowed the police to use the "leaping" loophole to justify warrantless searches of entire homes after the police arrested a suspect in his home. For example, federal agents purposely waited to arrest Anthony Brockington at home. The federal judges approved the warrantless search of his bedroom and his car, parked in his driveway. Needless to say, both his bedroom and his car were not within his leaping distance at the time of his arrest.[9]

Other judges refuse to stretch the "leaping" loophole beyond all recognition. The U.S. District of Columbia Court of Appeals, for instance, rejected the prosecutor's attempt to use the "leaping" loophole to justify a police search of Susan Lamont's attic after the police arrested her downstairs. These judges recognized that the attic was not within Lamont's leaping distance, and they also rejected the prosecutor's imaginative explanation that the police search was necessary to protect the police from a possible sniper in the attic.[10]

The "Searching for Suspects" Loophole. After the police make an arrest inside or immediately outside of your home, they can legally search it without a warrant by saying that they "needed" to search for other suspects who could shoot at them, run away with the marijuana, or simply escape. This legal loophole allowing searches without a warrant is used on a daily basis. Now and then when the police push it too far—that is, claim to be looking for suspects when there are obviously none present—judges have ruled that the searches are illegal and any evidence found must be suppressed. But most of the time, the majority of judges give great leeway to law enforcement officers who claim to be "searching for suspects."

NOTE: Obviously the police can only claim to be looking for suspects in places that are big enough to hold a suspect in the first place. Thus this excuse will not support warrantless searches of desk drawers, footlockers and old cookie tins. But as you now know, the "leaping" loophole can sometimes be used to justify a warrantless search of these places.

Remember, the easiest way to prevent the police from finding your marijuana during their search for suspects is routinely to keep it in a locked container, hidden away somewhere. None of the loopholes that allow police to conduct random searches without a warrant allow the search of a locked container in an out-of-the-way place.

EXAMPLE: Barbara's Speeding Tickets Catch Up with Her

Barbara is one of those people who file traffic tickets between the road map of New Hampshire and the old Milky Way wrappers at the bottom of her glove compartment. "I can't afford to pay them," she says. Unfortunately for her, she had to learn the hard way that she could not afford not to pay them.

"Knock, knock."
"Who's there?"
"The police."
"The police who?"
Barbara opened her door.
"Are you the Barbara Lashley who doesn't pay her traffic tickets? May we come in please?"
The police edged their way through the opened door.
"Who, me? Traffic tickets?"
The police stepped in, turning their attention to the living room.
"What's this here on the living room table?" one of the officers asked.
"A water pipe."
"What do you smoke in it?"
"I don't use it. It's a decoration."
"Someone uses it," said the officer, sniffing the bowl. "We have a warrant for your arrest for your unpaid traffic tickets. You're also under arrest for that water pipe. We won't handcuff you, but we have to search around you for our protection—just a formality."
"You can't search my house. I haven't done anything."
"Now, don't get excited lady, we better just look in this desk drawer."
"Ah . . . looks like hashish. Apparently you do use your water pipe. Any other hashish blowers in your home?"
"No, there's no one else home."
"We'll have to check just in case—this could be a dangerous situation."
The other officer quickly walked through the house.
"Didn't find any other suspects, lady, but I did find a couple of joints on your bedroom stand. Smells like marijuana to me. What are you, a drug addict?"

Question: Was the police entry legal?
Answer: Yes. The police had an arrest warrant and Barbara opened the

door and allowed the police to enter, even though they never asked if they could enter.

Question: Was Barbara's arrest legal?

Answer: Yes. The police had an arrest warrant.

Question: Could the State convict Barbara for possession of the water pipe?

Answer: Probably yes. The search was legal because the water pipe was in plain view. The conviction is legal as long as possession of "drug paraphernalia" is a crime, which it is in most states.

Question: Could the State convict Barbara for possession of hashish?

Answer: Probably yes. The "leaping" loophole could justify opening unlocked drawers within Barbara's leaping distance at the time of her arrest, without regard to actual necessity. The police could easily say that Barbara was standing next to the drawer.

Question: Could the State convict Barbara for possession of marijuana?

Answer: Probably, yes. The "searching for suspects" loophole will probably justify the police officer checking out the rooms and closets in the home and the "plain view nonsearch" justified the seizure of the joints.

HINT: Now that you see all the grief Barbara came to as a result of not paying her tickets, you may want to take a look in your glove compartment.

Is Police Misconduct Routine or Exceptional?

Police misconduct is an exception to the rule. But unfortunately, it isn't an uncommon exception. If you doubt this fact, read what Judge Ben Duniway of the U.S. Court of Appeals wrote in 1973 of a drug bust, when he and two other judges reversed the convictions of the victims of the following police conduct:

These appeals present a distressing picture of the notions of the agents of the Bureau of Narcotics and Dangerous Drugs of the Department of Justice who were involved in the case about the manner in which they are to perform their duties and their obligations toward citizens under the Constitution, and about their behavior toward the citizens with whom they become involved. We hope that the agents who testified in this case are not typical agents of the Bureau. If they are, we wonder what sort of training the Bureau gives its agents.

Two of the agents seem quite willing to make false affidavits, in which facts are distorted to achieve a result, such as a finding that seized evidence was in plain view. One agent, when confronted with the facts demonstrating that his affidavit was false, did not admit that it was false;

it was merely "inconsistent." These agents do not search a citizen; they "frisk" him, even if that involves fishing paper money out of his pocket and his wallet. Their fear for their own safety approaches paranoia. Even when six or eight agents, all armed, have a group of citizens herded into a room, a search of a citizen's wallet is justified on the ground that it might contain a razor blade. These agents do not break into a house without a warrant; they "secure" it, even if this means rushing in with drawn guns, rounding up everyone in the place and searching them all. They do this for their own protection. They seem to think that every citizen must carry some sort of identity card or paper, which they call "I.D.", and must display it to them on demand.[11]

The *"Let Me Get Your Coat" Loophole.* Another technique occasionally used by police to do legal warrantless searches of other places in your home after arresting you is to ask you pleasantly whether you want to put on other clothing or get your toothbrush before they take you to the station. If you agree to this sort of suggestion, the police may look for marijuana as they walk with you through your house to your closet or bathroom, and they may legally rummage through your belongings looking for any clothing you request. And any marijuana the police "innocently" come across can be used to convict you and will also enable the police to obtain a search warrant authorizing the complete search of your house for more marijuana later.

A True "John Sirica" Anecdote

Judge John Sirica of Watergate fame decided that it was legal for the police to open a suitcase in a closet simply because Daniel Margolin asked for his leather jacket. The U.S. District of Columbia Court of Appeals affirmed Judge Sirica's opinion of the matter, as many, if not most, courts in this country would have done. Chief Judge David Bazelon, however, dissented:

> At the time of the search [Margolin's] hands were handcuffed in front of him, an armed FBI agent was holding him, and a second armed agent stood between [Margolin] and the suitcase. The suitcase sat on a closet shelf at eye level, three to four feet away. Perhaps if [Margolin] had "been possessed of the skill of Houdini and the strength of Hercules," the court's conclusion [that Margolin might have leaped to the suitcase and opened it with his handcuffed hands] might be justifiable. But the court offers no evidence to "place him in such legendary company," nor does it explain how the mere "possibility of legerdemain" can justify a warrantless search.[12]

But Judge Bazelon is a rare judge, and Margolin remained in jail.

SELF-HELP NOTE: Obviously it's not possible to spend your entire life wearing clothes appropriate for a possible arrest, but if you are arrested in your home, it would seem to make excellent sense to go to jail in your night shirt rather than to ask the arresting officer to get you other clothes. In some situations (e.g., if you are without your shoes or pants), the police can look about your home to find them for you even without your permission. So if possible, should the police turn up at your door, take a moment to dress in appropriate attire before greeting them.

EXAMPLE: An Early Morning Soap Opera

Remember Barbara with the bad memory for traffic tickets? Well, unfortunately her recall didn't improve much and she forgot her court appearance.

Knock, knock. "Open up. Police officers." Tick, tick, crash, bang.

"You check upstairs." Leap. Bound. Thud. Thud. Thud. "I got her. Are you Barbara Lashley? We have a warrant for your arrest."

"What time is it? What did I do this time?"

"It's about 7 o'clock—time for you to get up, get dressed, and come down to the station. You missed your court appearance yesterday and the judge issued a bench warrant for your arrest."

"Yesterday! I thought the hearing was today!"

"Explain that to the judge."

"What's all the noise downstairs?"

"Just my partner doing his duty—checking for other suspects."

"But here I am."

"Don't tell us what to do, lady. We have to check out the entire house for our own protection. Where's your closet? What clothes do you want to wear to jail?"

"Can't I get dressed in private?"

"Lady, I can't let you leave my sight. Now, where's your closet?"

"Over there. Just throw me some clothes."

Rummage, rummage. "Here, is this okay?"

Rummage. "Hey, look what I found. Marijuana. You didn't even hide it. Right in plain view on your closet shelf."

Question: Was the police entry into Barbara's home legal?

Answer: No. Waiting a couple of seconds is not enough time to allow Barbara to open the door.

Question: Would most judges decide that the police entry was illegal?

Answer: Probably not, unless there were several reliable witnesses, such as neighbors, who would testify to the fact that the police didn't wait. The police are unlikely to admit breaking down the door without waiting. Remember, as Einstein proved, time is relative—the difference between two seconds and two minutes depends upon the unreliable mind; when given a choice, a judge is almost always going to give the police the benefit of any "relative" doubt. And if the police believe that someone has heard their announcement, then thirty seconds can seem like an eternity.

Question: Was the search for suspects legal?

Answer: Perhaps not—one officer was searching after the other officer had found Barbara, and Barbara's crime of missing a court appearance over unpaid traffic tickets does not suggest the presence of other dangerous criminals.

Question: But would most judges decide that this search for suspects was illegal?

Answer: Probably they would not, so long as the second officer testified to searching for Barbara without realizing that his partner had already discovered her in her bedroom.

Question: Was the search of Barbara's closet legal?

Answer: Probably yes. Obviously the police could not take Barbara to jail in her pajamas. Some judges, however, would rule that the police officer's conduct was illegal, because Barbara was obviously not a dangerous person, and the officer should have allowed her to dress on her own.

Protecting Your Rights in Your Home

Ask to See an Arrest Warrant

If the police come to your home and say that they are there to arrest you, ask to see an arrest warrant. If they show you one, then step quickly outside of the house. If they don't have an arrest warrant, don't open the door, and stay in the house. If the police do have an arrest warrant, it is more difficult to get arrested outside of your home than it might seem. The police are often trying to catch you inside the house because they want to search it but don't have probable cause to believe that you have marijuana.

In theory, the police are supposed to knock and announce who they are before breaking in. If they do knock, you may have a chance to step quickly outside. But again, judges have allowed police to break in almost immediately under the following circumstances:

- If they hear you running or making a lot of noise.
- If they hear any noises identifiable with flushing, burning, or otherwise destroying evidence.
- In some circumstances even if they hear no noise at all. Indeed, some judges have allowed break-ins after twenty seconds of silence.

You should probably not hide in the house if the police announce themselves at your door. If the police have bothered to come to your house in the first place, they will probably search it if they have any reason to believe that you are inside. Finding you in the house will make it easier for the police to justify their entry and search, even if they had no reason to believe you were inside before they entered.

If the police come with an arrest warrant to arrest anyone at your home, everyone in the house should quickly show up where the police can see them. Make it as obvious as possible that no one is hidden away. Even if the police break into your home before you have a chance to answer the door, everyone should join you in whichever room the police have gathered. The police may go ahead and search your entire home for suspects regardless of whether everyone has joined you, but if they don't find anyone, many judges will be suspicious of an officer's story that she heard noises and thus had to search the entire home for suspects. These judges may well suppress any illegally seized evidence found during such a random search. On the other hand, if the police find someone in another part of the house during their warrantless search, it is easy for them to use the "searching for suspects" loophole to justify their warrantless search.

Your Legal Rights Vis-à-Vis Sniffing Police Officers

Obviously, if you are smoking up a cloud of marijuana you would want to shut your windows to avoid alerting the nasal passages of passersby. If the police suddenly knock on your door one partying night to ask you to turn down the music, what do you do? You can't invite them into a room filled with marijuana smoke. One alternative is to turn down the music and ask the police what they want without opening the door. Remember that this situation is not a time to be too polite. If the police ask to come in, politely refuse. You are under no obligation to consent to a warrantless search (see Chapter 6). Of course, by refusing to open the door after the police knock, you risk making them suspicious enough to break down your door. If they enter with no warrant, they must at least prove that there was an emergency and that they had "probable cause" to enter, but the "smelly speculation" loophole is always available to them. The other alternative is quickly to step outside and close the door behind you. While it is less suspicious to talk to the police face to face, you risk having the police burst into your home or smell marijuana as soon as you open the door. It's a close decision that only you can make at the moment.

EXAMPLE: A Tale of a Blast That Turned into a Bust

Teresa likes parties and sometimes gets carried away. One Friday night the music became louder, the smoke thicker, and the laughter crazier. A little after midnight, one of Teresa's uninvited neighbors reached the boiling point and called the police to complain about the noise.

A partygoer saw the squad car pull up. Someone collected the marijuana and headed for the bathroom. Someone else turned down the music just in time to hear the ominous "knock, knock."

"Coming. Who's there?"
"The police. We've had a noise complaint."

Teresa opened the door, stepped outside, and quickly shut the door. One of her friends locked it behind her. The marijuana smell inside the apartment was still noticeable, but people scurried quietly about finding and flushing the last of the joints. Meanwhile, back in the hallway, Teresa was saying,

"Sorry about the music, officer, we will keep it down."
"Yes. You had better—it's late."

Teresa's eyes looked a little bloodshot and glazed to the officers and they had a hunch that there was some marijuana at the party, but as they had no hard evidence to justify an entry and they weren't particularly uptight about small amounts of grass, they left and everyone relaxed.

Now let's take the same example but change a few facts. This time the police knock on the door surprised a guest, who walked to the door to answer it thinking it was a late arriving friend.

"It's the cops," he yelled, as he slammed the door and ran to alert everyone. The partygoers squealed and scurried.

The police broke down the door, even though they did not smell any marijuana until they entered the house.

One officer yelled, "Don't move, you're all under arrest." Another officer ran to the back of the house to try to stop anyone from flushing drugs or climbing out the windows. Backup police arrived and everyone was searched.

Question: Was this warrantless search legal?

Answer: Technically perhaps not, but realistically, probably yes. The guest's reaction to finding the police at the door was suspicious, but it alone would not give the police "probable cause" to break down the door without knocking again and waiting. There was no real emergency which required the police to break down a door just to tell the owner of the house to stop "disturbing the peace." But the police are human and react to your reactions. In such situations some officers may casually wait at your front door and try to explain that they only dropped by to tell you to turn down the music. But after the police break into your home and find drugs, they are not likely to testify that they had no reason to do so. Indeed, after the exhilaration of busting down a door, the officers may truthfully believe that they smelled marijuana before, rather than after breaking in.

You Have No Right to Expect Privacy in Your Friend's Home

Keeping your marijuana in your friend's home is one of the worst ways to protect your privacy. Why? The U.S. Supreme Court has ruled that your protection from illegal searches and seizures extends only to your premises, not to your neighbors'. Thus, in most states, if the police find your marijuana during an illegal search of someone else's home, it can be used to help convict you (see Chapter 8 for a complete discussion of this legal loophole).

And now, after preparing you for the worse, here is a reminder that it's not always this bad—the high courts in some states take a more enlightened view of the Constitution and laws that protect our freedom and privacy. If you are arrested, you will want to be sure to investigate the specifics of the laws that affect you.

THE BEST YOU CAN EXPECT FROM A JUDGE

• In some states, judges frown upon police excuses for warrantless searches of homes and will condemn many of them.

• Some judges get less excited about "emergencies" than others, and will usually not accept this pretext as a justification for a warrantless "securing" or search of your home.

• Some state courts have not approved of the police stretching the "leaping" loophole to conduct warrantless searches of desk drawers and closed containers even within twenty feet of you after your arrest.

• In some states judges are concerned enough about the privacy of the home to question closely the need for the police to search your bedroom or closet for your clothes or to search your home for other suspects.

• A few judges, particularly in California, will not allow the State to use illegally seized evidence at all, even if the police illegally seized it from your friend's home.

CHAPTER **8**

Marijuana in Motor Vehicles

But man, proud man,
Dress'd in a little brief authority,
Most ignorant of what he's most assur'd,—
His glassy essence—like an angry ape,
Plays such fantastic tricks before high heaven
As make the angels weep."

William Shakespeare,
MEASURE FOR MEASURE, Act II, Scene 2

America—land of the freeway. Whether you think of motor vehicles as liberating us to explore the world or as enslaving us, the days when the world was measured by the perimeters of a small town or village are long gone. Now, at a moment's notice, we can rev up an engine and change our scenery dramatically. Indeed, more than a few contemporary Americans appear to find that peaceful, easy feeling while cruising the interstate in the fast lane and appear to suffer great anxiety when faced with the possibility that gasoline may become less available.

But whatever you think of the hustle of the 1980s, sooner or later, if you use or grow marijuana, you will transport it from one place to another. And while you may hop into your car with a joint in hand without much thought or planning, you should know that by transporting marijuana from one place to another, you are putting yourself in maximum legal jeopardy. Why? The legal rules that partially protect your privacy while you are in your own home or on your own land are fairer and firmer than those few that minimally protect you when marijuana is in your motor vehicle.

This chapter reviews in detail the constitutional rights that protect (or in many cases don't protect) you when you carry marijuana or any other contraband substance in an automobile. This information can be a bit dry and technical, but you

113

can cut through most of the complications by remembering one basic principle: *Only your locked personal luggage in the trunk or another closed compartment of your car is fully protected by the Fourth Amendment's search warrant requirement in all states and in nearly all situations.*

THUMBNAIL REVIEW
What the Police Can Do "Legally"

· The police must have a reasonable suspicion to stop your vehicle—that is, they cannot legally stop you just because they are "in the mood" to make a random check.

· Usually the police can legally justify stopping your car for a traffic or safety violation (or in other words, they don't need much of a reason).

· After the police legally stop your vehicle, they can often search any part of it toward which you make a "suspicious movement."

· After the police stop your car, they can seize any marijuana in plain (or sometimes not-so-plain) view.

· In most states, if the police arrest you for a traffic violation or any other crime, they can search everywhere within your reaching (leaping) distance, including handbags and briefcases, especially if they appear easy to open.

· Once the police stop your vehicle, they can immediately search your car for any marijuana they can smell, but they cannot open tightly-closed personal luggage.

· If the police find any marijuana in the interior of your car, they may be able legally to search the trunk without a warrant, but not any personal luggage in the trunk.

· If the police or a reliable informer see you place marijuana in your trunk, they can search for it without a search warrant.

· If the police tow your car, or order it towed to the police station for being illegally parked, they can routinely inventory the contents of the entire car, including the trunk, but not including the contents of locked personal luggage.

· In most states, if the police stop a car in which you are riding but do not own, you have no protection from an "illegal" search that turns up marijuana unless the marijuana is in your personal luggage. This legal loophole means that if the car isn't yours, the police can search it illegally and the State can convict you with the illegally seized marijuana if they can prove you possessed it.

What You Can Do to Protect Yourself

• Quite simply, the best way to protect yourself is *always to carry any marijuana in locked personal luggage and place the luggage in a locked compartment, preferably the trunk.* If this precaution is impossible, the next best self-protection plan is to carry marijuana in a tightly-closed and carefully secured container, such as a suitcase tied securely with rope.

• Be as inconspicuous as possible (for example, the police don't usually stop four-year-old Toyotas with all equipment in working order, driven by a reasonably respectable-looking sort who obeys traffic signals).

• Don't smoke marijuana or use any drug, including alcohol, while you drive or just before you drive.

• Never keep marijuana or other "illegal material" in the glove compartment or in the main portion of the vehicle.

• Don't throw marijuana or other contraband out a vehicle window when being followed by the police.

• If the police ask you to open your locked trunk, personal luggage, or other container, politely refuse and continue to refuse. Announce your refusal to witnesses if possible.

• Park your vehicle in a safe and secure place. Your private property—or the private property of a friend—is best. Next best is a private parking lot. Never leave a vehicle containing marijuana on the street or in any area where there is even a remote possibility that it can be towed.

• Never place your marijuana in the interior of a friend's car unless it is in *your locked personal luggage.*

• Minimize the time that marijuana is in any vehicle.

Powers of the Police
The Police Can Legally Search Your Car without a Search Warrant

The police are allowed to search your car without a search warrant in most circumstances because the U.S. Supreme Court believes that you have almost no reasonable expectation of privacy in your car when it is on the road. Furthermore, the Supreme Court does not consider it to be an illegal search when the police look through your car windows—even late at night with a flashlight. Indeed, the police can legally seize any marijuana they can spot lying around inside your car because looking for marijuana in "plain view" is not considered to be a search. The High Court has also determined that the Fourth Amendment warrant requirement (see Chapter 5) does not apply to your car if you are legally stopped or arrested. Why? Theoretically someone could drive the car away after the police stop it. Therefore the police can physically search through your entire car without a search warrant, as long as they say they had probable cause to believe that your car contained evidence of a crime.

Only Locked Personal Luggage Is Protected from Most Warrantless Car Searches

In years past, the U.S. Supreme Court justified routine warrantless searches of everything in your car simply because your car, unlike your home, is mobile. In 1979, the High Court ruled that closed personal luggage, such as suitcases and knapsacks, are protected by the Fourth Amendment, even if they are in your car.[1] In that case, the police searched a suitcase without a warrant and found nine pounds of marijuana. Seven of the nine Supreme Court justices agreed that the search was illegal because the suitcase couldn't drive away, and because an expectation of privacy in suitcases is reasonable. This rule of law means that the police can no longer use most of the car search loopholes discussed in detail in this chapter to justify searching a locked suitcase in the trunk of your car without a search warrant. Now the police must show probable cause and obtain a search warrant to legally open a locked suitcase in your car trunk.

It is important to realize, however, that some types of personal luggage stored in your trunk or a locked compartment on a pickup are better than others in discouraging warrantless searches. Here are some specifics:

A locked suitcase, or footlocker. These containers are the best insurance against a warrantless search as there is no possibility that the police could claim that a locked suitcase "popped open." If they break into it, you have the broken lock to prove it.

Tightly closed knapsack or duffle bag. As long as the pack is tightly tied shut, the police need a search warrant, although without a lock there is always a chance than an officer will get imaginative and claim that the pack "popped open."

Unlocked suitcase. Obviously not as good as a locked one, but in theory, the police still need a search warrant to open it. If the suitcase is roped, so much the better.

Box or bag. Here you are starting to tread on thin ice. The Supreme Court established protection specifically for *personal luggage.* Anything else has less protection and the police may well be able to justify searching it under one of the legal loopholes set out below.

But what is the rule if you place your personal luggage, such as a duffel bag, in the back seat of your car instead of in the trunk? As you will see in this chapter, the police may be able to justify the search by claiming that the bag was in an area where you could grab a weapon from it. This excuse is our old friend the "leaping" loophole. Although the U.S. Supreme Court has not yet directly ruled on this issue, many state and federal judges have used this loophole to approve unnecessary, warrantless searches of your hand bags. Some judges who appreciate privacy have said that the police only need to seize your knapsack, tote bag, or purse in order to protect themselves, and do not have a right to search through your personal containers. Nevertheless, if you must carry marijuana in your vehicle, you are best off if it is in locked luggage in the trunk, or in locked, personal baggage on a motorcycle.

Legal Seizure: The "Plain View" Loophole

Just as the police can legally grab any marijuana that is in "plain view" in your home or on your land, they can also legally seize any marijuana found in "plain view" in your motor vehicle. Therefore, because looking into a motor vehicle from the outside is not technically a "search," the police do not have to establish that they had probable cause. Not surprisingly, police officers tend to stretch this "plain view" exception to justify searches of suspicious objects, such as plastic baggies, even though they cannot see the marijuana inside the package and even though they do not have probable cause to believe that marijuana is contained within every plastic baggie in every American's glove compartment. Unfortunately, if a police officer claims that he could see marijuana inside a plastic or cellophane package or bag, most judges don't inquire very strictly and rule that the "plain view" loophole justifies the warrantless search. Judicial laxity has encouraged many law enforcement officers to develop what amounts to "X-ray vision."

Cellophane Wrapping Means Marijuana in Arizona

Officer Dade stopped Carlos Cooper near Wickenburg, Arizona for driving a "dirty, unwaxed" car with one bald tire. Supposedly, the officer saw the bald tire when the car was moving. The officer asked Cooper for the car registration and carefully watched him open the glove compartment. What did the officer see? Cellophane. "So what?" you ask. Well, Officer Dade testified that he saw a "brick-like cellophane covered object that appeared to be a kilo of marijuana" in the glove compartment. The judges of the Arizona Court of Appeals explained that the officer's vision and speculation were not to be doubted and they therefore decided that he had probable cause to make a warrantless search. "The officer had just received training in narcotics identification and had reason to believe that the object was marijuana," the judges wrote, affirming Cooper's conviction.[2]

The moral of this little story, and of other similar ones from around the country, is that you have little expectation of privacy in anything wrapped in cellophane, a plastic baggie, or silver foil. Judges and police all seem to know, millions of peanut butter and jelly sandwiches notwithstanding, that illicit drugs are always secreted within these packages.

Stopping Vehicles

Like it or not, it is usually not difficult for police officers to find a legal justification to stop your car. Once the car is stopped officers can look for and seize any contraband materials in plain view. Even if the marijuana isn't in plain view, the police can rely on several other justifications for searching the rest of the car. The important thing to understand is that the police do not have to see you using marijuana or even suspect that you are using it to stop your car legally. A muddy license plate or a missing tail light is reason enough to signal you to pull over.

On the optimistic side of what too often seems to be a pessimistic subject, there has been a slight improvement in your protection from random police checks. Until recently, the police could legally stop a car for no reason at all—simply on the pretext of checking a driver's license or car registration. Now, the police are permitted to check papers routinely only if they legally set up a roadblock for everyone. This new rule means that an officer can't legally flag you down just because he doesn't like your looks. If the police really want to stop you, however, they can use one of a variety of traffic violations, such as driving too fast, too slow, too close to the curb, or too close to the median line. Indeed, there are so many traffic rules that it's almost impossible for anyone to obey them all, especially when being tailed by an officer who is looking for an excuse to pull you over.

"Watch Him Until He Makes a Wrong Move"

The police in Fort Walton, Florida followed Anthony Nonet because they vaguely suspected that his car contained drugs. When the officers turned on their flashing blue lights to pull him over for an illegal right turn at a traffic light, Nonet stupidly threw his marijuana out of the car window. The police quickly retrieved the abandoned marijuana which lay in "plain view" by the side of the road. Nonet's precipitous action meant that the only issue the Florida judges had to decide was whether the police had reason to stop his car in the first place. They did, and Nonet was convicted. Because Nonet had in effect handed the police the marijuana, they didn't even need to think up a justification to search his car.[3]

Hint: Anything you throw out of a car is subject to immediate seizure because it is both abandoned and in plain view.

SELF-HELP NOTE: Protecting yourself from legitimate police stops is a simple matter of common sense: Keep your car in good working order, obey traffic laws, and stay straight while you drive. A quiet muffler and working exhaust system is a priority, both to prevent noise and air pollution and to avoid giving the police an obvious pretext to stop you and search your car. Making certain that your headlights, taillights, turn signals, and brakes are all in good working order is also advisable. And, you have an obligation to wait to get "high" until you are out of your car—for your own safety and the safety of everyone else on the road.

The police can quite properly stop you if they have reason to believe that you are intoxicated from the use of alcohol or drugs. Driving while you are intoxicated is already risky for you and others on the road, but it is particularly dangerous when you have some reason not to want the police searching your car. If the police suspect that you have been drinking or using drugs, they have a legally sufficient reason to stop your car, arrest you, and search both you and the interior of your car. And even if you are not intoxicated, the police may pull you over if they think that they have seen you drinking liquor or smoking marijuana at the wheel.

The police are also far more likely to stop you if you fit their stereotype of a likely "drug user" than if you are relatively inconspicuous. This observation doesn't mean that to avoid suspicion you should buy a new Buick and a tweed suit just to drive across town with two joints. But it should be obvious to you that you are more likely to be stopped by the police if you drive a 1948 International Harvester pickup truck which is painted like a psychedelic zebra and your clothing recalls the reincarnation of Sitting Bull or the Third Dalai Lama, than if you make a little effort to blend into the common herd of humanity.

To summarize, law enforcement officers only need a "reasonable suspicion" of any legal violation in order to stop your car, look through its windows, and question you. Thus they are usually able to cite you for a traffic violation to justify a stop if they find drugs during their encounter with you. Remember, most police officers have a great deal of experience (and training) in recounting events as they happened—and sometimes inventing things that didn't happen—and can usually convince a judge that their stop was justified.

EXAMPLE: Sarah Spaces Out at Twilight

Meet Sarah, a wonderful lady who trusts in rainbows, unicorns, and *The I Ching* and who has never won any awards for her practical approach to life. Sarah was driving along a country road at twilight with a couple of small bags of marijuana in her car. The sky was a wash of lavender, almost luminous, and she was enjoying the dusk so much that she forgot to turn on her lights. A few moments later, a police cruiser signaled her to pull over.

"Isn't it a beautiful evening officers? Is there something wrong?" Sarah asked with a big smile.

"You haven't turned on your lights. Can I see your registration?" replied Officer Frank Arrow.

"Sure," said Sarah. As she opened the glove compartment, the officer flashed his light into it, disclosing a small plastic bag.

"What do you have here, young lady?" Officer Joe Straight, asked. He reached in and picked up the baggie containing marijuana, smelled it, and arrested Sarah.

Question: Did Officer Straight legally seize the baggie and search it?

Answer: Probably yes. The bag was in plain view and the officer would surely testify that he knew that little plastic bags of that particular shape almost always contain marijuana. The officer would also very likely testify that he saw marijuana-type leaves in the bag.

Ways Police Legally Justify a Warrantless Car Search

Although the Fourth Amendment does not protect your car from a warrantless search, the police are legally required to have probable cause to believe your car contains contraband or other illegal material before they search it for hidden material. Remember, the judges do not consider it to be a car search when the police, from outside your car, spot and seize marijuana in plain view.

To refresh your memory of probable cause, a police officer must have a reasonable belief—not a "mere suspicion"—that you are hiding contraband in your car. A reasonable belief must be based on some "hard" evidence, such as a reliable informer's tip, or the sight or smell of marijuana. "Mere suspicion" can be hunches and intuitions based on someone's nervousness or long hair, or their hostile response to the police. Unfortunately, this area of the law is one where police often abuse the rules. Because they do not need to apply for a search warrant, they become the judges as to whether "probable cause" exists. The result is, of course, that they sometimes search vehicles on a hunch. If they find nothing, they know that you will probably not know enough (or care enough) to complain about their illegal search, and that even if you do, little is likely to be done about it. And if they do find marijuana, it is usually not difficult to fabricate circumstances that show they had probable cause before they searched. Even if the police distortion of the truth is fairly gross, you are placed in the difficult position of trying to convince a judge that the contraband material should not be placed "in evidence against you" because the police did not have probable cause before their illegal search (see Chapter 13). Thus it comes down to your word against the police officer's in a situation where the judge knows in advance that you did, in fact, possess illegal drugs. Guess whom the judges usually believe?

The following three sections discuss common ways police officers find probable cause to search your vehicle.

The Suspicious Movement Pretext

One of the ways police try to justify a warrantless search of your car is by claiming that you made a "suspicious movement" or "furtive gesture," leading them to suspect illegal activity. This suspicion can be based upon any movement you make as the police stop your car. You could be turning down the radio, turning around to look at the police, putting out a cigarette, reaching for your driver's license, or getting your registration out of the glove compartment, and many officers will swear in court that you made a "suspicious movement" and that, sure enough, when they searched, they found the marijuana right where you made your "suspicious move." But isn't a "suspicious movement" with no other evidence a pretty weak reason to show that probable cause existed, especially when you recall that the police officer who must justify the warrantless search is also the one who testifies to seeing the movement? Judges in a number of states agree that it is, and have interpreted their state constitutions to require something more than a "suspicious movement" to establish probable cause to justify a search. Thus, some state courts have also required an additional suspicious circumstance, such as lying to the police, driving without a license, or committing a traffic law infraction. But you cannot safely rely on this rule of law.

Justice Stanley Mosk of the California Supreme Court, in a decision which declared that a "furtive gesture" alone was not sufficient probable cause to justify the warrantless search of Martell Kaman's car, also recognized that, in practice, the suspicious movement pretext alone was enough to justify most warrantless car searches: "From a review of the cases and other authorities, we are constrained, unfortunately, to conclude that this rule [that something more than a furtive gesture is required] has more often than not been honored only in the breach."[4]

The "Leaping" Loophole

Many people believe that, while the police can find a legal justification to search the inside of their car if they are legally stopped, their constitutional right to privacy will at least protect any marijuana kept inside a purse, suitcase, or closed bag. Unfortunately, this bit of folk wisdom is very often not true. Remember the "leaping" loophole from Chapter 7? This loophole commonly makes it easy for the police to justify searching the interior of your car, including handbags and purses, after your arrest for any offense under the pretext of searching for weapons. While there may be some circumstances in which officers would have trouble justifying such a search (a tightly closed suitcase at the back end of a station wagon), many judges will give the police the benefit of the doubt if they claim that they felt that their safety required a search of your accessible personal belongings. This loophole has also justified the police in making a warrantless search of a cigarette pack after arresting a man for a traffic offense. While supposedly looking for razor blades, the police found a couple of joints. (For a more detailed description of this case, see Chapter 9.)

EXAMPLE: Sarah and the "Leaping" Loophole

Let's toss out our first little fantasy and give Sarah another chance. This time when she drove to town she had carefully remembered to turn on her lights. But unfortunately, Sarah—being Sarah—made a rolling stop downtown in front of the library, which just happened to be next to the police station. Officers Joe Straight and Frank Arrow were just pulling out of the station to start their rounds. In an instant, Straight had his lights flashing and poor Sarah was in the soup again.

"Step out of the car, Miss, and let's see your driver's license."

"What's the matter, Officer?"

"You didn't make a full stop at the stop sign by the library. Where's your car registration?"

"In the glove compartment."

"Joe, check the inside of the car for weapons—we wouldn't want this desperate-looking character to leap into the back seat for a gun. Check under the front seat also. I'm sure that I saw the lady hide something under the seat when we pulled her over. Lady, get the car registration out of the glove compartment and get out of the car."

"Looks like a joint to me, Frank. Found it in the lady's purse. There's nothing under the seat . . . but, wait a minute, yes, here's a few roaches in the ashtray."

"Arrest her, Joe."

Question: Was the warrantless search of the purse legal?

Answer: In some states, yes, if the police testified that the purse was within Sarah's leaping distance, whether or not they actually placed Sarah under arrest. In some states, the police could not use this loophole for minor traffic offenses, but only for misdemeanors or serious crimes for which they actually arrested the suspect. Therefore, in these states, a judge should rule that the "leaping" loophole search of Sarah's purse was an illegal pretext search. In most states, however, the police have the authority to arrest you and bring you to the police station for a traffic offense and therefore they can justify the "leaping" loophole search by arresting you for running the stop sign.

Question: Was the warrantless search of the car floor under the front seat legal?

Answer: Perhaps. The officer could say he had seen a "suspicious movement." But remember that in some states a "suspicious movement," at least in theory, is not by itself grounds for a warrantless search. In these states, an officer would have to testify to some other suspicious circumstance. And if the officer found nothing, he would not bother to think up other suspicious circumstances, as he wouldn't have to justify his search.

Question: Was the warrantless search of the ashtray legal?

Answer: Probably yes, if the police testified in court that the ashtray was open and "in plain view," or if they testified that they found marijuana in the purse before searching the ashtray (during their "leaping" loophole search) or perhaps even if they testified about a "suspicious movement" toward the ashtray.

Question: Was it legal for the police to order Sarah out of her car?

Answer: In most states, yes. If the police have reason to stop a car, they are almost always allowed to order the driver and any passengers out of the car.

The "Smelly Speculation" Loophole

Another way to justify a warrantless car search—that is, to establish probable cause—is for the police to claim that they smelled marijuana. As generations of high school students puffing away in school lavatories have learned—much to their

dismay—marijuana does have a distinctive odor. And judges have long been deciding that law enforcement (and school) authorities have the legal right to look for it if they can smell it. And just as the judges believe that police officers have extraordinary powers to *see* marijuana, it also seems to be judicially established that police have the noses of bloodhounds. By way of example, here's a story involving a Florida officer with a "super" sniffer.

A Florida Smelling Expedition

After the police arrested Dennis McGravey for drunk driving, an officer drove McGravey's car to the station and searched it, finding six pounds of marijuana. The officer justified this warrantless search by alleging that, upon entering McGravey's car to drive it away, he smelled marijuana, even though it was in a suitcase in the trunk. Although McGravey claimed that this feat of olfactory sleuthing was simply impossible, Florida judges believed the officer.[5]

> **NOTE:** Because of the recent Supreme Court case discussed in the beginning of this chapter, this sort of warrantless search would appear to be illegal because the marijuana was in McGravey's suitcase in the trunk. An officer's assertion that he could smell extraordinarily well, however,

would still justify a warrantless search of a box or a bag and would also be sufficient to establish the probable cause necessary to get a warrant to search the suitcase (see Chapter 5). The police could also have justified searching McGravey's trunk, but not the suitcase, with the inventory search loophole.

A Case of ESP (Extraordinary Smelling Powers)

Another story involving extraordinary smelling powers justified the search of David Geltmaker's motorcycle by three Fish and Wildlife Service agents. The agents followed Geltmaker into a restricted area of federal parklands, two miles north of the Mexican border, to ask him his purpose for being there. They found the motorcycle, but Geltmaker had taken a hike. The agents became curious about several bags tied onto the motorcycle, but as no laws had been violated, they needed a legal reason amounting to "probable cause" to justify a search of the bags. (The fact that all of this took place near the border was not a legally sufficient reason.) The agent who made the search testified at trial:

> You could smell the smell that I have smelled before which smelled like marijuana, and I took my knife out and cut one of the bags open, and there were several packages—well, in the bag that I opened up, and one of them was busted open and it was what looked to me to be marijuana since I had seen marijuana a few times before.[6]

Geltmaker's lawyer did not dispute that the agent truly smelled the odiferous marijuana, and Geltmaker was convicted. Indeed, it may be that everything occurred just as the officer testified, but the point of these stories is that smell is very subjective. In addition, there is no independent evidence to establish whether or not an officer truly got a whiff of marijuana or invented that reason later. This loophole, therefore, is another way that the police can subvert your constitutional right to privacy.

You Have Considerably More Legal Protection for Material in Your Car's Trunk

It's worth repeating that it is more difficult for the police to search your locked trunk without a warrant than most other places in your car. The police cannot claim that they feared that you could leap into a locked trunk to grab a gun; they cannot reasonably claim that they saw you make a "suspicious movement" to hide something in your locked trunk while you were driving; and even police with creative noses are usually unwilling to assert that the smell of marijuana was wafting from your trunk. Do these facts mean that you are completely safe if you put marijuana in your car trunk? No. As you will see, there is a big difference between increased protection and absolute, or even close to absolute, protection.

The police can still search your locked trunk without a search warrant if they can successfully convince a judge that they obtained probable cause in a way other than those last mentioned. How could they obtain probable cause, you ask? Well, finding some marijuana in the interior of your car is the easiest way for the police to establish a reasonable belief that you have more marijuana elsewhere in your vehicle. The judges in most states have decided that if police find any marijuana inside the car, they are justified in searching a locked trunk. Only some of the judges in a few states, including California and New Jersey, properly recognize that the finding of a joint or some marijuana seeds in the front seat does not give the police probable cause to believe that there is more marijuana in the car trunk, thus justifying its search.[7]

EXAMPLE: Sarah Revisited

Return with us now to the adventures of Sarah. This time Sarah was arrested by Officers Straight and Arrow when she made a left turn at 4:10 PM at a corner where left turns were prohibited between 4:00 and 7:00 PM.

"Don't you know that it's ten minutes after four, Miss?" Officer Joe Straight asked Sarah.

"No, Officer, I don't wear a watch. I believe that time is only an artificial mind constraint designed by people who mistakenly think schedules are important; and anyway, Officer, there is no one on the street but us."

"It makes no difference, Miss, so I'm afraid I will have to write you up. Let me see your registration."

When Sarah opened her glove compartment, Officer Frank Arrow spotted a small plastic bag and grabbed it. It contained marijuana. Although there was only enough grass in the bag to roll two joints, Officer Arrow asked Sarah for her keys. He then unlocked her car trunk and found another half-pound of marijuana inside a closed cardboard box.

Question: Could the officer legally search Sarah's trunk without a search warrant?

Answer: Probably yes. Most judges believe that an officer has probable cause to believe that anyone with a little marijuana in her glove compartment has more in the trunk. In this example, the officer's guess was right, but is it really reasonable to believe that all Americans probably have more marijuana in their trunk if they have a little in the glove compartment?

Question: If Sarah were arrested in a state which made the possession of a small amount of marijuana (usually less than one ounce) an infraction, would the officer still be able to search her trunk legally?

Answer: Yes. Either the judges of your state believe that a joint in a car means that there are probably two more in the trunk, or they don't. In a state where possession of a little marijuana is only subject to a small fine, the police are more likely to leave you alone, but it can still be used to justify a search of your trunk in many of these states. (In several states, including California and Colorado, the police are not authorized to arrest you and bring you to the police station for possession of less than an ounce of marijuana if you have identification and promise in writing to appear in court.)

EXAMPLE: Can the Change of a Single Fact Save Sarah?

Now let's assume that Sarah was stopped for driving with a broken tail-light (or for an illegal left turn or a rolling stop), but this time she had all of her marijuana carefully wrapped in her suitcase to hide any odor and locked in her trunk. This time when officers Straight and Arrow eyeballed the glove compartment, they saw nothing but roadmaps and a paperback collection of the writings of Alan Watts.

Question: Would the officers have a legal right to search the locked trunk?
Answer: No. If they had asked Sarah to open it, she should politely have refused and kept refusing. If they searched anyway and discovered the marijuana, most judges would rule that the evidence was illegal and not admissible in court.

Tips from Reliable Informers Can Give the Police Probable Cause

Another way the police can legally search your locked trunk without a warrant and without your permission is for an officer or an informer to see you place marijuana in your trunk. Robert Mason, carrying a paper bag, left a house that was under surveillance by police. He drove off in his car only to stop a block and a half away to place the bag in the trunk. It was this suspicious conduct, along with the suspicion that Mason and the owner of the house were drug dealers, that gave police probable cause to search Mason's trunk. They found cocaine and the State convicted him.[8]

The "Inventory Search" Loophole Justifies a Warrantless Search of Your Entire Car, Including Your Trunk

The police routinely search cars which they have towed to the police station because the U.S. Supreme Court recently approved the "inventory search" exception to the requirement that the police establish probable cause to justify a search. This loophole means that the police can automatically search any place in your car, including your locked trunk, for no reason except that it has properly been brought to the impoundment lot or police station. Whether your car was towed after you illegally parked it or after you were arrested for speeding is immaterial. If the police have a legal reason to tow your car, they can search it.

It's the Real Thing!

The South Dakota Supreme Court had decided that it was illegal for the police to break into Donald Oberlink's locked car after it was towed to the police station for being illegally parked. The police searched everywhere, including the glove compartment, where ownership and registration papers are usually kept, and where, as it happened, Oberlink kept a little marijuana. The U.S. Supreme Court reversed in a five to four decision. Chief Justice Warren Burger wrote that the warrantless, routine "inventory search" of Oberlink's car was reasonable and legal because the police were only exercising their "community caretaking functions" to protect personal belongings from theft, to protect society from thieves who steal guns from cars parked at police stations, and to protect the police from lawsuits for failing to protect personal belongings.[9]

This reasoning has seemed a bit specious to many observers for several reasons. The police, after all, do not go around breaking into cars legally parked on the street to protect personal belongings and certainly Oberlink's locked car was at least as safe in the police station as it had been on the street. Nevertheless, rather than simply locking your car, keeping it locked, or calling you to ask your permission to search, the police can now "inventory" your car after towing it. Though Oberlink arrived at the police station the same morning that his car was towed, the police had already completed their "protective inventory" search and Oberlink was convicted for possession of a little plastic baggie of marijuana.

> NOTE: The supreme courts of several states, including those of Wisconsin and California, have relied on their state constitutions to restrict the legal right of the state police—not the federal police—to undertake warrantless inventory searches of cars within their borders.

EXAMPLE: The Police Protect Sarah's Car from Thieves

"I can never find a parking place when people are waiting for me. Oh well, it's after five—I'll just leave it here in this loading zone since I'll be right back anyway," Sarah decided.

A few minutes later . . .

"Where is that Rambler anyway—I could have sworn that I left it right over there."

Later that evening at the police station . . .

"It looks like it's been a good day for illegally parked cars, Joe. Have you searched them all yet?"

"No, we've just towed some of them in, Frank. We always get a few between five and six."

"Well, search them and inventory their contents. We don't want anything stolen from locked cars in our police station parking lot before the owners come to claim them, now, do we?"

Later . . .

"Humm . . . looks like marijuana, Frank. Not much—mostly twigs and seeds in the corners of this box in her trunk. We had a little trouble with the lock, but we finally got it open."

Later, when Sarah arrived . . .

"You towed my car—the Rambler with the 'no nukes are good nukes' sign on the back. How much do I owe you?"

"We've been waiting for you, Sarah. Looks like you carry marijuana in the trunk of your car. We'd like to ask you a few questions."

"I want to talk with my lawyer."

"We're locking you up."

Question: What could Sarah's lawyer do about the inventory search?

Answer: In most states, nothing. The search was legal. It doesn't matter that even if a thief did steal something from the police parking lot, it's unlikely he would break into a car trunk to do it.

SELF-HELP NOTE: Avoid Giving the Police an Excuse to Tow Your Car. In most situations, if the police don't find any marijuana inside your car and don't have other reliable information, they will have no legal reason (probable cause) to search your locked trunk unless they can make an inventory search of the vehicle. Obviously, anyone with marijuana in the trunk will want to take steps to avoid this possibility. The easiest way to avoid giving the police an excuse to tow your car is not to park it illegally, and particularly not in a tow zone.

A more difficult problem involves preventing the police from towing your car after they stop you for a traffic offense and they arrest you for that offense or for some other reason, such as outstanding warrants. The police will routinely tow a car after an arrest if the car is not legally parked. So, whenever you see the police following you with their lights flashing, try to pull over to a place on the road where you can park your car legally. Naturally you cannot wait too long to pull over, but if you can quickly find a legal and safe place off the road to park your car, there is a good chance that a judge will not permit the police to use the "inventory search" loophole to justify towing your car to the station and searching it without probable cause or a search warrant.

Similarly, if the police ask you to drive your car to the police station and ask to search it first "for their own protection," you can refuse and ask that it be left or towed instead. Since some police departments restrict the use of the inventory search loophole, depending upon the city or state and the circumstances of the towing, it is always better to allow the police to tow your car than to give consent to a search.

The "Consent to be Towed" Case

When the police stopped Charles Choper for speeding, Raymond Mishkin, the passenger, panicked. He gave Choper, who was driving without a license, his own driver's license to show the police. After questioning Choper and Mishkin, the police arrested Choper for driving without a license and arrested Mishkin for permitting an unauthorized person to use his driver's license. The police told the two men that they would have to go to the station to post bond on the traffic tickets, but that in order to drive their car to the station, they would have to allow the police to search it. Instead of telling the patrolmen that they did not want their car searched and would rather that it be left by the side of the road and locked, Mishkin and Choper apparently believed that they had no choice but to consent. They "consented" and the police searched and found a boa constrictor, a gun, fifteen pills (later identified as LSD), and a suitcase. The police also used the "leaping" loophole to justify searching the car for their "protection." One officer placed the suitcase in the police car, supposedly at the request of Mishkin and Choper, who each wanted a change of clothing. On the way to the station, the police claimed they smelled marijuana in the suitcase and opened it, finding just what they allegedly smelled.[10] Though the police would probably have searched the car and everything in it even if Mishkin and Choper had said they would rather lock the car and leave it rather than consent to a search, a judge might have found such a search illegal. As it was, however, their consent ensured the legality of the search, even though the officer's story about Choper and Mishkin asking for a change of clothes from a suitcase stuffed with marijuana stretches the imagination.

A Guest in a Car Has Few Protections, or the "You Can't Complain" Loophole

A new exception to the Fourth Amendment's protection from unreasonable searches and seizures recently approved by the U.S. Supreme Court is the "you can't complain" loophole.[11] With this loophole, the police need not use any of the other pretexts in order to deprive you completely of your constitutional right to be free from unreasonable and warrantless searches. If you are a guest in a vehicle you are in danger. This new exception means that the police can admit that their search was unlawful and the State can still use the illegal evidence to obtain your conviction. Thus any marijuana the police find during an illegal search of a car can be used to convict you if you are *not the owner* of the car, unless the marijuana is placed within your own personal belongings, such as a backpack, suitcase, or purse, or on your person.

The owner of the car cannot be convicted with the evidence seized in the illegal search because the Fourth Amendment protects her rights in the car. But, somehow, the Fourth Amendment does not apply to a guest in the car. Why? The Supreme Court has concluded that a guest has no legal "standing" or right to object to an illegal search of someone else's car. Thus if you are a guest, you are almost defenseless against this loophole if marijuana is found in a car in which you are riding, unless the owner of the car is willing to admit to owning the marijuana and hiding it in her car without your knowledge. If the owner does not admit to owning the marijuana, you may be in trouble, at least if the State can prove that you possessed the forbidden flowers.

EXAMPLE: Ralph and the Hitchhikers

Ralph commonly picked up hitchhikers, especially in the country. Shortly after stopping for a couple of backpacking types one afternoon, he saw a police car in back of him, lights flashing. Ralph looked down the road, spotted an area where it was possible to pull off the road completely, and waited to stop until reaching the safe spot. At the last minute, he noticed one of the hitchhikers throw a baggie on the floor and kick it under the seat. Too late to do anything about that now, he thought.

"Driver's license. Car registration. Are these two friends of yours?" the officer asked.

"They're hitchhikers. It's legal to hitchhike, isn't it?"

"You all look like drug users to me. Get out of the car, all of you. Empty your knapsacks."

"What's wrong, officer? We don't have to do that. Are we under arrest?"

"Empty them. What's in the little bottle?"

"Eye drops."

"Put them in your eyes."

"I only use them before bed."

"Either you put them in your eyes, or I will run you to the station to check out the contents of that bottle."

"Okay, okay—watch."

"Frank, check the inside of that truck."

"Ah ha—here's some marijuana, Joe, right under the seat."

"The marijuana under the seat is ours," one of the hitchhikers said.

"Honest drug addicts, huh? Well, guys—you've just hitched a ride to jail."

At the court hearing to suppress evidence, Officers Straight and Arrow were completely honest. They explained how they could recognize drug user types and how they just had had a strong hunch that these people were holding marijuana. The judge was a little surprised. "You mean you didn't see a suspicious movement, you didn't see a marijuana seed on the floor, and you didn't smell marijuana in the truck?" he asked the officers.

"Your honor, our hunches are almost always right," Officer Frank Arrow replied. "We don't need to see or smell anything suspicious."

Question: Was the police search legal after this testimony?

Answer: No. As you should now understand, a hunch is not probable cause and the police officers did not even attempt to use any of the common loopholes to justify their search.

Question: Does this illegal search mean that the marijuana couldn't be entered as evidence against Ralph?

Answer: Yes. Ralph is off the hook even if the marijuana had been his own because his vehicle was searched illegally.

Question: But what about the hitchhikers? Could the State still use the illegally seized evidence to convict the hitchhikers?

Answer: Yes, in many states and in all federal courts. Here's how the judge explained the law to the hitchhikers:

Judge: You two hitchhikers must stand trial for possession of the marijuana the police found under the seat because neither of you has legal standing to complain about the illegal search of someone else's car. Because you admitted to the police that the marijuana was yours, you must suffer the consequences.

Hitchhikers: But your honor, you already ruled that it was an illegal search, which means the evidence is also illegal.

Judge: That's true, but it doesn't mean that the evidence can't be used against you. Let me explain the law one more time. Though the police seized your marijuana illegally, they did not violate your rights because they didn't illegally search your car. You have no legal right to care whether the police illegally search another person's car or home or whatever, as long as they leave you alone and respect your constitutional rights.

Hitchhikers: Wait a minute, your honor. I do care about the police respecting everyone's constitutional rights, and I must have a right to expect that the police won't use unconstitutional means to find evidence against me. How can you say we don't have the right to complain?

Judge: Under the law, you do have standing to object to an illegal search of your backpacks, but not the illegal search of someone else's car. And, what may be more surprising to you—if the police had found marijuana in one of your knapsacks during their illegal search, the prosecutor could use the illegal evidence to try to convict the person who had no marijuana in his sack.

Hitchhikers: But, for what crime?

Judge: Why, for possession of the marijuana. Of course, it would be a little more difficult for the prosecutor to prove knowledge of possession, but one of you would have no standing to object to the illegal search. Sorry boys, I'm not the U.S. Supreme Court. They make the rules and I just follow them.

The judge allowed the illegally-seized evidence to be used against the hitchhikers. They were tried and found guilty of possession of more than an ounce of marijuana—twenty-nine grams to be exact. The judge sentenced them to six months in jail (with three months suspended). Jail made them late for the start of the fall semester at college and they missed a course on the writings of Kafka, Camus, and Beckett, but some would argue that they had received a better education in the essential absurdity of it all, courtesy of county officials, than they ever would have received at the University.

SELF-HELP NOTE: If You Carry Marijuana in a Friend's Car, Place It in Your Personal Luggage. The only way to protect yourself and your constitutional rights from the "you can't complain" loophole when you carry marijuana in someone else's car is to keep it with your personal belongings. If the marijuana is in your own suitcase, you have legal standing to object to its search. In other words, although most judges will convict you for any marijuana that the police illegally search for and seize from under the seat or in the trunk of your friend's car, they will give you a right to object to an illegal search and seizure of *your* suitcase if you admit in court to owning the suitcase (see Chapter 11 for a surprising example of why you should remain silent and never deny owning your suitcase during its search).

IMPORTANT: If you have placed your personal belongings in *locked personal* luggage in your trunk, the police may still ask to search your luggage or car, threaten to arrest you, or say that they will simply hold you and your luggage while they obtain a search warrant. You should already know that it is your constitutional right not to consent to a search of any part of your car, and you should also know that it is in your interest to be patient while the police try to obtain a search warrant. Many people, falling victim to the American foibles of hurry and anxiety, end up giving the police permission to make a search for which they could never have obtained a warrant.

If the police insist on searching your car after you have refused consent and you believe the search to be illegal, you may want to call over a witness to establish that you have not consented to the search. But be careful and polite because you don't want to leave yourself open to a charge of resisting arrest or interfering with a police officer. If the police ask you for the key to your car trunk, you may want to refuse politely in order to make it more difficult for them to claim that you consented to their search. But never use physical force against an officer. If the police try to take the key from you, you have no legal choice but to submit.

EXAMPLE: Ralph Picks Up More Hitchhikers

Remember Ralph and his fondness for hitchhikers? The next week Ralph picked up another hitchhiker—this time a bicyclist with a flat tire. But Ralph's luck wasn't any better, and almost immediately the friendly neighborhood police cruiser was on his tail again. Ralph, it seems, didn't signal when he pulled back onto the highway after stopping for the hitchhiker. This time the police did not find any marijuana in the interior of the truck, but did find marijuana when they ordered the hitchhiker to empty her knapsack. On the flatbed portion of Ralph's pickup truck was a locked compartment.

"You there, driver, open this locked chest."
"No. You have no right to search my toolbox."
"Break the lock, Frank."
"Marijuana, Joe. Right in this little suitcase."
"Damn potheads, I can spot them every time."

Question: Was the search of the hitchhiker's knapsack legal?

Answer: Probably not. The police might try to justify the search by saying that the knapsack was within Ralph's or the hitchhiker's leaping distance, but most judges would not accept this excuse. In some states, the fact that Ralph and the hitchhiker were not placed under arrest for a traffic law infraction prevents the police from using the "leaping" loophole. And in all states, most judges would realize that ordering the hitchhiker to empty her own bag was obviously not the way for the police to prevent her from grabbing a gun or eating her marijuana.

Question: Was the search of Ralph's suitcase in his locked chest legal?

Answer: No. The U.S. Supreme Court says that the police almost always have to go through the formality of obtaining a search warrant to open personal luggage, even if it is in a motor vehicle, unless there is a true emergency. Ralph's suitcase and the hitchhiker's knapsack were personal luggage.

And now, after preparing you for the worst, here is a reminder that it's not always this bad—high courts in some states take a more enlightened view of the Constitution and the laws that protect our freedom and privacy.

THE BEST YOU CAN EXPECT FROM A JUDGE

• Some judges will be skeptical of a police story that you violated a traffic law if the police admit to following you around the town because they didn't like your looks.

• In some states, the law condemns a warrantless search of your car if justified only by a "suspicious movement."

• There are legal decisions in some states which restrict how far the "leaping" loophole can be stretched to justify a warrantless search of your handbag or briefcase in the interior of your car.

· Judges in some states, particularly in California, will not allow the police to make a warrantless search of your trunk solely because they found a joint in the interior of the car.

· In those few cities and states that do not permit a "routine inventory search" of your car after it is towed, most judges will condemn this type of warrantless search.

· In some states, judges will recognize that you do have a reasonable expectation of privacy concerning any bag in your car and any partially opened personal luggage and will, therefore, condemn a warrantless search of these containers.

· Some state courts will protect your reasonable expectation that the police will honor everyone's constitutional rights and will give you standing to object to the illegal seizure of anything which you own, including marijuana found in a friend's car.

CHAPTER **9**

Watch Your Step into Public View: Stops, Searches, and Arrests

MISTRESS OVERDONE: Nay, but I know 'tis so: I saw him arrested, saw him carried away, and, which is more, within these three days his head to be chopped off.

LUCIO: But, after all this fooling, I would not have it so. Art thou sure of this?

William Shakespeare,
MEASURE FOR MEASURE, Act I, Scene 2

How wonderful to be free to live out our dreams, make our mistakes, be on our own. Because the freedom to be left alone is such a precious quality of human life, the U.S. Supreme Court has decided that although it is not a constitutional right, the police *are* supposed to have a "good reason" before bothering you. What is a good reason for police interference? Well, what's a good wine, playmate, or song? We all have our own opinions, and so do the police and judges. The U.S. Supreme Court has tried to set some standards for "good reasons," but the police and lower court judges have been left a great deal of discretion. For example, the "good reason" standard usually depends upon the type of police intrusion. What may be a "good reason" for the police to stop you for a minute on the street may not be a good enough reason for them to search you. This chapter explains the escalating scale of "good reasons" necessary to justify different types of police intrusions, beginning with a police officer's friendly hello and concluding with rather uncivilized vaginal and anal searches. Your best protection is to try to avoid giving the police "good reasons" to increase the intensity of their intrusions. Unfortunately, however, you can usually only guess what reasons the police have, or can fabricate, to justify any particular intrusion, and thus even with the best information as to your rights, there are times when you will not be able to protect your legal rights. If you must carry marijuana in public, use a tightly-closed, preferably locked briefcase, knapsack, or handbag, never a paper bag or box.

THUMBNAIL REVIEW
What the Police Can Do "Legally"

• The police can always engage you in conversation by waving you over to them or *asking* you to stop.

• The police need "reasonable suspicion" of some criminal activity to demand that you stop, to stop you forcibly, or to insist upon identification.

• After stopping you, the police need "factual suspicion" that you are armed in order to "frisk" you by patting down your outer clothes. The police can seize any object that could possibly be a weapon. Depending on state law, police can either withdraw hard objects from your pockets or simply empty your pockets.

• Assuming the police have sufficient suspicion to stop and frisk, they may "ask" you, but not force you, to accompany them to the police station for further questioning.

• Then prior to taking you, voluntarily or otherwise, to the police station in their car, the police may frisk you and sometimes search all your personal belongings which are large enough to contain a razor blade.

• The police need probable cause to believe that you are in the process of committing any crime or have already committed a serious crime (felony) to arrest you. Since marijuana possession is a misdemeanor in most states, the police must see it or smell it before they can arrest you for possession in those states.

• The police need only a reasonable belief that you probably have more than a little marijuana in your pocket to arrest you in those states where possession of more than a small amount of marijuana is a felony (see the Appendix for state marijuana laws).

• After arresting you, the police may search your clothing, wallet, cigarette case, and sometimes even unlocked baggage within your leaping area, for weapons and marijuana.

• "Private" persons who are not employed by the State are not bound by the rules governing the police and other government agents. This rule of law means that even though private persons are supposed to leave you alone, they can search you for no reason if you allow them. If they search, even in an illegal manner, and discover marijuana or other evidence, the State can use it to convict you.

• After placing you under arrest and taking you to the police station, the police may strip search you before placing you in jail.

• After strip searching you, the police need "factual suspicion" to conduct vaginal and anal searches.

What You Can Do to Protect Yourself

• Stop when the police ask you to stop, and act respectfully even if they do not.

• Identify yourself if at all possible, even if you do not believe the police have "reasonable suspicion" to require you to do so.

• To avoid a frisk search, avoid the "armed and dangerous" look (whatever that is), do not make any quick movements with your hands, and do not reach into your jacket, coat, or pants pockets. If you must carry your marijuana on your person, use as small and soft a container as possible so that the police can't reasonably confuse it with a weapon.

• Never voluntarily accompany the police to the station for further questioning, but never resist arrest.

• To avoid giving the police probable cause to arrest you, do not smoke marijuana in public.

• Carry marijuana in tightly-closed, preferably locked, personal luggage, such as a briefcase, knapsack, or handbag.

• Try to avoid carrying marijuana on you, particularly in stores, schools, and private parks.

• After arrest, remain silent and insist upon seeing a lawyer.

THE FOURTH AMENDMENT AND STEPPING INTO PUBLIC VIEW

The Fourth Amendment specifically states: "The right of the people to be secure in their persons, houses, papers, and effects, against unreasonable searches and seizures, shall not be violated, and no Warrants shall issue, but upon probable cause . . . ."

But just as the Fourth Amendment does not protect your home or vehicle from many types of warrantless searches, it often does not protect your clothing, or even your body, from the intrusions of the State. The police can use many of the same legal loopholes to search your person that they use to justify the search of your land or your home. Indeed, when it comes to the bundle of blood and guts that you affectionately know as you, they even have a couple of additional reasons they can use to justify warrantless stops, searches, and arrests. In theory, the police need a specific factual foundation to justify stopping, searching, or arresting you without a warrant. Generally speaking, the more serious their search or seizure of your person, the better reasons the police need to justify it. For example, they can "seize" or stop you for ten or twenty minutes if they "reasonably suspect" that you are involved in a criminal activity, but they need to believe that you have "probably" committed a crime to arrest you. Unfortunately, many of the standards governing police conduct are so vague and so open to fabrication that there are many situations in which there is little that you can do to protect your constitutional right to be secure in your person. In the last analysis, your best protection when in public places may be to realize that the Fourth Amendment affords you only limited security and that it is wise to be cautious.

POWERS OF THE POLICE

The Police Can Legally Stop You For Any Reason— Or For No Reason At All

The police do not need probable cause to believe that you have committed, or are committing, a crime in order to stop you on the street or in a public place. In fact, no reason at all is legally required before the police can engage you in conversation, wave you over to them, or *ask* you to halt. Most judges simply believe that this type of stop is not a "seizure" in the Fourth Amendment sense. Of course, if this assumption were really true—that is, if you were not being seized and were really stopping to talk to an officer voluntarily—then you should be able to walk away without acknowledging the police if you feel like walking away. In reality, of course, you cannot safely ignore the police in this situation without risking arrest or worse, because in the best *Catch-22* tradition, the police will consider it suspicious if you assert your right to be left alone. Thus walking away from the police will usually allow them to justify stopping you forcibly. Indeed, people are stopped everyday on the basis that "they nervously turned and quickly walked away." Technically, however, the police need reasonable suspicion based on particular factual circumstances that "crime is afoot" to stop you.

Since there is little you can do to assert your right to be left alone, you should stop at the request of the police. In a sense, you are required to stop even if the police do not have reasonable suspicion that you are engaged in crime. *If you are carrying marijuana when the police ask you to stop, it is particularly important that you stop.* Walking or running may well give the police reason to frisk you, if not probable cause to arrest and search you. And even if you aren't arrested on the spot, the police have so many excuses which allow them to search you for marijuana without probable cause and without formally arresting you, that the less suspicious you make them, the better.

After the police stop you, they may ask you to identify yourself. In theory, you do not have to answer or give your name if the police do not have reasonable suspicion to stop you. But as you will not know if the police have legal cause to stop you, and because they can so easily fabricate "reasonable suspicion" if you remain silent, and because remaining silent may in and of itself justify more extreme police behavior, you should identify yourself. Similarly, if the police question you about an illegal activity or some other event with which you are not connected in anyway, answering truthfully is usually the best policy. There is no sense in risking an illegal arrest by refusing to talk with the police as a matter of principle. But it goes without saying that you should refuse to talk about anything vaguely related to marijuana and refuse to consent to any search of your clothes or belongings (see Chapter 11 for a discussion of the importance of remaining silent and allowing a lawyer to do your talking).

The Police Can Legally Search You for Weapons Without a Search Warrant

After the police stop you, they can search you for weapons without a warrant by patting down or frisking your body if they have factual suspicion that you are armed. This limited exception to the Fourth Amendment is understandable when it is genuinely used for the self-protection of the police. The problem is that often it is used simply as an excuse to search people. Since the suspicion necessary to justify the search can be based on such unreliable facts as acting nervously, refusing to stop, or having a bulge in your pocket it is easy to see how abuses can become rampant. Some state and federal courts even allow this purported search for weapons to extend to a pretext search for drugs, while a few state courts refuse to admit into evidence marijuana obtained in a weapons search if the drug container could not possibly feel like a weapon in a "pat-down" search. Therefore in such states as California, Illinois, and New York, marijuana found in a soft container or small pouch during a weapons frisk search is illegally obtained evidence and cannot be used to convict you. But a police officer in California can pick your pocket during a frisk so long as the officer suspects you are armed, and what he pulls out could possibly be a weapon. Anything else that gets stuck between his fingers will also be admissible in court. Thus, the officer looking for a person armed with a shotgun reached into Larry Acampora's pocket and pulled out a joint along with a lipstick container. Three judges of the California Court of Appeal decided that this search was legal because the officer said that he believed that the lipstick container might be a shotgun shell and the judges believed that Acampora could have exploded the shell in desperation.[1]

SELF-HELP NOTE: Avoid Carrying Hard Objects That Can Be Confused With Weapons. You are practically defenseless against the police unfairly using the weapons search to conduct a warrantless search for drugs. Naturally, your lawyer will have a better chance to convince a judge that the police illegally searched you on the pretext of searching you for weapons if you are not carrying any weapons or hard objects that feel like weapons. And you are more protected from a warrantless search if you do not look like "an armed and dangerous type." Realistically, however, your only guaranteed protection from a "stop and frisk" type search is not to carry any marijuana on you when you are outside. Again, if you are stopped, it is wise to treat the police with respect and to identify yourself. The police are less likely to search a person who is behaving in a friendly fashion. And if the police do search, they will find it more difficult to justify the search, especially if there are witnesses to the fact that you were behaving in a cooperative, nonthreatening manner.

Of course, if the police find a little marijuana in one of the eleven states that assess only a fine for the crime of possessing a small amount, usually under an ounce (see Appendix), they will often simply give you a ticket and let you go. The ticket procedure usually requires you to give proper identification and to promise in writing to appear in court or pay the fine by mail. Some officers, however, will use their discovery of a small amount of marijuana in your possession as an excuse to arrest you or to do further searching. While this book prepares you for the worst, you should still hope for the best.

EXAMPLE: Steve Steps Outside For a Smoke

The scene is a deserted street at midnight, a block away from a bar. Steve, who is standing by a fence, is greeted by a police officer.

"What are you doing out here?"
"Nothing."
"What did you throw over the fence?"
"Nothing."
"I saw you smoking from across the street."
"Ya, sure. I was smoking. I guess I threw the butt away."
"Let's see some identification."
"Why? What have I done?"
"Don't make trouble. Put your hands on the car. I'll have to frisk you. What's this lump in your pocket? I see it's a pouch. And what's this hard metal object? And what's in your pouch and this metal case?"

Question: Did the police officer legally question Steve?
Answer: Yes. Many judges would say that the officer needed no reason to ask Steve a question. Other judges would approve as long as the officer gave any plausible reason, such as the fact that Steve suspiciously threw

something over the fence, that he was looking around in a suspicious manner, or that what he was smoking smelled like marijuana.

Question: Did the police legally ask Steve for identification?

Answer: Yes. In nearly all states judges would require the officer to have a reason like one of those just listed, but wouldn't question the reason very closely.

Question: Did the police officer legally frisk Steve?

Answer: Probably yes. So long as the officer testified that Steve acted belligerently or that he noticed a "bulge" in Steve's pocket, most judges would approve the frisk. But some judges might say that under these circumstances the officer had no factual suspicion that Steve was armed, and rule that the search was illegal for this reason.

Question: Assuming that the frisk was legal, did the police officer legally withdraw the pouch from Steve's pocket?

Answer: Maybe, depending upon the state and the judge. Some judges would decide that the seizure was illegal because the pouch was soft and could not feel like a weapon. Some judges might decide that the search was legal because the pouch was large enough to contain a small weapon, such as a razor blade (for more information about legal decisions in this area, see the discussion on the "leaping" loophole in this chapter).

Question: Did the officer legally withdraw the metal case?

Answer: Yes. It could have been a weapon.

Question: Did the police officer legally look inside the pouch or the metal case?

Answer: Perhaps not. Judges in some states would realize that the officer could protect himself from any weapon inside by waiting to give them back to Steve until after he finished talking with him. Other judges would permit the officer to look for razor blades. The police officer, however, could make this search legal by testifying that he saw marijuana in a "half-opened" pouch or that the case popped open after he withdrew it. Of course, he would only bother to tell these fibs if, after opening them, he found marijuana in the pouch, or cocaine in the case.

The Police Can Do a Self-Protection Detention Search

After the police stop you, they can always "ask" you to go to the police station for further questioning. Usually the police will make this suggestion only if you have made them particularly suspicious. You may create suspicion by refusing to identify yourself, refusing to answer their questions, trying to avoid them, or because of your dress, way of speaking, or for any one of a dozen other reasons. If you refuse to go to the police station, the police may arrest you and force you to go. But in this situation, the law does partially protect you. The police need "probable cause" to arrest you and take you forcibly to the station. Without probable cause, your arrest is illegal and any marijuana the police subsequently find is illegal evidence that cannot be used to convict you. In contrast, if you "voluntarily" accompany the police to the station, they do not need probable cause to justify your voluntary detention.

Whether you are arrested, or you voluntarily accompany the police to the station, the police may now legally search you. This search is called a "self-protection" detention search and can occur as you get into a police vehicle or after you arrive at the police station. Normally, these searches are done as a matter of routine and have been approved by the courts with no requirement that the police have a specific reason to suspect that you have a weapon. Under these circumstances, any marijuana that the police "accidentally" find while looking for guns, knives, razor blades, or other weapons can be used to convict you.

This self-protection detention search might well be justifiable if the police told you that you have a right to refuse to go to the police station unless arrested and that if you agree to go, they will search you. Instead, if the police want to search you without a warrant, they will try to intimidate you into accompanying them voluntarily to the police station without telling you that once you consent to go with them, they may routinely search you for weapons (see Chapter 6 for the consent discussion). Only a few state courts have recognized that such detentions are really arrests, for which the police should have probable cause to believe that you have committed a crime (see Chapter 10).

SELF-HELP NOTE: Refuse to Accompany the Police Voluntarily Unless Arrested. If the police ever ask you to accompany them to the police station for questioning, you have the right to tell them that you do not want to go voluntarily, but that you will, of course, go peacefully if they arrest you. You should always try to be as cooperative as possible because the police have the armed power to do whatever they want. But if you are carrying marijuana or other *verboten* material, it is almost always better for you to refuse to accompany the police voluntarily. Forcing the police to choose between arresting you or letting you go is not itself suspicious conduct sufficient to justify an arrest. If you assert your rights, in some situations the police will let you go. In others, you may make the police suspicious or angry enough to arrest you and search you. This misfortune is still better than going with the officers voluntarily however, because before your trial for possession of the forbidden material, your lawyer will have an opportunity to show that the police illegally arrested you without probable cause. If your lawyer can convince the judge that the police acted illegally, the judge will exclude the illegally-seized evidence.

WARNING: Although you may think that you can avoid this entire scene by answering all police questions and talking your way out of trouble, it is critical that you remember that far more people have talked their way into jail than have ever talked their way out (see Chapter 11). As a general rule, it is unwise to lie to the police and even more unwise to talk to them about anything related to your private activities. If you do end up talking to the police who stop you and then arrest you, your lawyer may have a difficult time defending you. Since you will usually not know whether the police have a legal reason to stop you and detain you, it is a good idea to politely ask the police "Am I under arrest?" If they say "no," then tell them you want to go. If they say "yes," do not try to talk your way out of trouble. Shut up until you can talk to a lawyer or some other person with the knowledge necessary to help you. Even if the police find your marijuana, the judge may suppress the evidence if your lawyer can convince her that the police did not have reasonable suspicion to stop you, a sufficient reason to bring you to the station, or factual suspicion that you were armed.

The Police Can Use the "Leaping" Loophole to Justify a Warrantless Search

As you have seen, the police can do a search for self-protection if you accompany them voluntarily. If the police arrest you, they can use the "leaping" loophole to justify thoroughly searching you and everything within your leaping distance, including your clothing, wallet, and most hand baggage (see Chapter 7). Therefore, as long as the police have probable cause to arrest you for any crime, even a traffic offense, they can legally search you. They do not need to suspect that you are armed. On the other hand, when the police do not have probable cause to arrest you, they must have reasonable suspicion that you are armed in order to search you.

Creative Leaping—Or, the Supreme Court Protects the Police Against Imaginary Dangers

In one case, the U.S. Supreme Court ruled that it was legal for the police to open a cigarette box in which a couple of joints were contained. The only justification was that the box was within James Gieras's leaping distance when the police arrested him for driving without a license. In dissent, Justices Marshall and Brennan correctly pointed out that this search was completely unnecessary and unwarranted because it did not have anything to do with protecting the police:

> There was no reason to believe, and Officer Smith did not in fact believe, that [Gieras] was a dangerous person or that the package contained a weapon. The package's weight alone, no doubt, would have indicated that it did not contain a gun or knife. In any event, even were it possible that the package contained some sort of weapon—say a razor blade—there was no chance that [Gieras] could use it once it was in the officer's hands.[2]

In a similar case, Drug Enforcement Administration (DEA) agents arrested and handcuffed Jesse Vance Adams when he left an airplane. They then seized and searched the handbag he was carrying, finding a quantity of LSD. The U.S. Court of Appeals decided that the police were justified in making this warrantless search because Adams's suitcase was still within his leaping distance after his arrest. Only Judge Walter Ely honestly recognized the absurdity of stretching the "leaping" loophole to include this type of search:

> Here, the accused was handcuffed and arrested as soon as he stepped from the airplane. It is undeniable that he then, and thereafter, had no access to his suitcase. It is undeniable that the immediate search that followed his arrest was motivated neither by the possibility that the handbag or its contents constituted a threat to the officers, nor by the possibility that evidence contained therein was in danger of destruction.[3]

SELF-HELP NOTE: Avoid Giving the Police Probable Cause to Arrest You. Naturally, the easiest way to avoid giving the police probable cause

to arrest you is to follow the letter of the law. Once you bend the law, you leave yourself open for countless surprises. In order to establish probable cause to arrest, the police can use all the same loopholes that they use in connection with applying for search warrants (see Chapter 5). Indeed, fabricating probable cause is even easier for an arrest than a search, because a judge is almost never required to determine whether the facts known to the police before your arrest show probable cause. The judge sees the case only after the police have arrested you and charged you with a crime.

One bit of police misconduct that you should be on the alert for is the so-called dropsy story. When confronted by the police, the criminal supposedly "drops" the contraband at the officer's feet or into the gutter, thus justifying its seizure. Before a 1961 U.S. Supreme Court decision, the police seldom used this story because most state police could search persons on the street for almost any reason and use the evidence—even if it was illegally seized—to convict them. After the Warren Supreme Court decided that illegally obtained evidence must be excluded from both state and federal courts, however, the New York police "discovered" that nearly 50 percent of the drug criminals they stopped on the street threw their contraband on the ground in plain view, thus justifying its seizure and the criminals' arrest.[4] The only protection you have against this kind of trick is honest police and impartial witnesses. If you are being arrested after an illegal search, you may ask witnesses to contact your lawyer or a friend. If a friend is with you at the time of the arrest, she should avoid arrest by keeping quiet and out of the way. The possibility that an impartial witness who was not arrested may testify will encourage the police to be more honest.

> NOTE: The law also allows the prosecutor to use marijuana found on you during an illegal arrest as long as the police honestly mistook you for someone else for whom they did have probable cause to arrest.[5] Such honest mistakes of identity undoubtedly occur infrequently, but a single conviction based on an unlucky and illegal arrest is one too many.

Routine Warrantless Searches of Paper Bags are Now Legal

In an ominous development, a United States court of appeals ruled in December 1980 that you have no reasonable expectation of privacy for the paper bags which you carry. Notwithstanding the fact that nearly all Americans expect their shopping bags and lunch bags to be private and immune from warrantless intrusion, these judges simply decided that this expectation of privacy is unreasonable. The judges' reasoning tends to prove one of this book's theories: when our Fourth Amendment rights depend upon what judges believe to be our reasonable expectation of privacy, we will soon have little privacy. Here is why the judges believe you have no reasonable expectation of privacy in your lunch and shopping bags: "a paper bag is among the least private of containers. It is easily torn, it cannot be latched, and, to a greater extent than most containers, its contents can frequently be discerned merely by holding or feeling the container."[6]

Another federal court of appeals has said the same thing about a plastic bag. What this legal development means is that the police can routinely grab and search any paper bag you are carrying without a warrant. If they find your marijuana, the warrantless search is legal so long as the police, in their arrest report, can think up or explain sufficient reasons amounting to probable cause that the bag contained "forbidden fruits" before they searched it. The warrant requirement of the Fourth Amendment is conveniently ignored.

> SELF-HELP NOTE: In what do lawyers, businessmen, and respectable people carry their personal belongings? You guessed it: briefcases, purses, or portfolios. Briefcases, for example, are not easily torn, they can be

latched, and their contents cannot be easily felt by squeezing them. Therefore, judges will recognize that your expectation of privacy for these containers is reasonable. If you can't afford or don't care to wear three-piece suits to complement your $100 briefcase, you do have an alternative. While nothing is certain in these modern times, least of all your privacy, nearly all judges have recognized that you have a reasonable expectation of privacy for tote bags, knapsacks, and gym bags, at least if they are tightly closed.

Smoking Marijuana in Public is Asking for Trouble

Obviously, smoking marijuana in front of the police will usually guarantee your arrest. But what if you only smoke in public when your view is unspoiled by uniformed police? Aside from the possibility of plainclothes police officers, and police officers suddenly appearing from behind you or from around a corner, there are always good citizens ready to report criminal marijuana activities. Fortunately, in most states where marijuana possession is a misdemeanor (see the appendix), an informer's word alone is not enough for the police to arrest you. The police may stop and question you, but they themselves must see you smoking or possessing marijuana before they arrest you. If marijuana possession is a felony in your state, however, then a reliable informer's report that you were smoking marijuana is usually enough to justify your arrest and a body search.

One reaction to seeing a police officer walk or run in your direction when you are smoking a joint is to swallow it. What do you think you can expect some of our law enforcers to do when they see you put something suspicious into your mouth? In 1952, the U. S. Supreme Court unanimously decided that the police cannot stick their fingers down your throat to prevent you from swallowing a drug. In that case, three Los Angeles police officers entered Antonio Rehnquiest's home about nine o'clock in the morning without a warrant. Without knocking, they broke down his bedroom door, jumped on him, and tried to force open his mouth after he hurriedly put a couple of unidentified pills into his mouth. The police failed to prevent Rehnquiest from swallowing the pills so they took him, handcuffed, to a hospital where a doctor forced him to throw up. All the judges agreed that this type of search was unconstitutional because it "shocks the conscience."[7]

In later cases, California judges have recognized that if the police grab you by the throat and choke you, they are using similar tactics that are shocking and unconstitutional. A Texas judge in 1977, however, justified the following search by the honored judicial method of "distinguishing cases." What follows is the judge's complete opinion, with only the case citations omitted. And even though the case is about heroin, the law it establishes would apply to any illegal drug, including marijuana.

> This is an appeal from a conviction for possession of heroin. [Felix Hanson] was found guilty in a bench trial upon his plea of not guilty and his punishment was assessed at 20 years' confinement in the Texas Department of Corrections.

[Hanson's] sole complaint is that the manner in which the heroin was recovered "shocks the conscience." His motion to suppress [the evidence] was overruled.

The [trial] record reflects that as two San Antonio police officers who were acting on a tip that [Hanson] was in possession of heroin approached [him] they "saw his hand come to his mouth and try to put something in his mouth . . ." Believing [Hanson] to be secreting the heroin that they had been informed he was in possession of, the two officers rushed and wrestled him to the ground. While one officer held [his] arms, the other choked him until he spit out four balloons. Heroin was found in the balloons. California decisions notwithstanding, the law is well settled in this [State] that when an officer has probable cause to believe that an offense is being committed in his presence, he has the right to take reasonable measures to insure that the incriminating evidence is not destroyed and that reasonable physical contact is one of these measures.

[Hanson's] ground of error is overruled.

The judgment of the trial court is affirmed.[8]

The police in some circumstances may also forcibly take a blood sample if they have probable cause to arrest you for a crime, such as drunkenness or drug use, for which your blood content is evidence that will soon disappear. The police can even take blood samples to test for marijuana use, but usually don't. Some states now require that a judge must authorize such bodily invasions, and then only if there is probable cause to believe your body contains criminal evidence and there is no less intrusive way to get the evidence. In these states, the police are usually required to wait for natural processes to eliminate balloons of heroin which are allegedly swallowed, rather than to force you to submit to stomach pumping.

Private Persons Can Illegally Search You and the State Can Use the Evidence to Convict You or, the "I'm Completely Innocent" Loophole

People in authority, such as teachers, store detectives, park rangers, and airport officials often search people without a warrant, probable cause, or even suspicion in their respective private schools, stores, parks, and airports. From a Fourth Amendment point of view, these searches are often illegal. But here's the rub—even though the searches are illegal, the evidence can often be used to convict persons in criminal proceedings. Why? Because the police didn't participate in the original search, judges have decided that there is no reason to suppress the evidence. Sound crazy? Perhaps so, but that's the way it goes.

The dean of Elmira College in New York State, for example, went to Michael Howard's dormitory suite after hearing a rumor that he had marijuana in his room. The dean knocked on the suite door, opened it with his key, entered the room that Howard had just left, and found "what appeared to be marijuana lying openly on the floor." The dean told Howard to bring the "substance" to his office, and when he did, the dean called the police, who then came and arrested Howard. The New York judges approved the break-in and warrantless search by the dean because he had acted without police encouragement and because of the "dangerous drug prevalence in many schools." The State could use the illegal evidence, seized in violation of Howard's Fourth Amendment rights, to convict him because the State was "completely innocent" of the original wrongdoing, even though it was guilty of taking advantage of that illegality.[9]

> **NOTE OF CAUTION:**   Of course, you can legally refuse to let a private individual search you, at least if he is not a security guard, but if you are facing a six-foot goliath or a six-inch gun, you may wisely assume that your choices are limited.

EXAMPLE: Kathy and Mimi Go to the Store

It's a nice sunny morning when two college roommates go to Friendly's Camping Store to buy supplies for a backpacking trip.

In the store, a man approaches Kathy and Mimi and identifies himself as a store employee.

"Would you both follow me, please?"

"What's the matter?"

"I'll explain in the office upstairs." Once upstairs, the employee continued, "Lady, one of our clerks says that you placed a book in your handbag without paying for it."

"I did not."

"We'll see. Give me your purse. You sure have a lot of junk in here. No books, but what's in this baggie?"

"Trail mix. You know, nuts, raisins."

"Lucky for you it's not marijuana. I'd have to turn you over to the police."

"Is that why you searched us—for marijuana, not for stolen books?"

"No, but I could have, and you could be convicted with any marijuana I found."

"Do you mean that we have no constitutional rights once we walk into your store?"

"I don't know nothing about the Constitution, but I do know that the police and prosecutor don't care how I find marijuana or why I look for it. However, I am terribly sorry for the inconvenience. I only search when one of our clerks believes someone has stolen something."

Question: Did the store detective know what he was talking about?

Answer: Yes. Store detectives are only supposed to search you for a good reason, but if they search you for no reason and find marijuana, the State can use it to convict you. (All states have laws allowing store employees to detain customers.)

The Police Can Do Jail House and Strip Searches

Once under arrest at the police station, the police can strip search you as a routine matter before locking you up. The more intrusive anal and vaginal searches, however, usually require the police to have some suspicion based on facts that suggest you have concealed something in your body.

(NOTE: For information on strip searches at the border, see Chapter 10.)

SELF-HELP NOTE: As soon as you are arrested, you should politely insist that the police allow you to call a lawyer. The fact that your lawyer can complain about police misconduct more effectively than you can, may encourage the police to treat you more fairly. As long as the police do not question you, however, they are not constitutionally required to allow you to contact anyone until you are arraigned or placed in a line-up. Usually, however, the police will allow you to make at least one phone call. If you can afford your own lawyer, it is best to call her immediately. If not, you should call a friend who might be able to pay your bail and get you out of jail. At your arraignment, the judge will inform you of the crimes with which you are charged. You have a right to a lawyer at this hearing because the court will set the amount of your bail at this time (see Chapter 13 for a full discussion).

And now, after preparing you for the worst, here is a reminder that it's not always this bad—judicial rulings in some states take a more enlightened view of the Constitution and laws that protect our freedom and privacy.

THE BEST YOU CAN EXPECT FROM A JUDGE

• Some judges will be more alert than others about questionable "facts" that the police claim are sufficient to justify a frisk search and the opening up of both soft and hard containers looking for marijuana and razor blades.

• A few judges will realize that if you consented out of ignorance to accompany the police to the station, you did not also consent to having the police search you and your belongings.

• Judges in some states will condemn an unnecessary, warrantless search of your personal belongings on the pretext that you could grab a razor blade or a weapon, particularly after the police already have you in handcuffs.

• Judges in some states will recognize that Americans' expectation of privacy in their shopping bags and lunch bags is reasonable, and will give these containers Fourth Amendment protection.

• Most judges will condemn police tactics that include strangling you to prevent you from swallowing a joint.

• High court rulings in some states do not allow the State to take advantage of illegal conduct by private persons, particularly security guards.

• A few state courts require the police to have some reason to conduct a strip search before you are jailed.

CHAPTER 10

Special Searches, including Airport, Boat, Customs, and Mail Searches

SIR TOBY: Excellent! I smell a device.

SIR ANDREW: I have't in my nose too.

SIR TOBY: He shall think, by the letters that thou wilt drop, that they come from my niece, and that she's in love with him.

MARIA: My purpose is, indeed, a horse of that colour.

SIR ANDREW: And your horse now would make him an ass.

MARIA: Ass, I doubt not.

SIR ANDREW: O, 'twill be admirable!

William Shakespeare,
TWELFTH-NIGHT; OR, WHAT YOU WILL, Act II, Scene 3

Perhaps you'll agree that we have muddled through fairly well in most areas of our national life in the nearly 200 years since the American revolutionaries banded together to adopt our Constitution and Bill of Rights. Granted the American Dream has changed more than a little in the intervening years—in the 1780s we Americans were goggle-eyed at the new model buggies, while today if it doesn't whiz through space it's hardly worth a glance. Yet with all these changes, we have the same old Constitution, and judges have the often difficult job of applying its meaning to new technologies.

When faced with new situations, courts have tended to respond as government institutions almost always do—conservatively. This chapter will examine what has happened to our Fourth Amendment protections in the light of new technologies and phenomena, such as airplanes and rock concerts. Special situations have tended to result in special exceptions to our Fourth Amendment rights. As you read this chapter, don't bother trying to rationalize or harmonize these rules—there's no rhyme and little reason for their existence.

THUMBNAIL REVIEW
What the Police Can Do "Legally"

· The police or private security guards can routinely search you and your belongings before allowing you to enter courtrooms, federal buildings, concert halls, or commercial airliners. They do not need probable cause or even suspicion that you have committed a crime to make these searches.

· Police dogs can routinely sniff your airplane luggage.

· The police can legally stop you anywhere in airports with little reason and can often search you for drugs without a search warrant.

· Customs officers can routinely open and search all your international luggage and international mail, but are not supposed to read your mail without a warrant.

· The police can search your plane or boat without a warrant if they have a "reasonable certainty" that it has crossed an international border. The Coast Guard can do a routine documentation and safety check of your boat on any occasion, and can use this check as a pretext to search your boat.

· The police can strip you during a customs search if they have suspicion, and they can examine your inner body if they have a "clear indication" that you are hiding drugs.

· The police can search all domestic mail without a warrant except items mailed first class via the U.S. Post Office.

· Private mail companies can search all your mail without any reason, and turn over any illegal drugs to the police.

· The police can record without a warrant the type of mail you receive, including return addresses and postmarks.

· The police can inspect your bank records without a warrant and without probable cause to suspect you of wrongdoing.

· With a search warrant the police can read your most personal mail, diary, or journal.

· The State may terminate your welfare benefits if you unreasonably refuse to allow a social worker into your home.

· The State can do a routine health, safety, or fire inspection of your home without probable cause, but you can demand a convenient time or a search warrant.

· The State can confiscate any vehicle, boat, or plane that has transported marijuana.

What You Can Do to Protect Yourself

· You can avoid courtroom, concert hall, and commercial airline searches by not entering these restricted areas when you are carrying marijuana.

· You can prevent sniffing drughounds from smelling your dope by not checking any luggage containing marijuana at an airport.

· At airports you can avoid the drug enforcement police and their tricks by looking cool and acting straight, and by refusing to consent to searches or to accompany them "voluntarily" anywhere.

· You should send all your mail, packages and all, first class via the United States Postal Service—*not* the United Parcel Service (UPS), or airfreight companies—to assure it the greatest protection from warrantless searches.

· To avoid being set up for a bust via the mail, do not open suspicious packages.

· Be careful about writing down information about marijuana in your letters or your diary.

· Don't make any bank deposits that you can't explain.

· Relocate your favorite plants before inviting a social worker into your home.

· Refuse to admit a health inspector into your home until you have had time to remove your plants, but avoid insisting upon a search warrant.

· Because your vehicle will be subject to confiscation if marijuana is found in it, you may want to transport marijuana in a less expensive vehicle.

SPECIAL SEARCHES

Special dangers have been cited to justify routine warrantless searches of everyone who enters certain courtrooms, federal buildings, concert halls, and almost all commercial airplanes. For example, previous incidents of violence in some courtrooms and federal buildings has been used to justify protective searches in all such areas. Similarly, violence during rock concerts has led to the legal searching of almost everyone who enters certain auditoriums. And the serious danger of airplane hijacking has been deemed a legally sufficient reason to justify special procedures used at airports to screen everyone boarding a commercial airplane. While these searches are undoubtedly a reasonable response to increasing violence, many officials, particularly at rock concerts, use their right to search for weapons as a pretext to search for marijuana and other contraband.

> **NOTE:** Recently many private businesses have also instituted controlled access procedures for entrance onto their premises. Thus newspaper offices, radio and TV stations, and increasing numbers of other enterprises require identification or a search of bags, boxes, and clothing before letting you enter their property. These searches are legal because judges assume that you voluntarily consent to them.

> **SELF-HELP NOTE: You Can Avoid These Searches by Not Entering Restricted Areas.** Of course, you can avoid being searched by not taking a commercial airplane, entering a courtroom or federal building, going to a rock concert, or entering other places where you must submit to a routine, warrantless search. You should always have an opportunity to decide whether or not to submit to such a search; officials are supposed to warn you about them. Furthermore, because the officials are not supposed to search selectively, you should notice others being searched and have plenty of time to leave the area before being searched. In some places, such as federal buildings, you may have a choice of allowing the officials to search your handbag or briefcase, or of leaving it at a checkpoint without it being searched.

If you are ever surprised by an official who wants to search you, do not panic. Simply say that you did not know that you had to be searched before entering the building and that you would prefer to leave rather than to submit to a search. If the official is not a police officer, she will probably allow you to leave. Of course, once the officials have already begun to search and are about to discover your marijuana, it may be too late to refuse consent. For example, if a metal object that you carelessly packed along with your marijuana sets off the magnetometer at an airport checkpoint, the guards are quite likely to discover both the metal and the marijuana during their search for weapons. And once they are in the middle of a search they are unlikely to let you go.

Airports
Police Dogs Can Easily Sniff Your Luggage

Your constitutional rights are particularly likely to be violated at airports, where numerous plainclothes police, usually DEA agents, loiter about looking for suspicious people carrying illegal drugs. To confirm even a vague suspicion, the police can use their dope-sniffing dogs to smell any luggage you check or even

carry-on luggage. Because many judges do not consider canine dope sniffing to be a search, the police need no reason or suspicion to sic dogs on your luggage. Therefore, you can never be sure when the police will have their dogs perform a nonsearch of your bags. Any drugs in your luggage which the dogs detect can be seized by the police and used to convict you. Of course, these judges who declare that dog searches are not subject to the Fourth Amendment because they are not really searches have probably never witnessed the East German police routinely using dogs to search westbound trains for people trying to leave the "worker's paradise."

Drug Enforcement Agents Can Legally Stop You in Airports without Good Reason

Drug enforcement officers are commonly quite active in airports and some judges permit them wide latitude in this setting. Other judges are more vigilant about protecting your rights, but this area of law is one that depends in large part upon the particular facts and the particular judges. Legally, drug enforcement officers need some factual suspicion to stop and seize you, but in practice they can often justify stopping you by saying that you fit a "drug carrier profile."[1] Unfortunately, some of the profile characteristics are so general as to fit almost anyone, while others are difficult to dispute in court. Thus, judges may approve a stop if the police testify that you fit several of the following criteria:

You are "visibly" nervous or anxiously looking around

You have little or no luggage, lock your luggage with a padlock, or do not have an FAA required name tag on your luggage

You are black or Hispanic or young

You travel to and return from a "known drug center" within several days (almost any major city can qualify as a known drug center, including New York, Chicago, Detroit, Houston, Miami, Los Angeles, San Diego and San Francisco)

You change planes en route or take a circuitous route

You travel under an alias or use a false telephone number to make airline reservations

You make a phone call immediately after arriving at the airport

You leave the airport at an exit where there is no public transportation

You are the last person off the plane

You walk quickly or run in the airport (watch out O.J.!)

You enter a restroom for a short time

You do not have a ticket folder

You possess a lot of cash

You pay for the plane ticket with small bills or large bills

You travel alone and are met by no one at the airport

You travel with someone who walks behind you.[2]

Drug Enforcement Agents Can Legally Search You in an Airport without a Search Warrant

Though the police can stop you almost at will by saying that you fit the drug carrier profile, they cannot legally search you without probable cause to believe you are committing a crime. Probable cause requires more facts than the suspicion needed to stop you, though the police are often able to exaggerate the probable cause circumstances. Because the police often need no warrant to search you at an airport, there is no independent check or restraint on their decision that sufficient probable cause existed to justify a search. For instance, according to police testimony, when the police stopped Endia Aronovsky and questioned the validity of her identification, she "became extremely nervous and began shouting incoherently." The police noticed that the name on her suitcase was that of a "documented" large-scale drug dealer. Consequently, they went ahead and searched Aronovsky over her objections. As there was no requirement that the police obtain a search warrant, they were the ones who decided that probable cause existed for the search. Judges entered the picture only later, after drugs were found. At that point, they decided that the police had engaged in a legal search.[3]

Usually, however, the police do not have probable cause to search you after stopping you at an airport. Remember, suspicion alone does not legally justify a search. Therefore, the police may try to persuade you to consent to a search. When the police casually asked Erma Secord if they could search her purse, she tried to bluff by consenting and saying that she had nothing to hide. The police found a little marijuana, which justified her immediate arrest. Incident to her arrest, the police searched her body, uncovering additional drugs.[4]

The police found it more difficult to convince Luis Finnegan and Maria Vetter to consent to a search. When the agents threatened to apply for a search warrant, however, Finnegan and Vetter ensured their convictions by consenting to a search of their luggage, which contained illegal drugs.[5]

A "Voluntary" Strip Search

In 1980, five of the nine justices of the U.S. Supreme Court, including all four of Nixon's appointees, approved federal Drug Enforcement Administration methods designed to trick people into surrendering their constitutional right to be free from warrantless searches. DEA agents stopped Sylvia Michand, a 22-year-old black woman, because she flew from Los Angeles to Detroit, left the plane after the other passengers, "appeared to be very nervous," did not claim any luggage, and was transferring to an airplane bound for Pittsburgh. The agents asked to see her identification and her airplane ticket—which, it turned out, had not been issued under her name. She told the agent that she had been in California for only two days. According to Agent Kennedy, Ms. Michand "became quite shaken, extremely nervous," when he identified himself as a narcotics agent. He asked her if she would accompany him to the airport DEA office for further questions. According to his testimony, she went along voluntarily and at the office agreed to submit to a search of her body and purse. She then, according to Agent Kennedy, voluntarily handed him her purse and stripped for a policewoman in a private room. While removing her clothes, she expressed concern about missing her plane. The policewoman reassured her that she would make the plane in time so long as she did not have narcotics. Before removing her final pieces of clothing, she handed the policewoman two small packages containing drugs.

At trial Agent Kennedy testified that he had told Ms. Michand that she did not have to consent. He also testified that he would have detained her forcibly if she had refused to come with him. Michand argued that Kennedy did detain her when he tricked her into cooperating to avoid drawing further suspicion upon herself, and that it was unlikely that she would have volunteered to stand cold and defenseless in her underwear in an airport search room had she been informed of her rights. Nevertheless, the High Court upheld Michand's conviction.[6]

You Can Refuse to Consent to Searches or to Accompany the Police "Voluntarily"

Some people have successfully defended themselves against police tricks. When DEA agents stopped Paula Halback in the airport, she showed proper identification and firmly refused to consent to a search. The agents searched anyway, finding illegal drugs, but the judges decided that the search was illegal because the agents did not have probable cause to believe that Halback had drugs and she had refused to consent to the search.[7]

In another case, the police stopped Trent Carter and tried to trick him into voluntarily accompanying them to an office for further questioning in the hope of obtaining probable cause to arrest him. They began to escort Carter to their interrogation room. At this point, many judges would have been willing to say that Carter was voluntarily accompanying the police or, at best, that the police were only making a temporary stop, for which only factual suspicion is required. Carter luckily showed the falsity of these theories, though in a foolish way—he ran. The police caught him, but because now there was no question that the police had forcibly detained him without probable cause before he ran, their subsequent search of his luggage—which revealed drugs—was illegal. Ironically, if Carter had run before the agents stopped him, then the search would have been legal because running away would have given the police "probable cause." Because in both cases the searches were illegal, however, the judges excluded the illegally obtained evidence and Halback and Carter were released.[8]

> **SELF-HELP NOTE:** Even if the police have reason to stop you, they cannot legally search you or hold you against your will for more than ten or twenty minutes—though some judges say that an hour-long detention is acceptable—without probable cause or your consent. A method of showing your refusal to accompany the police that is less risky than running is simply to ask, "Am I under arrest?" and then verbally refuse to go along unless you are. Of course, never physically resist the police if you value your health. If the police illegally hold you or search you anyway, any marijuana they find should not be used in court to convict you, particularly if you were carrying it in locked baggage.

Customs Searches At Borders and Airports

The State Can Routinely Search Everything that Enters the Country

The U.S. Supreme Court has always declared that routine, warrantless searches of everything that enters the country are legal. These searches are exceptions to the Fourth Amendment because they are "necessary and reasonable," and because if you do not want to be searched, you do not have to reenter the country. Therefore, you can expect a complete search of everything—you, your car, boat, plane, mail, and personal luggage—that enters the United States from foreign lands. Judges accept this rule of law, even though many historians believe that the American revolutionaries, some of whom were smugglers themselves, enacted the Fourth Amendment to prevent customs searches similar to those carried out by the British that were authorized by general warrants (see Chapter 2).

When you land in this country aboard an international flight, you are subject to customs and you and your luggage can be thoroughly searched. No suspicion is necessary. The officials can also order you to strip if they have "reasonable suspicion." In various cases, judges have decided that one or more of the following circumstances justified a strip search:

- Excessive nervousness
- Unusual conduct
- An informer's tip
- Computerized information showing pertinent criminal propensities
- Loose-fitting or bulky clothing
- An itinerary suggestive of wrongdoing (going to New York, Colombia, etc.)
- Discovery of incriminating matter during routine searches
- Lack of employment or a claim of self-employment
- Needle marks or other indications of drug addiction
- Information derived from the search or conduct of a traveling companion
- Inadequate luggage
- Evasive or contradictory answers[9]

Recently, some major international airports have installed X-ray machines to check your inner body for drugs, though the courts have not yet decided whether the officers need more than suspicion to justify this type of search.

If you fly your own plane into an airport from foreign lands, you and your plane are also subject to a customs search. If you have not reported leaving the country, the police must have a *reasonable certainty* or a *firm belief* that your plane has crossed an international border in order to do a customs search. Radar tracking, alert airport officials, and talkative friends are some of the ways customs officials can establish a reasonable certainty that your plane has crossed an international border. Of course, if the police have probable cause to believe your plane contains marijuana, they can search it regardless of the reasonable certainty requirement. And, if they also have reason to believe that you could escape, the police may be able to search your plane without a warrant.

Free Flying Planes versus Government Surveillance

This true story begins with a U.S. Customs pilot flying around the British West Indies looking for private planes. After spotting Johnnie Simpson's plane on a small island, the customs officer radioed Miami Customs warning them to be on the lookout for it. Shortly afterwards, at 4 AM, local police became suspicious when they saw a plane landing at Zephyrhills, Florida. They called Customs who confirmed by computer that Simpson's plane had indeed been outside of the country and had not landed elsewhere in America. At 5:30 AM customs agents arrived on the scene to make their routine customs search and found twenty-seven burlap bales containing 2100 pounds of marijuana. Because there was a high probability that the plane had crossed a border, Zephyrhills Airport became the functional equivalent of a border at which such customs searches are perfectly legal.[10]

In another Florida case, customs agent Grady found an informer after nosing around for a month. Based on this informer's tip, U.S. Customs installed a mechanical device called a "transponder" to follow the route of Mike Carlson's plane. The plane left the country, picked up six tons of marijuana, and returned to Mount Pocono Airport. To the surprise of Carlson, customs officials appeared and searched the plane. The "transponder" gave customs officials a reasonable certainty that the plane had landed at a "functional equivalent of a border" and, therefore, needed a routine customs search.[11]

In a recent case, a U.S. Customs radar operator at a naval air station in the San Diego area was monitoring his radar screen for planes crossing the border from Mexico. At 8:21 PM he observed an airplane about twenty miles south of the border; he watched it cross the border at 8:26 PM; and he tracked it until it landed at Palomar Airfield at 9:00 PM. Apparently alerted by the radar operator, the airport police "detained" Duennebier and Dickens until a customs officer arrived to do a routine customs search. The customs officer found thirty-six duffle bags containing about 1000 pounds of marijuana. The judges ruled that the search was legal, because Customs had a firm belief and a reasonable certainty that the plane had just crossed the border.[12]

Boats

State Officials Can Do a Routine Safety Inspection of Your Boat as a Pretext to Search It for Drugs

The Coast Guard, police, or customs officials can also search your boat without probable cause or a search warrant if they have a *reasonable certainty* that your boat has recently returned from foreign waters.

Because pleasure boats do *not* have to report to Customs upon arrival in the United States from foreign lands unless they have something to declare, it is quite difficult for the authorities to establish with reasonable certainty that they are subject to a customs search. Satellite tracking, talkative friends, and Coast Guard surveillance are some of the ways in which Customs can establish a reasonable certainty that a boat has left the country, thus justifying a routine customs search. Customs officials can only undertake a customs search within twelve miles of the U.S. coast or at port, but the Coast Guard can search anywhere on the high seas.

By stretching the customs search loophole beyond recognition, federal judges have also authorized warrantless safety and identification inspections of boats anywhere in the Gulf of Mexico and most of the Atlantic Ocean, but not the Pacific Ocean, at least after dark. As a result, in the waters bordering much of America, your boat is not protected by the Fourth Amendment at all. The Coast Guard can conduct this search anywhere on the high seas, even by boarding a boat registered in a foreign country in violation of international law. The Coast Guard or the police can board your boat for a routine documentation inspection without a warrant or even suspicion that you are smuggling. The Coast Guard specifically keeps a watch out for boats that fit the "smuggling ship profile." The profile characteristics include "improper markings; no permanently attached name or home port; failure to fly a flag; failure of the boat to identify itself; the condition of the boat; and unusual activities aboard the boat."[13]

Once the police arbitrarily board your boat on the pretext of checking identification, they can say they saw or smelled marijuana to justify further search of your boat. In one case, the Coast Guard justified a search by saying that "one of the officers with a keen sense of smell thought he detected 'the faint odor of marijuana' in the forward hold." Lo and behold, when he searched, he found some.[14]

In another case, when the police pulled alongside Gerald Witherspoon's boat to check it out, one officer said he smelled a "strong odor" and another officer thought he smelled marijuana. Once on deck, they observed "marijuana residue" which allowed them to justify a warrantless search. They uncovered more than 9000 pounds of marijuana.[15] Since warrantless and unannounced safety inspections of cars and planes are illegal, one judge pointed out: "I do not think the craft's watery location of itself distinguishes a vessel from a land vehicle or a plane. The Fourth Amendment makes no such distinction."[16] Although the United States Court of Appeals for the western part of the country has ruled that these pretext inspection searches are illegal in the Pacific Ocean, at least after dark, the Coast Guard continues to do these searches.[17]

A Coast Guard Boarding Officer's Practical Advice

In a confidential interview, a San Diego Coast Guard officer, who will be called Gary Cummings, made the following observations about his job. Each month Gary receives a list of the names of about forty boats that are "suspect drug-running vessels." A private agency called El Paso Information Center (EPIC) compiles these computerized profiles based on reports, tips, and observations— such as a report that a boat loaded with provisions left a harbor at night (*under cover of darkness* in law enforcement lingo). Cummings has standing orders to board and check any boat on the list. He has boarded many such boats in the last several years, and has yet to find any drugs. Most days his orders are to board every fourth boat entering the harbor. Recently, he received orders to board every boat entering the harbor for two weeks, supposedly to check for documentation, but in reality because the authorities had a tip that a drug smuggling boat was due to arrive. During each routine documentation check of any boat over five gross tons (as small as thirty feet long), Cummings must walk through its private cabin—a temporary home—to check the registration number on the main beam inside the boat. For smaller boats that are registered with the state and have their identification numbers on the outside of the boat, Cummings has the option of turning the five minute documentation check into a thirty minute safety check. If the boat owner is uncooperative, if the boat's documentation is not proper, or if something else arouses his suspicions, Cummings will search the entire boat to make certain that it has running night lights, life preservers (called "personal flotation devices" (PFD) in Coast Guard lingo), fire extinguishers, proper sewage disposal, and emergency equipment.

This abuse of power does not mean that the Coast Guard has no legitimate responsibilities on the sea. Cummings helps many people in trouble and he boards boats with visible safety violations. Unfortunately, most federal judges permit routine documentation checks, which are unavoidably used as a pretext to search your boat without probable cause or a search warrant.

Border Crossings By Land

Strip or Else

The most arbitrary searches occur as you cross the United States border by land. At the border, as in an international airport, however, the police need some suspicion before they can order you to strip and they need a "clear indication" to delve deeper. In addition to the same reasons that justify a strip search, the customs officials are on the lookout for Vaseline and prophylactics in suitcases, a stiff and uncomfortable walk, or a greasy ass as a "clear indication" that your body contains illegal drugs. In 1968, however, a doctor who did hundreds of anal and vaginal searches estimated that more than 80 percent of these degrading searches produced nothing but humiliation.[18]

Two Out of Three Judges Recognize Outrageousness

One of the more sickening searches that uncovered heroin occurred in May, 1966 at the San Ysidro, California border crossing. Customs agents ordered Oscar Reagan, a Los Angeles citizen, to strip because his eyes appeared to be "glassy and pinpointed." When they allegedly saw "needle marks on his arms" and a "greasy substance" on his ass, they brought him to a baggage room. Dr. Critzer, who testified that there was no "lubrication" in the buttock area, proceeded to insert his finger into Reagan, "but when the doctor persisted in the 'digital manipulation,' [Reagan] vehemently protested" and began to struggle. "The agents handcuffed [Reagan] and threw him onto a table." Eventually, the agents were able "to break [Reagan's] will" so that the doctor could extract four packets of heroin as the agents held Reagan down and laughed. Because "there was no emergency necessitating or justifying the brutal force process to which [Reagan] was subjected in the conduct of the intrusive rectal cavity invasion," two of the three judges decided that the search was illegal.[19]

There is absolutely nothing that you can do to protect yourself from strip searches as you cross a border except to be so wealthy or influential that the customs officials would not dare to order you to strip and bend over. Of course, you can avoid leaving the country and avoid conforming to any of the above mentioned "suspicious characteristics."

EXAMPLE: Peter Crosses the Canadian-American Border

Peter, age twenty-eight and driving a 1971 MG, approaches the border confidently, on the way home from a visit to Canada. He smoked his last joint the day before and has nothing to fear. Peter is met by a customs officer who says, "Please pull over here. Step out of your car, please, so that we can search it. Also, we would like you to come inside our office. We suspect that you are a drug user. You will have to strip and bend over."

"No. I haven't done anything." Peter asserts.

"Either you take off your clothes, or we will do it for you. There is no turning back now—you're in U.S. territory—so bend over," the agent insisted.

Dogs and customs officials sniff and search everywhere, but find no drugs.

Peter, feeling furious and violated, goes along with the search, vowing to protest this disgusting violation of his privacy as soon as he gets home.

Question: Would Peter's protests do any good?

Answer: Probably not. The customs officer made a legal search.

A Border is Not a Place, It's a State of Mind

The police can do a complete customs search of you and your vehicle at any so-called functional equivalent of the border. Such a delayed customs search is permitted anywhere in the United States so long as the police have a reasonable certainty that you have not stopped and picked up what they are looking for after you have crossed the border. Usually, the police use this concept to justify their warrantless car searches for illegal aliens within several hundred miles of the Mexican border. In one case, however, a truck with a hidden compartment carrying marijuana crossed the Mexican border and the police waited five days to do the customs search, until it arrived in San Antonio, Texas, 150 miles from the border. The warrantless search was legal because San Antonio became a functional equivalent of a border, and because "the concept of the border is an elastic one."[20]

SELF-HELP NOTE: If you are so lucky as to succeed in smuggling marijuana across the border, don't begin to celebrate until the border is far behind you. You are safe from a warrantless "functional equivalent" customs search only after law enforcement officials no longer have a reasonable certainty that any marijuana in your car crossed the border.

Mail: It's Not as Private as You Think

The State Can Routinely Search International Mail

Just like a border search, customs officials can search without probable cause or suspicion all packages mailed from foreign countries. Even first-class letters from foreign countries can be searched without probable cause, although the customs inspectors do need a reasonable suspicion that the letters contain contraband or merchandise subject to duty. The enclosure of any material besides a piece of paper is sufficient to support this suspicion. Letters from countries such as Thailand, Nepal, and Colombia are suspect, particularly if they are bulky or weigh more than a normal first-class letter. State officials cannot open international mail to read a letter without a search warrant, but as you doubtlessly know, there is abundant evidence that the CIA and other federal agencies ignore this rule of law.[21]

First-Class Domestic Mail is Protected from Most Warrantless Searches

Only if you send your mail first-class via the U.S. Postal Service does the Constitution protect it against warrantless searches. You must affix first-class postage to any package or letter that you do not want the post office to open, and to be on the safe side, also mark "First-Class". If you take this precaution, then the only way the State can legally open your mail is with a search warrant based on probable cause that it contains criminal evidence or contraband. The State can legally hold up even your first-class mail in transit for a day, while officers investigate to try to obtain a search warrant. Recently, the post office has established "priority" and "express" mail categories. These more costly types of mail are also given the same constitutional protection as regular first-class mail.

If you are so foolish as to send your packages or mail second-, third-, or fourth-class mail, post office officials can often search them without a warrant or probable cause. The State justifies these routine searches as necessary to ensure that proper postage rates are paid.

Second- and third-class mail offers service at a reduced rate for printed materials and other kinds of letters and packages. Because judges cannot agree about second- and third-class mail, these types of mail occupy a twilight zone where they may be vulnerable to legal warrantless searches. At present, some legal decisions offer some protection and others offer none. Again, don't take a chance—pay a little extra for first class.

Fourth-class mail, the cheapest rate to send packages, has, by agreement of all judges, no constitutional protection.

Private Mail or Package Delivery Companies Offer No Legal Protection

Your packages have virtually no legal protection if you mail them via the United Parcel Service (UPS) or a private airfreight or truck company, no matter how much you pay for "top-class" service. Privately employed persons can violate your constitutional rights at will, and any evidence discovered can be turned over to the police and used to convict you. Private mail companies routinely open packages to ensure against fraudulent insurance claims or to check the proper routing of the package. Sometimes inspectors employed by private companies also search packages deposited with them by "suspicious" persons. Because these searches are usually done by a private employee without police involvement, any evidence discovered can be used against you, while the same evidence discovered by the police as part of a warrantless search would be thrown out of court. The general rule is that as long as the private postal or airfreight inspectors are not working under the direction of the police, any marijuana they find while checking your packages can be used by the State to convict you.

After the private company turns your marijuana over to the police, the police will probably make a "controlled delivery" of the package to your home, having already obtained a warrant to search your home to be executed after they deliver the marijuana. An undercover agent in a deliveryman's uniform will deliver the package, leave, and probably wait long enough for you to open it. Then, other officers will announce themselves at your door with a search warrant in hand.

The Police Can Legally Order a Mail Cover
Without a Warrant but can fuck you in your booty!

The police can order a routine "mail cover" of your mail without probable cause or a search warrant. A mail cover is conducted by a postal employee who copies the names and addresses of everyone who sends you mail, and notes the class of the mail and any other information contained on the outside of the letter or package. In one case police agents told the local post office to notify a postal inspector upon receipt of any package addressed to Glenn Filer's home. Several weeks later, the post office notified the inspector of a package. Even though it had airmail postage, the inspector opened it without probable cause or a search warrant, found cocaine packed in a doll, and called the police. The police carefully put the package back together, obtained a search warrant, and delivered it to Filer's home. After the delivery, they searched the house, again finding the cocaine. Since the airmail postage exceeded the first-class rate, the judges decided that the post office searches were illegal, thus making the home search illegal also.[22] If the package had been posted with a few cents less, the search and arrest would probably have been legal. The moral of the story is that you can often protect yourself for just pennies more.

Don't Open Suspicious Packages

It may be extremely unlikely that anyone (the police, a police informer, or some-one who has it in for you) will ship drugs to you without your knowledge. But unlikely or not, it has happened. Unfortunately, just as you probably believe that no one would set you up, most juries will also doubt that you were innocently set up if the police find drugs in your home.

If you receive a suspicious package for which you cannot account, the best bet is not to open it for at least several days. If you are really concerned, call your lawyer or another responsible person. This person can at least testify to your concern if need be. You will probably be left to decide whether to return the package unopened to the mail service or to open it. If you open it and find drugs, you can destroy them immediately or report your discovery to the police. If your greed gets the better of your fear and you decide to risk keeping them, remember that it's rare that one gets something for nothing in this world and if, in fact, you have been set up, you are going to have a hard time convincing anyone of it after you bake the marijuana into brownies and the crumbs are still clinging to your shirt at the time of your arrest.

EXAMPLE: Too Many Birthday Surprises

The scene is rural Montana. It's Mary Ellen's birthday and she has just finished a breakfast of fresh orange juice and whole wheat waffle with a fried egg on the side.

"Here are a couple of presents that came in the mail, Mary Ellen."

"I wonder what's in this parcel post package from Hawaii. Maybe it's from Carey or Esther. It sure is carefully wrapped in a lot of plastic. Wow! I hit the jackpot—sinsemilla! It must be from Esther."

"There's one more package. One of those airfreight outfits delivered it earlier today."

"Peyote! And here's a note. 'Respect our sacramental host.'"

"Remember that Indian who stayed for a weekend last summer? Didn't he belong to the American Indian Church whose members can legally use peyote in their religious ceremonies?"

"Mary Ellen, all these drugs in the mail—I know it's your birthday, but it's pretty weird."

"Gifts from the gods?"

Soon there is a knock at the door.

"Who's there?"

"Happy birthday—it's the FBI."

At the evidence suppression hearing before Mary Ellen's trial, the FBI explained that a post office employee opened the fourth-class package from Hawaii and that an employee of an airfreight outfit opened the other package because she did not like the looks of the Indian who mailed it. They both informed the FBI of their discoveries.

Question: Are these searches legal?

Answer: Yes. Re-read the last section if you answered "no."

The Police Can Read Your Personal Mail, Diary, or Journal if They Have a Search Warrant

The police can read your personal mail, including first-class mail sent within the United States, if they obtain a search warrant. They can obtain a search warrant if they can demonstrate that they have probable cause to believe your letter contains criminal evidence. Similarly, the police can also obtain a search warrant for your diary, journal or other personal papers. Indeed, if the police have probable cause to read your diary and have reason to believe you are about to destroy it, they can seize it immediately, even without a search warrant.

That the State can seize a person's mail and most personal papers and delve into their most private thoughts and fantasies is quite simply immoral. As is so often the case, however, morality and legality are not the same thing; unfortunately, this sort of snooping is legal. Therefore from a legal point of view, you should avoid writing anything in your diary or in your letters that you would not want a prosecutor to read to a judge or jury. Sure, this advice may sound a little absurd, since the reason many people keep a diary is to have at least one place where they can be completely open and honest. But even so, do be careful what you write and where you write it.

Bank Records Aren't Private

Some of your other private records are not even protected by the search warrant and probable cause requirements of the Fourth Amendment. For instance, the U.S. Supreme Court has declared that your bank records are not private. The police can walk into your bank and look at your bank account and cancelled checks without a search warrant or probable cause or even suspicion.[23] Creditors and government agencies also have access to your financial history that has been computerized by private companies.

> **SELF-HELP NOTE:** People who grow and sell marijuana often get fairly large amounts of money at a time. If somehow the police get wind of a person's illegal activities concerning marijuana, they are almost sure to check bank accounts to see if there are large unexplained deposits. Under certain conditions, the Government can confiscate all your money and property that it can trace to certain illegal activities, including marijuana cultivation. (See the discussion of forfeiture at the end of this chapter.) These deposits can also be of interest to federal and state tax authorities. Once you realize that American bank accounts are open to routine checks by the authorities, you need no further legal information to act wisely.

Inspections
Social Workers

To receive welfare, you must be willing at various times to open your home to a welfare worker. These inspections are not legally classified as searches. Instead, the home visit is considered a necessary administrative procedure to determine whether you are eligible for government assistance and whether you are properly spending the money under applicable guidelines. In many states, the law requires that you be given advance notice of the visit. If this is true in your area, you should be able to protect your privacy. Advance notice should give you plenty of time to round up your favorite plants and put them in a secure, out-of-the-way place. The welfare worker is not visiting your home to search for marijuana, but she can "innocently" find it when she is observing your home for evidence of child neglect. Therefore if you do not have advance notice of the visit, you should feel free to tell the welfare worker to come back later. There are many legitimate reasons why you may not be able or willing to invite someone into your home at a moment's notice. A social worker can never enter your home without your permission and cannot obtain a search warrant for your home. Only the police can obtain a search warrant, and only if they have probable cause to believe you have engaged in welfare fraud or some other crime.

But what if you refuse to admit the welfare worker without a legitimate reason? In some situations, the State can cut off your financial assistance, although you have a right to contest the action at a hearing. In most situations, your best bet is to ask the social worker to come back in a few minutes (or hours). As long as you are polite and agree to meet with the worker fairly promptly, you are unlikely to face a cut-off.

The Tarantula Gambit

Here's a true story about Jim, who received Aid to Families with Dependent Children (AFDC) and had a small greenhouse filled with marijuana plants attached to the side of his house. Now and then he also had a few plants in the house. Naturally, he was unenthusiastic about having his social worker pay him unannounced visits. Jim solved his privacy problem by getting several large tarantulas and putting them in a glass-fronted case immediately next to the front door. He then told the social worker that occasionally he let his pets out for exercise and put a sign on the door warning people about the poisonous spiders. Jim reported that his social worker always called and made appointments well in advance and would never enter the house until he was assured that it was safe to do so.

Health, Fire, and Safety Inspectors

Your home is subject to routine health, safety or fire inspections. While these searches may not be routine in your area, they are always possible, especially if a public agency receives a complaint. Although the inspection is supposed to be limited to a search for possible health, safety, or fire violations, you are unlikely to know where the inspector will want to search. In some rural areas where many buildings do not conform to building codes, these inspections are a real danger.

Some cities and counties will give you advance notice of these inspections. If your city or county does not, you should ask the inspector to come back later in the day or the week if you need time to relocate marijuana plants. You have the right to refuse entry to the inspector whether or not she has a search warrant. You should realize, however, that it is only a formality for the inspector to obtain a warrant and get the police. Probable cause that your house is a health, safety, or fire hazard is unnecessary for the issuance of an inspector's warrant. A showing that the city is doing a routine inspection of your neighborhood is sufficient. Furthermore, although you have a legal right to force the inspectors to obtain a search warrant, it is unwise to antagonize them. The inspectors will simply come back with a search warrant, and an angry inspector is likely to search considerably more aggressively and thoroughly than is one whom you have treated politely. Naturally, an inspector can also report to the police any information about marijuana discovered during any search.

EXAMPLE: Dick and the Pushy Building Inspector

"Who's knocking at the door now?"

Dick puts on his pants and walks outside. "What's the problem?"

"Building inspector. I have a warrant to check your home for building code violations."

"You're going to have to come back later. My house is a mess and I'm going out soon. Tomorrow afternoon is a good time for me. Is that okay?"

"No. I'd like to search your home now. I have a warrant."

"Are you a cop?"

"No."

"Well, come back later. The warrant may give you the authority to search my house, but it doesn't give you the power. You're going to need the police for that."

"I'll be back, wise-guy."

Betty and Dick cleaned up their home quickly, emptied their greenhouse and trimmed the marijuana growing behind the corn, a few hundred yards behind the house. Although the inspector could have asked the police for help, he decided to come back the next day. He inspected Betty's and Dick's home carefully and began to walk outside toward the greenhouse and garden.

"Hey, I don't want you out here. No one lives in the greenhouse."

"What are you so nervous about?"

"We value our privacy."

"I don't know why you live without indoor plumbing or electricity, but your home looks solid. You have one month to fix the foundation under that ramshackle back room, however. Here's the citation."

"How did you get a search warrant, anyway? You didn't have probable cause to believe that something was wrong with my home."

"I inspect all newly built homes and all older homes every five or ten years for health, safety, or fire violations. I don't need probable cause, just so long as I search everyone's home every five or ten years."

Question: Was the building inspector correct?

Answer: Yes. A nondiscriminatory routine makes these kinds of searches "reasonable" without the requirement of establishing probable cause.

Forfeiture

The State Can Confiscate Your Car, Boat, or Plane if They Can Show that You Transported Illegal Drugs in It

If you are ever caught transporting illegal drugs in your car, boat, or plane, you will not only lose your drugs, but you may also lose, or in legal lingo, "forfeit," your vehicle to the state or federal government. Even if you loan your car or boat to a friend who is caught transporting marijuana or other illicit substances *without* your knowledge or permission, the State can nevertheless confiscate your car or boat. Furthermore, you have no right to a hearing to challenge the confiscation. Still, you should ask nicely for it to be returned, and perhaps file a lawsuit if you are desperate. Sometimes the state or federal officials will return your vehicle, but you should not expect them to do so.

The following section of the United States code explains what property is subject to forfeiture by the United States government:

Forfeitures—Property subject

(a) The following shall be subject to forfeiture to the United States and no property right shall exist in them:

    (1) All controlled substances [marijuana, cocaine, opium, etc.] which have been manufactured, distributed, dispensed, or acquired [illegally].

    (2) All raw materials, products, and equipment of any kind which are used, or intended for use, in manufacturing, compounding, processing, delivering, importing, or exporting any controlled substance [illegally].

    (3) All property which is used, or intended for use, as a container for property described in paragraph (1) or (2).

    (4) All conveyances, including aircraft, vehicles, or vessels, which are used, or are intended for use, to transport, or in any manner to facilitate the transportation, sale, receipt, possession, or concealment of property described in paragraph (1) or (2). . .

    (5) All books, records, and research, including formulas, microfilm, tapes, and data which are used, or intended for use [in connection with controlled substances].[24]

The Government Gets a Jeep and a Boat, but Not an Airplane

During a warrantless "routine inspection of incoming foreign mail," a customs officer opened a small package mailed from Colombia. He found 350 grams of cocaine. Customs contacted the Drug Enforcement Administration (DEA), and DEA agents took it from there. DEA agents sent a pickup notice to Virginia Hodovan, the person to whom the package was addressed. Hodovan arrived at the post office in her jeep, picked up her package and drove home. On the way, DEA agents stopped the jeep, arrested her, seized the cocaine in the package, and also seized the jeep. Even though Hodovan complained in court that the DEA agents set her up by purposely allowing her to transport the package in her vehicle, the judges let the government confiscate the jeep as well as the coke.[25]

On the night of September 8, 1975, the Coast Guard boarded a sailboat that was sailing without any lights, fifteen miles west of Cuba. When Coast Guard officers boarded the boat, they smelled marijuana, searched, and found 2,030 pounds of it. They seized both the marijuana and the boat and brought them back to America. Even though the boat was not seized in American waters, the U.S. government got the boat by winning the forfeiture proceedings.[26]

Edwin Degnan sold a plane to Stephen Remmers and then told Customs that he suspected Remmers would fly it to Mexico to pick up marijuana. Remmers did take a trip somewhere, and when he arrived back at the Bermuda Dunes Airport in California, customs officials were there to greet him. They searched his plane from cockpit to tailpit and found only three flakes of marijuana. Later in the laboratory, during the process of analyzing the three flakes, they were destroyed. But the agents had their proof. After Remmers apparently got away with importing marijuana, the federal government filed suit to claim forfeiture of his plane for transporting three flakes of marijuana. There was no question in court about the right of the government to take away Remmers' plane for transporting only three flakes of marijuana. (Recently, the government confiscated a Porsche for transporting .226 grams of marijuana, which is almost invisible.) But the judge decided that the customs officials made an illegal, warrantless search of the plane because they did not have a "reasonable basis"—some judges would say "reasonable certainty"—for believing that Remmers had flown nonstop from Mexico to Bermuda Dunes Airport. Since the government did not have any "independent," legally acquired evidence that showed probable cause to seize the plane, Remmers got his plane back.[27]

NOTE: Under some circumstances, which are too detailed and complex to explain here, the State can also confiscate your business property, land, and money. The primary requirement for forfeiture is proof that you acquired the property, at least in part, through marijuana or other drug profits. The DEA has recently begun to use this law against marijuana cultivators, although the law was originally aimed at organized crime syndicates. Suffice it to say that it is wise to be an inconspicuous consumer after a bountiful harvest.

And now, after preparing you for the worst, here is a reminder again that it's not always this bad—high courts in some states take a more enlightened view of the Constitution and laws that protect our privacy and freedom.

THE BEST YOU CAN EXPECT FROM A JUDGE

• Judges in some states will not allow the police to let their dogs sniff your luggage without some factual suspicion.

• A few judges will realize that persons carrying drugs rarely consent in a truly voluntary way to accompany the police to an interrogation room, to open their drug-filled suitcase, or to take off their clothes.

• Some federal judges, particularly on the West Coast, will not allow the Coast Guard to stop and search boats on the pretext of making a routine documentation and safety check, at least if it's after dark.

• Some federal judges are more concerned about unnecessary strip searches at the border than others, and will condemn them unless the customs police had good reason to subject the suspects to this experience.

• A few judges will recognize that you have a reasonable expectation of privacy in other classes of mail than first class.

• Judges in some states, such as California, will condemn warrantless searches of your bank records by state police.

CHAPTER **11**

Silence is Golden: Let Your Lawyer Do Your Talking

Silence that fellow: I would he had some cause
To prattle for himself.

William Shakespeare,
MEASURE FOR MEASURE, Act V, Scene 1

Why is it that most people are resistant to the "silence is golden" rule when dealing with the police? Perhaps it is just that humans, being the animals who invented conversation and music so we wouldn't have to pad about the planet in silence, love to make noise. Certainly for most of us, talk is an intrinsic part of daily life and is especially important when we are excited or under stress.

Communication may be a balm to the spirit, but it rarely does people much good when they are talking to the police about marijuana. For no matter how sympathetic an officer pretends to be, her role is not to forgive, console, and understand you, but to administer the criminal law, which, at least in the case of marijuana, is unsympathetic to your interests.

Unfortunately, the police are skilled at getting people to talk. One very effective technique that is often used to loosen people up is "accusation." Accusation, the police have learned, inspires denial almost automatically:

"You did it!"
"No, I didn't!"

"Yes, you did!"
"No, I didn't!"

Now, alone and of itself, denial of an accusation is not unwise and, in fact, judges sometimes consider that no denial is as good as an admission of guilt. But the great danger here is that denial of guilt is frequently followed by an explanation, and once the police have you trying to explain your actions, they often have you on a slippery slide that leads straight to your conviction.

And in case you imagine that this scenario is an exaggeration and believe that you are intelligent enough to fence verbally with the police without saying the wrong things, this chapter should go a long way toward convincing you that you are wrong, wrong, wrong. If you are arrested or detained, your best strategy is quite simple—shut up and call a lawyer. If you have any doubt about the validity of this advice, read the rest of this chapter, which discusses your Fifth Amendment right to be silent, as well as the complicated and unfair legal loopholes judges have invented to frustrate this right.

THUMBNAIL REVIEW
What the Police Can Do "Legally"

• The police must inform you of your rights to remain silent and to see a lawyer if they arrest you and wish to interrogate you.

• But the police do not have to tell you of your rights to remain silent and to see a lawyer before taking you into custody during an investigation.

• And the police do not have to tell you of your rights to remain silent and to see a lawyer even after arresting you if they do not interrogate you about your suspected crime. Even if the police arrest you and interrogate you without telling you of these rights, the State can use your "voluntary" statements to call you a liar *if* you protest your innocence at trial.

• Also, if the police illegally pressure you to talk after you say you want to remain silent, the State can use your "voluntary" statements to call you a liar if you protest your innocence at your trial.

• And even if the police illegally refuse to allow you to see a lawyer and continue to question you after you say that you want to speak to a lawyer, the State can use your "voluntary" statements to call you a liar if you protest your innocence at your trial.

• In addition, there are many ways that the police can legally trick you into talking by lying to you or appealing to your conscience after you say that you want to remain silent and see a lawyer, as long as they do so without directly questioning you.

• The police can legally use jail house informers to encourage you to talk while in jail as long as the informers are not paid to trick you into talking.

• Finally, the police can sometimes pressure you to talk by holding you in jail for days and by questioning you for hours without a lawyer, but they cannot beat or torture you in an attempt to make you confess.

What You Can Do to Protect Yourself

• After you are accused of a crime, you can simply deny it by insisting: "I'm innocent," or "You're crazy."

• In the face of an accusation, you should refrain from explaining or justifying your statement of innocence and remain silent.

• If the police question you about the weather or about an activity that has absolutely no connection with you, you may want to answer as long as you can be completely honest.

• If the police question you about any activity that remotely connects you with marijuana or ask you about your personal life, you should remain absolutely silent and ask for a lawyer. You have a right to a lawyer whether or not you can afford one.

• You should remember your rights to remain silent and to see a lawyer because the police will not remind you of these rights in many situations.

• It is almost always better to remain silent than to speak and *always* better to remain silent than to lie.

◦ Even if you are innocent and have a good explanation, it often makes sense to allow your lawyer to tell it to the police just in case someone is trying to set you up. This precaution is especially true if you or a friend might be compromised by your explanation in any way.

• If you believe that the police may accuse you of a crime, consult a lawyer immediately. In limited circumstances, after you have consulted a lawyer, it may be wise for you to turn yourself in to the police and claim you are innocent even before the police arrest you.

• If the police begin to question you without telling you your right to remain silent, ask them if you have a right to remain silent before refusing to answer.

• Wait to talk to your lawyer even if the police try to trick you into talking by pressuring you, promising you deals, or appealing to your conscience. If the lawyer isn't immediately available, shut up and be patient.

• Do not talk to anyone about your "crimes," particularly fellow prisoners in your jail cell.

• Go ahead and talk if the police threaten to physically abuse you. Silence is not *that* important.

Your Right to Silence
People Commonly Convict Themselves by Talking

Trying to talk ourselves out of trouble is a habit most of us developed in early childhood—and some of us have gotten quite good at it. But whether we are adept at it or not, such childhood maneuvers are rarely effective in the adult world—especially when dealing with the police or judges.

The Fifth Amendment establishes the right of every American to remain silent in the face of accusers: "No person . . . shall be compelled in any criminal case to be a witness against himself." A criminal case begins as soon as the police begin to question you. If you do not exercise your right to remain silent at this time, whatever you say can be used against you at trial and often is—in ways you might never have imagined. The general rule is that even if you are innocent and feel completely safe, it is better not to talk about yourself to any law enforcement official. A simple denial, such as "I'm innocent" or "You're crazy," will suffice and beyond that it makes sense to button up your lip.

Answering Innocent Questions Honestly is Usually Appropriate

If the police are asking you about the weather or who won a particular football game, it is usually fine to talk to them. You must be careful, however, because a seemingly innocent fact can be used against you. Thus as soon as a police officer asks questions that show an interest in you, your friends, or your marijuana, your answer, no matter how innocent-sounding, can get you and your friends into a lot of trouble. And it may not become clear what information the police are really after until the conversation begins. But you can be sure of one thing—if the police are bothering to talk to you at all, they are almost certainly after some information, and that information is extremely unlikely to be used in your behalf. So, unless you are certain that you can give a completely honest answer to an officer's questions without connecting yourself in any way to marijuana smoking or other illicit activity, and unless you are certain that no one is setting you up, simply say "I'm sorry, but do I have the right to remain silent? I believe that I do and I want to talk to a lawyer." If the police continue to pressure you, keep on repeating the above sentence. Don't let the police intimidate you with statements like: "You must be guilty or you would talk to us," or, "What do you have to hide?" or "No, you have no right to remain silent."

Remember Your Right to Remain Silent because the Police May Not Remind You

As many of you probably know, the police are supposed to tell you that you have a right to remain silent; that anything you say can and will be used as evidence against you in court; that you have a right to a lawyer; and that the State will

provide a public defender or other lawyer if you cannot afford to hire your own attorney.

In the 1966 *Miranda v. Arizona* case, the United States Supreme Court decided that if the police do not tell you of your rights—they are now commonly called "Miranda rights"—anything you say constitutes illegally obtained evidence and cannot be used in court to convict you.[1] But what many people who get their information courtesy of "Barney Miller" or "Starsky and Hutch" reruns don't realize is that the police are required to advise you of these rights only if you are officially in custody and only if they want to "interrogate" you. If you are not in custody, no warnings are mandatory. And it does not matter whether you believed that you were in custody when the police were questioning you—it's entirely up to the judge to decide whether or not the police began "custodial interrogation" before telling you of your rights. In theory, you are in "custody" when you are under the "control" of the police, but who is to say at exactly what moment this control begins? For example, many judges believe that the police may legally stop you, question you, and search you for weapons without taking you into custody. Therefore, the police need not tell you of your rights under these circumstances as long as they do not admit to planning your immediate arrest.

Similarly, judges may define "interrogation" quite narrowly. Thus in one situation, Officer Collins of the Los Angeles Police Department arrested Clarence Johnson for possession of drugs. There was no doubt that Johnson was in custody when the police officer began to question him without first telling him that he had the rights to remain silent and to consult a lawyer. The officer had just broken the window of the car in which Johnson sat and dragged Johnson out of it. Officer Collins accused Johnson of swallowing several balloons of heroin and told him that he could die if the balloons broke inside his stomach. The officer then asked Johnson whether he wanted to have his stomach pumped to make sure that the balloons did not burst and kill him. Instead of holding his tongue, Johnson angrily answered: "Let me die." Whether the officer's statement was in fact true or false, Johnson's response implied that he had swallowed heroin. And because the judges ruled that this conversation didn't constitute an "interrogation," the prosecutor was able to introduce Johnson's statement at trial, even though he had not been told his Miranda rights. The State successfully convicted Johnson.[2]

Even when the police should remind you of your rights prior to custodial interrogation, they may not, fearing that if they do you will assert your rights to remain silent and to talk with a lawyer. It is even possible—though not probable—that the police will later lie and say that they did tell you of your rights, and they usually win "swearing contests" in court when it is their word against yours. So don't talk to the police even if you feel that they have made a mistake. The best general rule to follow is to assume that, no matter what the circumstances, anything you say can be used against you.

> **WARNING!** Some people believe that failure to talk to the police can result in their becoming more suspicious, and that a person is more likely to be arrested if he refuses to answer questions. As a general rule, this assumption isn't true. If the authorities have enough evidence to arrest you when they begin talking to you, they will probably do so no matter what you say or don't say. If they don't have enough evidence, chances are they will let you go. A thoughtless lie, however, may have extremely damaging consequences. For example, even if you make a statement that isn't true about something that has nothing to do with marijuana, the prosecutor can use your lie to demonstrate to the jury that you are an untrustworthy witness. Thus a short conversation can sometimes result in a long sentence.

Convicted by a Spontaneous Lie

In one case, James Jones's spontaneous denial of guilt caused his conviction. One morning, drug enforcement agents followed Jones from his apartment to an airport terminal. When he got out of his car with a suitcase and began walking, an agent said, "Federal Narcotics agent—I'd like to talk to you," and a policeman said "Police." Jones looked back, immediately dropped his suitcase, and continued to walk away. After Jones took about three steps, the police arrested him and took him to a police car. Although the police told him of his rights to remain silent and to consult a lawyer, Jones foolishly agreed to talk. He then foolishly lied by denying that he dropped the suitcase and by saying that it was not his and that he had never seen it before. The police illegally searched the suitcase and found illegal drugs. The judges decided that Jones could not object to the introduction of the unconstitutionally seized evidence because he had lied to the police by saying that it was not his suitcase, and therefore "lacked standing to object to its search." Jones lacked standing to object only because he had lied about not owning the suitcase and, as a result, the State convicted him for possession of the drugs found in the suitcase. It is quite likely that Jones would not have been convicted if he had not talked to the police, or if he had talked first to a lawyer, or if he had not lied, or even if he had not tried to abandon his suitcase.[3]

Lying to a Federal Agent is Illegal

If a government agent who works for a federal agency such as the FBI, IRS, DEA, or the Social Security Administration ever questions you, it is particularly important that you remain silent rather than lie. Usually, when these government agents question you, they will not have you in "custody," and therefore they do not need to remind you of your right to remain silent. If you lie to *any* Federal government agent, you can theoretically be imprisoned for up to five years and fined up to $10,000.[4]

EXAMPLE: Heidi Experiences "Friendly" Police Questioning

This little drama begins with police investigators in plainclothes pulling up in front of Heidi's home in an unmarked car. This time, the story involves grass of a different sort than you have come to expect. But obviously, this sort of police questioning could as easily occur in a case involving marijuana.

"Excuse me, Miss, do you live here?"

"Yes. Is anything wrong?"

"Oh, no. We're just here to check out a complaint. I'm sure there's no truth to it, but, you know, we have to check these things out. We've had some reports of people running around without their clothes in the meadow down the way. Since your home is close to the meadow, we thought that you might have seen these people."

"Oh, is it illegal to dance nude in the meadow?"

"Oh, no, Miss. That meadow is far from a public area. Only public nudity is against the law. For example, it would be perfectly legal for you to run naked in your meadow. That's not hurting anyone. But these people running around in your meadow may have been trespassing on your land."

"Oh, I wouldn't care about that. But, you know, this silly rumor could have been about me and my boyfriend. David and I sometimes dance and run naked in our meadow. Naturally, we didn't think anyone was watching."

"Naturally. Okay, that's fine. You know, I'll be honest with you. We suspected that you and your friend might be the free-spirited dancers in the meadow, but we don't like to jump to conclusions or accuse people."

"It's nice to hear that Officer."

"Now, I remember when I was young, and I wouldn't be surprised if you and David have made love in the meadow—maybe on some of the same days that you were running about naked."

"Well, sure. We sometimes like to make love in the sunshine, and the meadow is wonderful."

"Okay, Miss — now I'm going to read you your rights. This is just a formality, but we're supposed to do it before asking you some more personal questions that I really don't like asking."

"Oh, I've heard those rights before; you don't have to repeat them."

"I'm sorry, I think this is silly too, but it's just something we have to do. It'll just take a minute. You have the right to remain silent. Anything you say can and will be used against you in court. You have the right to a lawyer. A lawyer will be provided to you free of charge if you cannot afford one. With these rights in mind, do you freely and voluntarily consent to talk with us?"

"Why are you doing this now? What's the matter. I was talking with you all along."

"Everything's fine. Just sign this card and we can finish our little talk. We don't want to have to take you to the station."

"Take me to the station? I haven't done anything!"

"Miss, we'd like to finish talking to you to clear everything up, but we can't unless you sign this card."

"No, I won't sign it, but I'll talk to you—maybe. What's really going on here?"

"We're just doing our job. We really hate to get into personal questions and we certainly don't want to take you to the station. I'll come right to the point. Do you and David kiss each other around the genitals?"

"Why are you asking me that? Is it illegal?"

"It's better to be honest. You have been very helpful so far. Don't hold anything back. It'll be much easier on you if you'll just answer the question."

"So, it is illegal. Well, I'm not going to say another word. I know my rights."

At the court hearing before trial to determine the legality of the police questioning, the detectives explained that they had been checking out the heated complaints of a neighbor who reported that he had seen Heidi and a young man run naked in a meadow and then lie down on a mattress and commit unspeakable crimes against nature. The neighbor insisted that the police do something because Heidi was only seventeen years old, which meant that her obviously older boyfriend was committing statutory rape. As it turned out, the concerned neighbor was the old man across the street who spent much of his day looking through his telescope.

Question: Did the police legally question Heidi?

Answer: Yes. Judges consider this type of questioning to be friendly investigation, since Heidi was not in "custody." Nor were the police obligated to tell Heidi their true purpose in questioning her.

Question: Would the police questioning of Heidi have been legal if they had had photographic evidence of her sexual crime rather than just an informer's story.

Answer: Maybe not. Such evidence would probably give the police probable cause to arrest Heidi and some judges would require that the police tell Heidi of her Miranda rights if they had probable cause to arrest her and, in fact, planned to arrest her. Most judges, however, would approve of the police questioning because the police had not yet taken Heidi physically into custody. Furthermore, even if the police had questioned Heidi illegally, the State could use her statements to convict David of statutory rape and oral sex. The important lesson here is that you have no way of knowing what information the police have or don't have, and therefore you take a great risk by talking to them about yourself or your friends.

Question: Were the police required to tell Heidi of her rights as soon as they did?

Answer: Probably not. But for those few judges who require the police to give Miranda rights after they have probable cause to arrest, the police played it safe. Heidi's admission to having done everything but the lovemaking crime confirmed the informer's story and most likely gave the police probable cause to arrest her at that point.

Question: Did it matter that Heidi refused to sign the card saying that she had been informed of her rights to remain silent and to see a lawyer?

Answer: No. Asking her to sign a card was simply an attempt to obtain additional proof that the police obeyed the law and told Heidi of her rights. It is not necessary for the police to have such proof.

Insist on Your Right to Talk to a Lawyer

Not only should you refuse to talk to the police about your personal conduct, it is often critical that you insist upon speaking to a lawyer. While this book gives you information that will help you to help yourself, it is no substitute for a lawyer if you are arrested. Even if you believe that you know how to protect yourself from the questions of the police, your answers to police questions are more likely to be appropriate if you have had time for reflection and an opportunity to discuss the matter with an objective and experienced person. Holding your tongue also gives you an opportunity to organize your story, emphasizing certain points and de-emphasizing others, before you talk to the police. Once you talk to an officer, you cannot tell your story differently at trial without damaging your credibility. That is, the prosecutor can call you a liar — called *impeaching your testimony* in legal lingo — if you relate the details of your story differently at trial than you did at the police station.

Even if you are completely innocent of the crime of which the police accuse you and even if your story is completely true, you should still hesitate to tell it to the police, at least until you have talked to a lawyer. It is not unheard of for paid informers and the police to try to set you up and later lie about it; and, if the prosecutor knows every detail of your defense in advance, he can better use whatever evidence he already has to make it appear that you are guilty.

The U.S. Supreme Court Protects Us Against the "Possibility of Perjury"

In the most famous case in this "impeachment" area of law, the police arrested Viven Hernandez, a heroin addict, the day after he supposedly sold two "glassine bags" of heroin for $12 to an undercover agent. (Even though this example doesn't involve marijuana, the legal principles involved would, of course, be exactly the same if it did.) The police did not follow the law and explain to Hernandez that he had a right to a lawyer, and within one hour of his arrest, he talked. Hernandez told the police that everybody in his area of New York City was selling drugs and that he needed heroin for his habit. He said that the undercover agent set him up by promising to give him a little heroin and $12 in exchange for buying some heroin for the agent. When Hernandez testified at his trial, however, he told a different story to the jury than he had told to the police. He told the jury that he had sold two "glassine bags" to the agent for $12 which contained nothing more than baking powder that looked like heroin.

By testifying to his innocence, Hernandez opened himself up to be "impeached" or discredited, and the prosecutor was able to tell the jury the story Hernandez had told to the police the day of his arrest. The prosecutor was able to impeach Hernandez's credibility with his own prior statements to the police, even though *illegally* obtained in violation of *Miranda,* on the theory that no one has a right to commit perjury. Hernandez was convicted and sentenced to prison for six to eight years.[5] Thus even though Hernandez's story in court may have been the truth and his first story to the police a lie, the U.S. Supreme Court ruled that it was more important to guard against the commission of perjury by criminals than to ensure that the police obey the law and tell you of your constitutional rights.

If Hernandez had known enough to remain silent, even though the police had not told him of his Miranda rights, the jury might have believed his story and acquitted him.

EXAMPLE: Brendan Forgets His Vow of Silence

Two uniformed police officers arrived in their car at Brendan's country home.

"Hi. Do you mind if we ask you a couple of questions? Have you seen anyone hanging out in the woods up the road?"

"No. What's up?"

"We understand that's your land up there and that your truck has been parked up there regularly for several months."

"Yeah. I've been clearing some brush."

"Listen, buddy. We found a little marijuana garden up there. You have some explaining to do."

"I don't know anything about it."

"The garden was fenced and there's a water system. Somebody has been taking care of it. We also found some tools. Are you missing a shovel and a pickax?"

"I don't want to talk to you. You can't prove that's my patch."

"Brendan, we know you smoke marijuana."

"Yeah. So what?"

"So, we think you grow it. That's your garden up there, isn't it?"

"You can't prove it."

"We're taking you down for fingerprinting. We'll see if we can't prove it."

"No. That garden could be anyone's. I don't have to go."

"Either you come voluntarily or we'll arrest you."

"I'm not going."

"You're under arrest. Hands on the car. Spread your legs. What's this in your pocket? Looks like a bag of grass to me. Okay. Hands behind your back. Into the car. And listen buddy, let me give you some advice. If you confess, the judge will be easy on you. Everyone grows a little marijuana around here. No one cares. I just do this as part of my job. Anyway, we have you for this grass. You don't want to go through this fingerprinting stuff. If you admit it, we'll book you and let you go. No bail or anything. You'll get a trial date, plead guilty, first offense—it's just probation. Save yourself a hassle."

"I don't know. I'd like to talk to my lawyer."

"Ah, your lawyer. You know what he'll say? Don't talk, fight it. And then he'll bill you. He's not cheap, is he? You'll pay for listening to your lawyer. I've seen lawyers screw so many nice guys like you who could have gotten off with probation or a little fine."

"Okay. The hell with him. You really found fingerprints on my tools, huh?"

"Yeah, we sure did. I have to read you your rights now. Then you can sign this form and just write down that you grew the marijuana."

"Okay, where do I sign?"

Question: Did the police legally obtain Brendan's statement that he worked in the woods by the marijuana and that he smoked marijuana?

Answer: Probably yes. A few judges, however, might decide otherwise. They would reason that the police already had probable cause to arrest Brendan and that the police must inform a suspect of his rights as soon as they have probable cause to make an arrest, or even after their suspicion has focused on a particular person.

Question: Did the police legally obtain Brendan's written confession?

Answer: No. Brendan confessed after they took him into custody and after he asked for a lawyer and was refused (or talked out of it). In this situation, however, it wouldn't be unusual for the police to develop a selective memory as to what was said.

Question: If the police are honest, could the prosecutor use Brendan's illegally obtained confession to call him a liar if Brendan testifies to his innocence?

Answer: Yes, except in a few states.

Question: Could the prosecutor convict Brendan for possession of the bag of marijuana?

Answer: Maybe yes, so long as the police claim that they had probable cause to arrest. The police may not want to say that they had probable cause in this situation, however, because they will want to be sure that Brendan's later statements would be legally admissible (see the first question above).

REMINDER: You can avoid all of these dangers and technicalities by simply being patient enough to tell your story to your lawyer first. Often, your lawyer will counsel you not to say things that appear to you to be harmless. A prosecutor is not allowed to tell the jury that you refused to talk to the police or that you insisted upon talking to a lawyer after your arrest, with one possible exception.

A Dastardly Exception

In the summer of 1980, the Supreme Court dreamed up yet another way to subvert our Fifth Amendment right to remain silent. The prosecutor can now tell the jury that you remained silent before the police arrested you and told you your rights.[6] Even though this loophole is simply another attempt by the Supreme Court to deprive you of your right to remain silent, you are still more likely to avoid a trial and conviction by standing on your rights and buttoning your lip. If you are forced to trial and the prosecutor tries to suggest that you are lying because you didn't tell your story immediately to the police, stand up and tell the jury and the prosecutor why you remained silent. Being as cool as possible under the circumstances, you or your lawyer can explain that you were under the misconception that there was a Fifth Amendment in our Constitution that gave you the right to remain silent without fear that a jury would be told that silence implies deception and guilt.

> **SELF-HELP NOTE:** As soon as the police begin to question you, *ask* them if you have a right to remain silent. Whether they say yes or no, their response may protect you from this new loophole, either because the police would have told you about your right to remain silent, or because they would have lied. If you believe that the police may accuse you of a crime, consult a lawyer immediately. In limited circumstances, after you have consulted a lawyer, it may be wise for you to turn yourself in to the police and claim you are innocent even before the police arrest you.

Always Remember—the Police Have a Strong Incentive to Pressure You to Talk

When the police realize that they cannot get you to talk about your marijuana activities, they will often be forced to let you go because they do not have enough evidence to arrest you. Indeed, if the police have a conclusive case against you, they are unlikely to put much effort into getting you to provide them with additional evidence. As a general rule, they are most anxious to get you to talk when they have a weak case. Reasoning along this line, it is easy to understand that police questioning is frequently designed to catch you in a lie—any lie—to weaken your psychological defenses and convince you to confess. Your best defense against these tactics is, of course, to keep your mouth shut until you see a lawyer. No matter how "glib," "streetwise," or "legally sophisticated" you are, you place yourself in a position of extreme legal and psychological jeopardy by trying to spar verbally with the police.

Here is something else to watch out for. Although by law the police must stop badgering you to talk once you assert your constitutional right to remain silent and request a lawyer, in practice they often do not. Or, to state the matter more forcefully, the police frequently violate the law by trying to convince you to talk even after you have asked for a lawyer, because at this point they have little to lose by violating your constitutional rights. They know that the first thing a competent lawyer will tell you is "Do not talk to the police or anyone else." If the police have a fairly weak case, they know that they will be less able to convict you if they can't convince you to talk. But the police also know that if they are only able to convince you to talk after you have asked for a lawyer, anything you say can't be used as part of the prosecution's direct case against you at trial.

Since this rule is the law, why do the police continue to pressure you to talk? Ah, ha! Now you'll see just how tricky and unfair the law can be. The police know that while they can't use the statements you make after you ask for a lawyer as part of their direct case against you, they are permitted to use these statements to "impeach" your testimony at trial. Anticipating abuses, Justices William Brennan and Thurgood Marshall of the U.S. Supreme Court warned that "after today's decision, if an individual states that he wants an attorney, police interrogation will doubtless be vigorously pressed to obtain statements [in violation of the law] before the attorney arrives."[7]

EXAMPLE: Paul Stands Up to the Police

Knock, knock.

"It's the police."

Paul stepped outside and closed the door behind him.

"Last night there was a burglary next door. We suspect that the burglar was looking for drugs. Do you know anything about that?"

"No, I don't."

"Do you mind if we check your back yard?"

"What's the matter?"

"Do you have friends who live out by the coast?"

"I'm sorry. My lawyer has told me never to answer police questions concerning my personal life."

"We'll have to take you down to the station if you're not cooperative."

"Am I under arrest? What for? I want to speak to my lawyer."

"Okay. Up against the wall. Spread your legs. You're clean. Listen, we don't want to take you to the station, strip search you, and put you in jail for the weekend. Your lawyer can't help you, but if you'll only answer a few questions, we'll let you go."

"No. I know my rights."

The police jailed Paul. At 11 PM, 5 AM, 7 AM and 11 AM the police brought him to their interrogation room, but Paul refused to talk. Finally they let him call a lawyer.

Question: Did the police legally arrest and jail Paul?

Answer: No. These facts do not show probable cause to arrest.

Question: If Paul had talked because of the threat of the illegal arrest and jailing, could the State use anything he said to convict him?

Answer: Not as part of their direct case against him but they could use his statements to impeach him if he testified to his innocence at his trial.

Question: If Paul had talked at one of the early morning interrogation sessions, could the State use anything he said to convict him?

Answer: Again, at least to impeach him, so long as the judge decided that his statements were "voluntary." The police tape-record virtually all of these interrogation sessions and are almost always sure to tape themselves giving the *Miranda* warnings. If Paul said on tape that he voluntarily gave up his rights to remain silent and to see a lawyer, the police may also conveniently forget that he ever asked for a lawyer so that they can introduce Paul's statements directly at trial rather than simply use them for impeachment purposes if Paul testifies to his innocence.

Stand Up to Police Pressure and Persuasion, and Remain Silent No Matter What They Say

If the police tell you that "Your partner has confessed" or "We won't arrest your wife if you talk" or "We'll go easy on you if you make it easy for us by talking," you should realize that your need to remain silent and consult with a lawyer is probably even greater than you thought. Again, remember that the police are probably applying pressure to convince you to talk because they do not otherwise have enough evidence to convict you. If you do talk under such circumstances, many judges will not permit what you say to be used against you at your trial, but you cannot depend on it.

Two Tricky But Legal Confessions

Although Joseph Kadish's lawyer warned him not to talk, Kadish, unable to resist, asked Sergeant Anderson about his case. The sergeant lied and said that two people had said they saw him in the area of the crime in question that day. Though it was the officer's lie that led Kadish to confess, the confession was still admitted at trial because it was "free and voluntary."[8]

In another case, a seventeen-year-old with a seventh-grade education was led to confess after the police told him that an accomplice had confessed. The Pennsylvania Supreme Court decided that the confession was admissible because "we are not convinced that the alleged fabrication concerning the [accomplice's] confession was likely to cause an untrustworthy confession. Nor do we find it so reprehensible as to invalidate the confession as offensive to basic notions of fairness." One judge dissented.[9]

It is a common belief in the United States that confessions obtained as a result of heavy-handed interrogation techniques by police cannot be used against a person in court. While this belief is true up to a point, judges are the ultimate arbiters of what is unacceptable police behavior. Some people have confessed after being subjected to what they considered to be outrageous police misconduct, only to learn that a judge had a different definition of "outrageous" and allowed the confession to be admitted into evidence against them.

Police persecution must be quite severe before you can rely on a judge to rule that the police forced you to talk. Usually, therefore, you should keep your peace and quiet, even if you are threatened. Good advice, however, can be taken too far, so if the police threaten to physically abuse you, you should cooperate. Under the law, judges should not admit your coerced confession into evidence. But be wary. In 1967, for example, the U.S. Supreme Court had to overturn a decision of the Alabama Supreme Court that permitted the prosecutor to use a second confession obtained from a hospitalized suspect five days after the police used the following persuasion: "The police chief . . . said, 'If you don't tell the truth, I am going to kill you.' The other officer then fired his rifle next to the suspect's ear and [he] immediately confessed."[10]

If the police beat you, a judge will almost always rule that your confession is involuntary and therefore unreliable. Not unexpectedly, however, the police rarely admit that they have beaten people to force them to talk. For instance, David Grady testified that "his confession was procured by torture and brutality." The judges of the Florida Supreme Court did not believe him, even though the police held him for fifty-three hours in jail before his seven and one-half hour interrogation without a lawyer.[11]

Close Your Mouth in the Jail House

After you are arrested and jailed you must be extremely careful not to talk about your case to fellow prisoners. Many prisoners will gladly accept a plea bargain on their own cases in return for repeating to the jury at your trial whatever you have told them. In 1980, the U.S. Supreme Court finally did prohibit the most outrageous uses of inmate informers.[12] Now other inmates or undercover police who have "deliberately" tricked you into talking about your crime while you are in jail *and* charged with a crime, and who are rewarded on the basis of how much "useful information" they gather, cannot testify in court about what you have told them. This sort of testimony is discouraged, in part, because it is often highly unreliable. People who stand to get a reduced sentence or perhaps even a release from prison obviously have a considerable incentive to lie. The Supreme Court, however, has only outlawed this one kind of informer testimony. For example, in a situation in which you talk to a fellow inmate voluntarily (he has not deliberately sought to trick you), your conversation can be used against you. So please realize that it is utter foolishness to talk about your crime to anyone but your lawyer, at least until you have been convicted and have no more rights to appeal.

Conclusion

No matter how badly the police abuse you or violate your constitutional rights, there is often a loophole in the law big enough to make you wish that you had not talked. Judges are reluctant to release a "guilty" person simply because her constitutional rights were violated. Therefore, you had better keep your vow of silence.

And now, after preparing you for the worst, remember that it's not always this bad—appellate court judges in some states take a more enlightened view of the Constitution and laws that protect our privacy and freedom.

THE BEST YOU CAN EXPECT FROM A JUDGE

• Some judges will be more willing than others to recognize that the police had you in custody and questioned you before telling you of your Miranda rights.

• In some states, judges will require the police to tell you of your Miranda rights after they have focused their investigation upon you.

• In a few states, judges will not allow the prosecutor to use an illegally obtained statement in any way at your trial.

• Some judges will not allow the State to use statements you have made after the police have lied to you, held you in jail for hours, or questioned you for hours without a lawyer under questionable circumstances.

CHAPTER 12

The Call of the Grand Juries

Why, thou unreverend and unhallowed friar,
Is't not enough thou hast suborned these women
To accuse this worthy man, but, in foul mouth,
And in the witness of his proper ear,
To call him villain? And then to glance from him
To th' Duke himself, to tax him with injustice?

William Shakespeare,
MEASURE FOR MEASURE, Act V, Scene 1

Protecting society from violence and crime while at the same time protecting the innocent from violations of their privacy by the police is no easy task. In a sense, the individual is threatened simultaneously by an absence and an excess of law. In parts of this country, trying to defend oneself against criminals is a major preoccupation, but even at its worst it is probably not as scary as being victimized by a lawless police investigation or an unfair prosecution.

The problem of protecting the innocent from both criminals and the State isn't a new one—it was around at the time our country was founded and our Constitution was written. Indeed, the solution that our ancestors adopted had already been used for centuries in England: the grand jury.

In a nutshell, the grand jury is supposed to be twelve (or seventeen, twenty-three, or twenty-four) good, fair, honorable, independent, freedom-loving American men and women whose job is to protect the innocent from unfair accusations of the State and at the same time see that the guilty are pursued and punished without fear or favor. Unfortunately, the grand jury has become little more than a secret inquisition controlled by the State's prosecutors with the power to imprison folks who refuse to confess their crimes or those of their friends.

THUMBNAIL REVIEW
What the Grand Jury Can Do "Legally"

• The grand jury can accuse you of a crime, investigate your activities, and force you to answer its questions.

• The grand jury can order you to appear before it to answer its questions on threat of imprisonment if you refuse to appear.

• The order to appear can be based on vague suspicions or rumors.

• When you are summoned before it, a grand jury does not have to tell you the purpose of its investigation or whether you are a prime suspect or an innocent witness.

• In addition, the grand jury does not have to remind you of your Fifth Amendment right to remain silent or inform you that you might give up your Fifth Amendment right to remain silent if you even begin to answer the grand jury's questions about the subject of its investigation.

• The grand jury does not have to provide you with a lawyer if you are too poor to afford one, and even if you can afford a lawyer, your lawyer cannot enter the grand jury chambers with you.

• If you refuse to talk by asserting the Fifth Amendment, the grand jury may order you to talk by promising not to use your testimony to convict you (called *use immunity* in legal lingo) and may imprison you if you continue to refuse to talk.

• The grand jury may also imprison you if you refuse to talk about the activities of your friends or family (including parents, children, and lovers, but not spouses) as long as your testimony would not incriminate you; or even if it would incriminate you, after the grand jury promises not to use your testimony against you by granting you immunity from prosecution.

• The grand jury can accuse you of a crime based on illegally obtained evidence, or secondhand ("hearsay") evidence, though not on evidence derived from an illegal wiretap.

What You Can Do to Protect Yourself

• If you are ever called before a grand jury, see a lawyer immediately to learn how to deal with what can almost amount to a Star Chamber type of proceeding.

• Assert your Fifth Amendment right to remain silent if your answers to grand jury questions could in any way link you (or even possibly link you) to a crime.

• Never lie to the grand jury. Bad memories, however, are sometimes unavoidable.

• If the grand jury promises not to use your testimony to convict you, you have lost your constitutional right to remain silent. You must choose jail or submit to the humiliation of confessing and possibly implicating your close friends.

• You can legally refuse to answer any grand jury questions that involve your spouse.

• In addition you may refuse to answer any grand jury questions about conversations that have been illegally wiretapped; and you may refuse to answer questions about areas that are irrelevent to the purposes of its investigation, if you can figure out what those purposes are.

• You can try your best to serve on the grand jury and encourage your neighbors to do the same, so that you and your neighbors are in a position to protect Americans from arbitrary and abusive State power.

ALL ABOUT THE GRAND JURY

If you assert your Fifth Amendment right to remain silent, the grand jury can promise not to use your answers to convict you and then order you to answer its questions or face prison. If you and a friend are both ordered to testify, the State can use what each of you say to convict the other. If, after being offered immunity, you still refuse to talk, the State can imprison you for up to eighteen months or for as long as that particular grand jury is meeting, without a trial, a jury verdict, or proof of any crime, except the crime of refusing to talk to the grand jury. There are some who believe that this sort of grand jury *Catch-22* threatens to become a modern equivalent of the torture chambers of the Middle Ages. Even if you think this sort of analogy is a little strong, it is indisputable that the power of the grand jury can—and has—led to dangerous abrogations of individual freedom.

The grand jury has two functions.[1] The Fifth Amendment established one of these roles in 1791:

> No person shall be held to answer for a capital, or otherwise infamous
> crime, unless on a presentment or indictment of a Grand Jury, except in
> cases arising in the land or naval forces, or in the Militia, when in actual
> service in time of War or public danger . . .

Translated into modern English, this part of the Fifth Amendment means that you have a constitutional right to have a grand jury determine whether or not you should stand trial for a *serious* crime.

An "indictment of a grand jury" is a written announcement that formally accuses someone of committing a crime or crimes, thus authorizing his arrest and trial. The theory behind a grand jury indictment is that the grand jury protects you from false or baseless criminal accusations. In reality, most prosecutors have almost complete control over the grand jury, and thus most of the time its indictments constitute little more than formal approval of a prosecutor's decision to prosecute.

In most states, if the authorities give you a choice between a grand jury indictment and a preliminary hearing, you should "waive," that is give up, your right to be indicted by the grand jury (see Chapter 13). In those states that have no state constitutional right to a grand jury indictment in the first place, this choice will not be an issue. Why? A grand jury indictment is not considered a "fundamental" right under the U.S. Constitution, and except for certain "fundamental" rights, the Bill of Rights of our Constitution does not apply to the actions of the state and local governments, but only to the actions of the federal government (see Chapter 2). In summary, grand juries no longer serve their original constitutional function to protect people from false accusations.

The second and more dangerous role of the grand jury is to investigate crime secretly, behind closed doors. It is here that a grand jury has the power to force you to talk with a possible penalty of imprisonment if you refuse. For example, a grand jury might be impaneled to investigate "organized crime" or "political corruption" or "marijuana and drug traffic" within a certain local jurisdiction. In deciding what, whom, and how to investigate, the grand jury is supposed to protect you from unfair prosecutions by acting independently of the prosecutor. In reality, however, the prosecutor commonly controls the grand jury's power to call and question witnesses, and to indict or accuse people of crimes. There have been situations of independent-minded grand juries who have gone against the mandate of the local establishment, but unfortunately this sort of behavior is rare.

The grand jury is also supposed to represent a cross section of the entire community, but in fact, this goal is rarely achieved. In many areas, the selection process has worked to overrepresent white, affluent men and women, while ordinary working people, even when selected, have been discouraged from serving by the fact that the grand jury often meets during working hours for at least several months and sometimes for as long as three years.

How does a grand jury proceed? Usually as part of a criminal investigation, the grand jury calls witnesses to testify before it. Witnesses are called to testify by serving them with a *subpoena,* often by mail. The subpoena, which literally means "under pain of punishment," will order you to appear before the grand jury at a certain place on a certain date. Occasionally, it is possible to be ordered to appear far from your home on short notice. If you fail to show up, you can be punished—arrested and jailed on a charge of contempt of court. If the grand jury wants you to bring some of your papers or other personal evidence with you, it will mail you a *subpoena duces tecum* which orders you to bring certain documents. (Literally it means "under pain of punishment you shall take it with you.") If you refuse willfully to bring evidence that you have under your control, you can be arrested and jailed. Only if you or your lawyer can convince a judge that your subpoena is unreasonable or oppressive, will the judge "quash" or revoke it. Judges tend to believe that grand jury subpoenas are not unreasonable or oppressive.

If the Grand Jury Calls You, See a Lawyer (If You Can Afford One)

You should see an experienced criminal lawyer if you are called before a grand jury. You should seek legal advice even if you feel that you personally have nothing to fear. Think about it for a moment. How many of us can answer every possible question about our activities (or those of our friends) without the risk of giving a grand jury a reason to ask the district attorney to prosecute?

Ordinarily, you cannot refuse to appear before the grand jury whether it is investigating your marijuana activities or for any other reason. If you are sick, of course, you can postpone your appearance, but you must notify the grand jury immediately and be prepared to have a doctor confirm your illness. If the grand jury tells you to appear at an unacceptable time or on short notice, you can insist upon a more convenient time; if it orders you to appear far from your home, you can request that it pay for your transportation, particularly if you are poor. To avoid arrest for failure to comply with the court's subpoena, however, you must convince the grand jury to grant such reasonable requests. Your lawyer will probably be better able to convince the grand jury to change your appearance date or to pay for unusual transportation costs. Experienced criminal defense lawyers, however, tend to be expensive, and you must pay for one yourself or do without.

The State will not provide you with a lawyer to discuss the legality of the grand jury subpoena, to advise you about the great dangers of testifying before a grand jury, or to help you through the hassle. The U.S. Supreme Court has declared that you have no legal right to consult a lawyer about the grand jury, and, therefore, it is "too bad" if you cannot afford to pay a lawyer to help you. If you ask, some grand juries will provide you with a lawyer out of a sense of fairness. And, in most major cities, the National Lawyers Guild may give grand jury advice for little or no fee, depending upon your income. Do not be concerned that paying for a lawyer's advice about your grand jury appearance will prevent you from qualifying for a free lawyer at your trial if you are charged with a crime. If you are poor enough (before or after you pay for a grand jury lawyer), you can still qualify for a public defender or a state-appointed lawyer to represent you at your trial if you are charged with an offense after your grand jury testimony (see Chapter 13).

The Grand Jury Can Order You to Testify About Rumors

It is legal for the grand jury to order you to appear before it to testify about marijuana, even if you do nothing more than smoke it, or you are rumored to grow it. The grand jury can claim that it wants to make certain that you do not cultivate or sell marijuana or that it wants to ask you the name of your supplier. In other words, the grand jury can call you as a witness on the basis of rumors that would not be sufficient legal justification for a police officer to stop you on the street.

In addition, when the grand jury calls you, it does not have to tell you whether you are an innocent witness. The grand jury can investigate any crime the prosecutor suggests, and it can order you to testify even if the prosecutor already has enough information to charge you with a crime. That some grand juries act more fairly than they are legally required to act is nice, but that fact is little comfort when grand juries act as unfairly as the law allows.

Usually, however, before a grand jury will call you for interrogation purposes, someone in law enforcement must seriously believe that you are part of a large group dealing with marijuana. Recently, for example, a Florida grand jury investigated the members of an Ethiopian Zion Coptic Church located on an island off the coast of Florida who not only openly smoked marijuana as part of their religious ceremonies, but also smoked it throughout the day and freely allowed children to smoke it. Finally, the Florida Supreme Court decided that because the location of the church violated zoning ordinances, it could not be used as a church, and because the members of the church used marijuana indiscriminately, they could not lawfully use the substance at all.[2]

Refuse to Answer All Incriminating Questions

"Silence is golden" when dealing with the grand jury for most of the same reasons that it's "golden" if you are arrested (see Chapter 11). By talking to the grand jury, you may unknowingly provide information that is innocent on its face but which connects you or a friend with marijuana or other contraband when added to other evidence that the State possesses. Also, by talking in a situation where you have no right of legal representation and where you are likely to be intimidated, you may impulsively or thoughtlessly lie, thus allowing the prosecutor to charge you with the serious crime of perjury. And even if you don't incriminate yourself, testifying before a grand jury can lead to later problems because anything you say can be used to impeach or contradict your testimony should you be charged with a crime and brought to trial.

You should always refuse to answer any questions relating in any conceivable way to your marijuana or other "criminal" activity. You should also refuse to answer any questions when you are unsure of the effect of your answer. Technically, you can refuse to answer *only* by invoking your Fifth Amendment privilege to remain silent on the grounds that anything you say might incriminate you. It is up to you to assert your rights. Neither the prosecutor nor the foreman of the grand jury has any legal responsibility to tell you that you have a right to remain silent, that anything you say can be used to convict you, or that you have a right to consult with a lawyer if you can afford one.

Even if you doubt that a particular bit of testimony would qualify for your Fifth Amendment right not to incriminate yourself, it's still better to remain silent even in the face of a contempt citation—until you can talk the problem over with a lawyer. You will be given time to consult with a lawyer before being jailed for refusing to testify.

The "It's Too Late to Take the Fifth" Loophole

Watch it! The prosecutor may try to trick you into answering seemingly innocent questions about the general subject matter of the investigation with the idea of getting you to give up your Fifth Amendment privileges. These preliminary questions may seem so innocent and unconnected to any dealings with "criminal" activity that you will be tempted to answer them. But there may be a surprise consequence of answering any of the inquisitor's questions beyond your name and address. A legal rule says that if you answer any questions about the general subject matter of the grand jury's investigation, it may be too late for you to claim your right to remain silent. Thus, because you have answered some of the prosecutor's questions, some judges may rule that you have "waived" or given up your right to refuse to answer the rest of the prosecutor's questions on the same subject. To be sure to avoid the "It's too late to take the Fifth" loophole, you must assert your Fifth Amendment right to remain silent almost immediately.

Remember, only you are allowed into the grand jury's chambers to answer the questions of the prosecutor. Consequently, you should not hesitate to demand to see your lawyer, if you have one, whenever you have the slightest doubt about the wisdom of answering a certain question. If you need to, you can ask to leave the grand jury room after every question to ask your lawyer's advice outside of the grand jury room.

Testifying before the grand jury can become particularly troublesome if you learn that the grand jury is more interested in your friend's marijuana activity than in your own. Why? Unfortunately, you have no constitutional right to refuse to answer a prosecutor's question by invoking the Fifth Amendment on the grounds that your answer may get a friend into trouble. In this situation, however, a lawyer could help you determine whether answering a question about your friend's marijuana activities might not also incriminate you. If you do not have a lawyer and are at all unsure, you should refuse to talk about a friend's activities on the grounds that your answer might possibly incriminate you.

EXAMPLE: **Trusting Jerry Responds to a Grand Jury Subpoena**

"Joan, I received some sort of subpoena from the grand jury over at the county building. Listen to this:

" 'Jerry Munoz, you are hereby ordered to appear before the Essex County grand jury on September 29. Failure to appear may result in your imprisonment for contempt of court.' "

"I received one too. My date with the grand jury is October 15."

September 29th arrived and Joan and Jerry went to the courthouse in town. When they got to the appointed room, they were met by a deputy sheriff who, after asking for identification, said:

"Miss, you must wait out here. Only the witness can go inside the grand jury room."

In a few minutes the proceeding got under way.

"Jerry, do you swear to tell the whole truth and nothing but the truth, so help you God?"

"Sure."

"Answer yes or no, please."

"Yes."

"Mr. Munoz, I am the special prosecutor. I will ask the questions. These twenty-three ladies and gentlemen are members of our community and have been appointed to serve on this grand jury."

"I thought that a grand jury was supposed to be made up of my peers. Everyone here seems to be twice my age and white. Where are my brothers?"

"We do have older and mature members of our community on the grand jury. They have more free time than most people. Unless you or your lawyer have filed papers challenging this panel, we will proceed.

"Where do you live, Mr. Munoz, and with whom?"

"I live with Joan Allison out in the hills, several miles back on Prairie Meadow Road."

"Why do you live so far away from other people?"

"We like the peace and quiet and privacy."

"You don't have anything to hide, do you, Mr. Munoz?"

"No, I have a right to live in the country, don't I?"

"You don't have the right to break the law. It would appear that living so far away from the rest of us tempts you to flout our laws."

"I don't understand. Are you accusing me of something?"

"We know that you people out in the hills grow marijuana. Do you grow marijuana, Mr. Munoz?"

"No, we grow vegetables, fruit trees, and flowers."

"Are we supposed to believe you?"

"Yes. I don't even smoke marijuana."

"*You* don't even smoke it? Well, who does smoke it, Mr. Munoz?"

"Lots of people, I imagine."

"There is no need to be sarcastic—we know that you know the names of some of your neighbors who smoke marijuana. You have a legal duty to tell us their names."

"I can't do that. They're my friends."

"Ah, ha. So you admit that you know the names of *friends* who smoke marijuana. I am afraid you are legally required to tell us their names or you will go to jail for contempt of this proceeding."

"Go to jail? What do you mean? I haven't done anything."

"You are withholding the names of lawbreakers—people who cultivate, smoke, and sell marijuana."

"But I have the right to remain silent. That's my constitutional right. I refuse to answer any more of your questions."

"You misunderstand the Constitution, young man. You have no right to hide the criminal acts of others. It's as simple as this. If you do not answer all of our questions about criminal activities in this county, we will have to put you in jail until you do. That's the Constitution. I'm the lawyer here. I know."

"I won't rat on my friends."

"Sheriff, escort Mr. Munoz to jail and let's see if a few days behind bars doesn't loosen his tongue."

Question: Was the prosecutor legally required to tell Jerry about his right to remain silent?

Answer: No.

Question: How long could the State keep Jerry in jail for refusing to talk about his friends?

Answer: Usually for the life of the particular grand jury investigation. His imprisonment could easily last months and as long as a year and a half.

Question: Could Jerry get out of jail if he explained that he had refused to answer because his answer might have incriminated him, or have been used against him as evidence?

Answer: No. The "It's too late to take the Fifth" loophole prevents Jerry from asserting his Fifth Amendment right to remain silent because he "waived " his right by talking in the first place beyond giving his name and address.

The Grand Jury Can Force You to Talk by Giving You "Immunity"

If you refuse to talk about anything on the Fifth Amendment ground that your words could incriminate you, the grand jury may order you to talk by granting you "immunity" from prosecution. "Immunity" should mean just that—complete protection from having any criminal action brought against you that is related to the testimony for which you are granted immunity. But in many courts, grand jury immunity does not offer you complete protection. And just as with some diseases, where immunity comes only after the pain of an injection, pain often accompanies a grant of immunity from prosecution. This time the pain isn't physical. Rather, it's the emotional grief that can accompany the knowledge that your words may not only implicate another person, perhaps even a friend, but yourself. It's not a pleasant predicament. If you refuse to talk, you can be imprisoned for as long as the grand jury remains in session. If you do talk, another person or persons may end up in jail.

In some circumstances, going to jail rather than testifying may be your best choice. Why? First, there is a possibility that the authorities may not jail you for refusing to talk. Second, the promise of "immunity" for you may not be as ironclad as it is supposed to be. For example, the State can convict you for the same marijuana activity about which it has forced you to testify (and about which it has granted you immunity) by showing that it found the evidence that it introduced at your trial "independently" of your testimony. In practice, this so-called use immunity can allow a prosecutor to ask questions about your life in order to find an independent source of evidence with which to convict you, or use the "independent" evidence of a friend who is forced to testify before the grand jury.

NOTE: Some states, such as California and New York, recognize the unfairness of this "use immunity" doctrine and grant broader "transactional immunity" to all witnesses who are forced to testify after asserting their Fifth Amendment right to remain silent. This type of immunity means that the State cannot prosecute you for any crime about which it forces you to talk, regardless of whether the State's agents gather evidence from a so-called independent source. Because this area of the law is so tricky, see an attorney, if at all possible.

Both types of immunities are objectionable, however, because both are designed to force you to talk against your will and both are used to try to get you to testify against your friends. It even happens that the State will try to force you to turn "State's evidence" against your friends when it knows that you are not guilty of any crime yourself.

One of the worst reactions to this "go to jail or rat on your friends" dilemma is to lie to the grand jury. In fact, the prosecutor may put to you this difficult choice in the hope of encouraging you to lie to protect your friends. If you do lie, and the prosecutor finds sufficient evidence to document your lie, you are likely to face a charge of perjury. Usually prosecutors only resort to this sort of trick when they believe you are guilty of a crime that they cannot prove. Their cynical theory is that it's their duty to imprison you, even if they have to manipulate the law to do it. If you do feel that you must bend the truth, the "I don't recall" answer made famous by so many of the Watergate conspirators is a prevarication that's difficult to prove false, because it might not be.

An Informer Gets His Deserts, Justly or Otherwise

In return for freedom and a promise of confidentiality, Richard Jasen provided Drug Enforcement Agency officers with information about his friends and associates involved in a cocaine deal. Apparently, DEA agents made arrests in the case, but couldn't find out where the stash was hidden. Jasen wouldn't talk any more because he had his freedom and had kept his part of the sleazy bargain. Jasen had also assumed that his bargain with the DEA agents meant that he was truly free and would not be harassed any more, but he assumed wrongly. The DEA agents thought otherwise. They explained their little problem to a federal grand jury in California and the grand jury ordered Jasen to talk. When Jasen asserted his Fifth Amendment right to remain silent, a judge gave him "immunity" and told him to testify before the grand jury the next day. Jasen refused, but as he had been granted immunity, he no longer had a constitutional right to remain silent. On August 11, 1980, federal district court Judge Manuel Real found Jasen in contempt of court and ordered him jailed until he decided to talk or "for the life of the grand jury, whichever is shortest." One month later, three judges of the U.S. Court of Appeals approved. They decided that Jasen's agreement with the DEA did not include a promise not to force him to talk before the grand jury.[3]

A Few Defenses against Grand Jury Procedures

By this time you are probably convinced that no one has any real rights when faced with a grand jury investigation. Well, surprise! You do have a few. For example, the State cannot force you to testify against your husband or wife. While the spousal relationship is considered sacred or special enough to warrant this exception, your parents, children, brothers, sisters, best friends, and lovers do not qualify. But many of your confidential communications with a psychiatrist, lawyer, doctor, or member of the clergy do qualify. A lawyer can tell you more about these areas of immunity.

Theoretically, you may also refuse to answer a question on the ground that it is irrelevant, but irrelevancy is extremely difficult to establish. All questions asked in the grand jury room are considered relevant so long as they have any conceivable relation to the subject under investigation. Since the grand jury need not even tell you what it is investigating, you may risk jail for refusing to answer seemingly irrelevant questions. Still, after consultation with a lawyer, irrelevancy may be an objection that's worth raising. In any case, you are unlikely to be jailed until a court passes on the question of relevance.

EXAMPLE: Joan Learns from Jerry's Mistake

Now, to continue the little story begun earlier in this chapter. As you will recall, Joan's hearing date before the grand jury was a couple of weeks after Jerry's. Seeing the trouble that Jerry had had, Joan wisely decided that she had better get some expert advice. She borrowed enough money for a two-hour consultation with a local attorney who had a reputation for handling marijuana cases honestly and well. Joan began the conversation.

"Jerry's in jail and now I must appear before the same grand jury on October 15. I don't want to involve my friends either, but I really don't smoke much marijuana and I don't grow or sell it at all. It seems pretty dumb to end up in jail. How can I use my Fifth Amendment right to refuse to talk so that I don't end up in the kind of trouble Jerry did?"

"Joan, telling the grand jury the names of your friends who smoke or grow marijuana could in theory incriminate you. If you have smoked marijuana or ever had a little around the house, you have been guilty of a crime. If your activities and those of your neighbors are related, you are entitled to assert your right to remain silent. You could remain silent even if you didn't smoke dope, so long as you have been at a party where marijuana was smoked or you have passed a joint to a friend."

At the first hearing, Joan refused to talk by taking the Fifth.

The prosecutor then asked a judge for permission to grant Joan "use immunity" from prosecution. The judge agreed, and the prosecutor mailed Joan another subpoena. Joan again arrived to testify and the questioning began.

"Ms. Allison, as you know you have been granted immunity from prosecution for any responsive answers to my questions. You must now answer. You can no longer legally assert the Fifth Amendment and if you do, you will be imprisoned for contempt of court. Do you understand?"

"Yes, but I didn't ask for and don't want immunity from prosecution. I'm not talking about any activities of Jerry Munoz or anyone else."

"Have you ever seen Jerry Munoz or anyone else grow, sell, or smoke marijuana?"

"I refuse to answer on the grounds that it is none of your business."

"Drug crimes are our business, even if there are no victims."

"But Jerry's my longtime companion, best friend, and lover. He's been just like a husband for the past five years. I must have some sort of immunity from testifying against him."

"If he's not your legal husband, you must talk."

"No. I refuse to answer on the moral grounds that friendships are a necessary part of my life and I would rather go to jail than betray my friends."

"There are no such things as moral grounds or the Fifth Amendment after the State gives you immunity from prosecution, young lady. It's speak up or go to jail."
"I'd rather go to jail."
"So be it."

Question: If Jerry and Joan actually grew marijuana and both admitted to it after being given "immunity," could the State use Jerry's testimony to help convict Joan and use Joan's testimony to help convict Jerry for marijuana cultivation?

Answer: Yes, in most states and in federal courts that give only "use immunity." Such evidence is "independent" of the testimony that each was forced to give, and thus the State would have kept its promise not to use Joan's forced confession to convict Joan or Jerry's forced confession to convict Jerry.

Other Unfair Grand Jury Procedures

There are a number of other practices engaged in by grand juries that some people consider to be particularly unfair. These include:

Questions Based on Illegally Seized Evidence. You cannot refuse to answer a grand jury's questions because they are based on evidence that has been illegally seized. This rule of law means, for example, that the police can illegally break into your home and the grand jury can force you to talk about anything the police illegally discovered before a judge throws the evidence out of court. The grand jury can even charge you with a crime based on illegal evidence in a situation in which you will later succeed in challenging the use of the evidence at a suppression hearing before your trial (see Chapter 13). The Supreme Court believes that this loophole is fair and necessary because it would be too inconvenient for the State to determine the legality of all the evidence presented to the grand jury *before* it accuses you of a crime.[4] The only exception to this rule is that the State cannot force you to testify about your conversations overheard in an illegal wiretap.

Hearsay Evidence. The grand jury can also charge you with a crime based solely on secondhand or "hearsay" evidence which would be insufficient to convict you at trial.

No Defense Allowed. The prosecutor does not have to present the grand jury with any witnesses who might testify in your favor, and you have no right to testify before the grand jury to try to convince it that you are innocent of any crime. The Supreme Court justifies these unfair practices by saying that it does not matter whether or not the grand jury proceeding is fair, so long as you ultimately get a fair trial.

SELF-HELP NOTE: To ensure that you do eventually get a fair trial, you are well-advised to write down everything you tell the grand jury. Why? Although the State can give you a transcript of your grand jury testimony if it desires, it sometimes has the power to arbitrarily deny you a copy of the hearing, and it does not have to record the grand jury hearing in the first place. Unless you have this information, however, it will be easier for the prosecutor to call you a liar at trial if you forget the exact words you used before the grand jury. For the same reason, you should also photocopy any records or papers that the grand jury tells you to bring to the hearing, per order of a *subpoena duces tecum*.

EXAMPLE: Denis and Toni before the Grand Jury

Denis consulted Susan, his lawyer, after receiving a grand jury subpoena. Susan told him to ask to be excused in order to consult with her after every question was asked and before answering it. Denis went into the grand jury's chambers, stated his name and decided to wait to consult Susan until the prosecutor asked him a question even vaguely connected with marijuana.

"Where do you live, Mr. Sullenger?"

"I live in the hills, about three miles from Salmon Creek County Road."

"Do you know a woman named Toni Hearsh in the city?"

"Yes. She's a friend of a friend and I've seen her a few times."

"Do you sell her marijuana?"

"I take the Fifth. That question asks me to confess to a crime."

"Do you grow marijuana?"

"I refuse to answer. There's a constitutional principle called the Fifth Amendment in our country."

"You're dismissed."

A little later, Toni was called to testify before the same grand jury.

"Do you know the suspected marijuana grower, Denis Sullenger, who lives in the hills several miles from Salmon Creek County Road?"

"No."

"No? Are you sure?"

"Yes."

"He says that he knows you."

"Well, it's not true."

"I'll show you the transcript of his hearing; Denis Sullenger admits to knowing you right here.

"Does he sell marijuana to you?"

"I take the Fifth Amendment and refuse to answer on the grounds that it might incriminate me."

"Where did you obtain this marijuana that the police found in your home?"

"That was an illegal search. They just broke in. They had no search warrant or other excuse. I take the Fifth Amendment again."

"Ms. Hearsh, we will give you immunity from prosecution for your testimony about marijuana. You will then have to talk to us about the activities of Denis Sullenger."

Several hours later, after a judge authorized use immunity, questioning continued.

"Okay—Denis did sell me some marijuana."

Question: Did the prosecutor legally ask Toni about the marijuana found in an illegal search?

Answer: Yes, as long as a judge has not yet decided that the search was illegal.

Question: Could the State prosecute Denis for the sale of marijuana on the basis of Toni's testimony?

Answer: Yes. But if Denis had consulted his lawyer and had refused to answer the prosecutor's seemingly innocent question as to whether he knew Toni until *after* the prosecutor had granted him immunity from prosecution, then the State might not have had any "independent" evidence with which to convict Denis.

Question: Could the State prosecute Toni on the basis of Denis's testimony even after giving Toni immunity from prosecution?

Answer: In theory, the State could prosecute—for perjury—as she had lied about not knowing Denis. Although the State could not convict Toni for perjury by using her own admission of knowing Denis after it had given her immunity, the State could convict her with Denis's testimony and any other independent evidence that it could gather. Although it would be unlikely that a prosecutor would bother to file charges for this little lie after Toni cooperated, it is wise to remember that when the State promises you immunity from prosecution, the immunity covers *only* the statements you make from that time on. Even then, you only have immunity from prosecution for telling the truth, never for lying.

Serve on the Grand Jury if Possible

One of the best things that you can do to protect all Americans against the secret inquisitions of the grand juries is to try your best to serve on one, and to encourage your neighbors to do the same. For the grand jury to represent a cross section of society, you or a neighbor should be on it. In most states, only registered voters are given the opportunity to be on the grand jury, so you should register to vote.

Even though the prosecutor usually dominates the grand jury by calling the witnesses and asking all the questions, a single independent-minded juror can exert considerable influence by trying to persuade a majority of the grand jurors to act independently. The grand jury is not supposed to be a weapon of the prosecutor, but instead a protector of the American people from arbitrary and abusive State power. Grand jury members should insist upon asking their own questions; they should demand that actual informers testify rather than accept the "hearsay" evidence presented by the police; they should refuse to charge people on evidence which is obviously weak or illegally obtained; they should refuse to subpoena witnesses unnecessarily; they should refuse to investigate unimportant matters; and they should refuse to charge persons with most "victimless crimes," such as those related to marijuana.

And now, after preparing you for the worst, here is that reminder that it's not always this bad—the judges in some states take a more enlightened view of the Constitution and laws that protect our privacy and freedom.

THE BEST YOU CAN EXPECT FROM A JUDGE

• In some states and federal courts, judges will require the grand jury to tell you the purpose of its investigation and whether you are a suspect or an innocent witness.

• Some judges will require the grand jury to tell you of your right to remain silent.

• Some judges will require the grand jury to provide you with a lawyer if you cannot afford one.

• Some judges will allow you to "take the Fifth" even after you have begun to answer the grand jury's questions.

• In a few states, judges will require that the grand jury give you "transactional immunity," which gives you complete protection against conviction for what you are forced to confess.

• A few judges will scrutinize possible grand jury harassment, including forcing you to testify against your family, forcing you to answer irrelevant questions, or forcing you to answer questions about obviously illegally obtained evidence.

CHAPTER **13**

Lawyers and the Criminal Justice Process

QUEEN ELIZABETH: My words are dull; O, quicken them with thine!

QUEEN MARGARET: They woes will make them sharp and pierce like mine.

DUCHESS OF YORK: Why should calamity be full of words?

QUEEN ELIZABETH: Windy attorneys to their client's woes.
Airy succeeders of intestate joy,
Poor breathing orators of miseries,
Let them have scope! Though what they will impart
Help nothing else, yet do they ease the heart.

William Shakespeare,
THE TRAGEDY OF RICHARD THE THIRD, Act IV, Scene 4

The planet Earth is obviously not the residence of perfect people. We all screw up from time to time, even if it's nothing more than being unkind to a friend. While we are left to handle most of our small mistakes ourselves, society has developed a criminal justice system to determine guilt or innocence for certain types of major deviations from accepted behavior. In recognition of the fact that judges are not gods, capable of infallibly determining guilt or innocence, society has included a number of procedures and safeguards in the criminal justice system to attempt to protect the rights of accused individuals.

While there is a great debate about the extent to which complex procedures are necessary to ensure fair and accurate trials, there is no question that the American judicial system is complicated. The fact that it takes at least three years of specialized study after college to become a lawyer is some evidence of how difficult and overly complicated the law has become. While making law too complicated for the average person to understand is obviously not a healthy development for society, there are so many technical rules that can influence the outcome of even the simplest criminal case that you probably will have little choice but to get a lawyer if you are arrested and charged with a crime.

This chapter introduces you to the many procedures that you face after an arrest. It also explains why you will probably need a legal friend to help you and how, in some limited circumstances, you may be able to act as your own lawyer. Certainly by familiarizing yourself with postarrest procedures, you should have less reason to be fearful, anxious, or paranoid if you are arrested, and should be better able to deal with your own lawyer. But please understand that reading this chapter will not make you a lawyer and will not by itself qualify you to handle your own criminal case.

LAWYERS

Choosing the Right Legal Help

Before discussing the details of the criminal justice process, the next couple of sections examine your options concerning legal help. Normally, if you are arrested, the single most important thing for you to do is to find a competent local lawyer specializing in criminal law. Even if you have represented yourself in civil proceedings such as a divorce, adoption, or name change, and happen to know something about criminal law, it is normally not wise to enter court as your own lawyer when you are charged with a crime. This principle is true even if the crime with which you are charged is relatively minor, such as possession of a small amount of marijuana. Even in minor cases, the consequences of any criminal conviction can be serious. In many situations a conviction can mean imprisonment or a fine. But even if you are given a suspended sentence, a conviction can get you deported if you are not a citizen, can cause you to lose your license to practice a profession or can make you ineligible for certain other jobs. Furthermore, if you are convicted of a second crime, it is likely that your punishment will be more severe than if you had a "clean" record.

Unlike other less important legal matters, you have a constitutional right to a lawyer in any criminal case for which you could be imprisoned. But you also have a constitutional right to act as your own lawyer at your criminal trial. For those of you who are determined to represent yourselves, this chapter will discuss how to approach it.

The "Rich Man's Choice": A Private Defense Attorney

If you are financially comfortable you can hire a competent criminal defense lawyer, using the same sorts of common sense techniques that you use to find quality services in other areas. Start by asking a lawyer you know, a friend, or a business associate for a referral to a good criminal defense lawyer who practices locally. You will want to seek out a person who spends at least 50 percent of her time on criminal cases because a "full-time" criminal lawyer is more likely to know all the subtleties of the most recent criminal cases. You should also try to find a local lawyer because she will be in a position to know the idiosyncrasies of the judges and prosecutors who will handle your case and who have great discretion in disposing of it.

Once you have the name of a lawyer or, preferably, several lawyers who handle criminal cases, you will want to meet them and see if you feel comfortable with their approach. Remember, it's your case—not the lawyer's—and you want to be sure to hire a person whom you respect and who will respect you enough to explain fully what is going on at all times. If a lawyer is not open and frank with you at the first interview, it is unlikely that her communication skills will improve later. Remember, the Latin root of the word client is "to hear, to obey." It is easy to find a lawyer who encourages that kind of relationship, but if you want some say in your own case, you will have to be a bit more choosy.

Probably the best way to approach payment with a lawyer you don't know is to agree on a price for an initial consultation. Some lawyers will briefly discuss your case for free, or for as little as $15 for half an hour. For a more detailed discussion of the facts of an average marijuana case and the lawyer's suggestions about a defense strategy, something in the range of $50 to $100 would seem fair. If you don't like the lawyer, you haven't wasted much money. One way to judge whether a lawyer will satisfy you in the long run is to pay attention to how straightforward she is willing to be at the beginning.

The "Poor Man's Choice": A Public Defender

If you cannot afford the hundreds or thousands of dollars for a criminal defense attorney, you can request of the judge that the public defender represent you. In some states, such as California, you simply make an appointment to discuss your case and financial situation at the county public defender's office. In other states, a judge will appoint a state public defender or a private member of the bar to represent you, payment being made by the State. The legal determination of whether or not you can afford a lawyer depends upon the requirements specified by the particular county or state in which you live and upon the crime with which you are charged. If you have a relatively low-paying job, or no job, if your family is living on a tight budget, and if you do not have a savings account large enough to pay a lawyer to represent you, then most counties, states, or judges will allow the public defender to represent you or will authorize a private attorney to do so.

Even if you do have some financial resources, but not thousands of dollars, the State will practically always provide you a lawyer if you are charged with a sufficiently serious crime—one which will cost the State tens of thousands of dollars to prosecute. The State does not want to risk having to convict you a second time if appellate judges determine later that you could not afford a lawyer and thus were deprived of your constitutional right to counsel at your first trial. Thus if you insist that you cannot afford a lawyer, the State will usually provide you with one. In some states, such as California, however, the State can require you to pay back the cost of your legal services after your trial, using a fee schedule based on your income.

Trying to qualify as indigent so that the public defender can represent you is often a sensible way to proceed. Although there are some incompetent public defenders or appointed lawyers with little or no experience in criminal law, by and large the public defender system is better than you might think. Many public defenders choose their careers because they genuinely want to help people. As a result of handling so many criminal cases, they are generally both experienced and competent. Indeed, you have a far greater chance of finding a lousy lawyer by looking blindly through the Yellow Pages than you do by consulting a public defender. Even if you do not qualify for free representation, the public defender's office may refer you to a relatively inexpensive, but competent private criminal defense lawyer if you ask.

Perhaps the biggest drawback of being unable to afford a criminal defense attorney is that you risk getting an appointed lawyer to represent you with little experience or interest in criminal law. Another less serious disadvantage of having public representation is that public defenders are almost always overworked and may not give your case—especially if it is a minor one—the attention that you feel it deserves. If you don't think that your case is getting enough attention or that it is being handled with sufficient care, ask the lawyer to explain to you exactly what is being done. If her explanation doesn't satisfy you, try to get another lawyer.

NOTE: You do *not* have a right to a lawyer paid by the State if you are charged with a petty crime for which you cannot be imprisoned. For example, if you are arrested for possession of less than an ounce of marijuana in one of the states that assess only a fine for this crime, the State is not required to provide you a lawyer. Under these circumstances, it is still a good idea to talk to a judge or a public defender to make certain that the crime with which you are charged cannot result in your imprisonment or other penalties. Even in these cases, you may want to hire your own lawyer.

The "Gambler's Choice": Self-Representation

Representing yourself at your own criminal trial is a gamble. To save the money that it costs to hire a lawyer, you risk a conviction or a stiffer sentence which you might have avoided if you had been represented by an experienced criminal defense lawyer. Self-representation makes sense if you are charged with a relatively minor crime such as possession of a small amount of marijuana in a state where penalties are light, but if you are charged with a felony, you have so much to lose that gambling on your ability to act effectively as your own lawyer is almost always foolish.

Is this legal fact of life fair? No, of course not. Our legal system should be simple and straightforward enough so that most people would not need a mouth-piece. But instead, the existing system is not only complex, but prosecutors often will not treat you the same way that they would treat defense lawyers. Unfortunately, they are likely to take advantage of your ignorance and punish you for not going along with the system. And most judges will not and, indeed, cannot help you to act as your own lawyer or advise you that you're making stupid decisions. In short, if you make a wrong choice while you are playing lawyer, you may have to live with it for a long time. In contrast, if your lawyer makes an outrageously stupid move that no reasonably competent lawyer would have made and you are convicted in part because of the lawyer's mistake, some judges will grant you a second trial with a competent lawyer. If you do decide to represent yourself, you at least need to talk to a local lawyer to find out:
1) if there is a fairly standard disposition or plea bargain for the type of crime you are charged with;
2) if you are eligible for a diversion program;
3) if you are eligible for diversion, what are the pros and cons of the diversion program;
4) what are the possibilities that a lawyer can get you a better result than you can get yourself, and at what cost.

A Word About Lawyers

Once a lawyer agrees to represent you, she has a duty to represent you to the best of her ability, whether or not you are guilty. Indeed, except under the most unusual circumstances, a criminal defense lawyer has a moral responsibility to continue to defend you, even if you say that you have committed the act with which you are charged. Because your lawyer is not the judge or the jury, she cannot rely on her "opinion" of your guilt or even on your own "opinion" of whether you are guilty. Unless you want to plead guilty, the attorney's job is to provide you with the best possible defense.

It is important to emphasize again that if you want to participate in your defense, you should make this agreement with your lawyer *before* she begins to represent you. If you are a participating type, you should try to find a lawyer who feels comfortable explaining to you the legal aspects of your case and consulting you about your case. There are some decisions, such as whether to object to evidence or how to cross-examine a witness, which are appropriate for the lawyer to make. There are other choices, such as whether to plead guilty or accept a plea bargain, that should be yours. As a general rule, tactical decisions about procedure should be explained to you, but you should be willing to pay close attention to your lawyer's advice. Think of it this way—if you hire a carpenter to build a bookshelf, you will want to go over the plans carefully, but you will probably rely on the carpenter's experience when it comes to choosing the nails.

There is no substitute for finding a lawyer whom you can honestly trust. Honesty is important because to defend you against the State's prosecution, your lawyer must know the whole truth about your illegal activities. For example, you should be ready to tell your lawyer—and only your lawyer—all the details about your growing marijuana, even if you were only arrested for possession of a couple of ounces. If you cannot be completely honest and forthright with your lawyer, then find another one. Finding another lawyer is easy if you can afford to hire one, but if the State has appointed you a lawyer, then you must convince a judge to appoint a different one. Often, to persuade a judge, you will have to give specific reasons why you do not want to work with the lawyer. The fact that she is not spending enough time on your case is a good reason.

CAUTION: Only your *confidential* conversations with your lawyer are forbidden from being used against you in court. If you talk to her about your case in front of an undercover agent, this person can repeat, in court, what you told your lawyer. Therefore, you should only talk to your lawyer in private.

THE CRIMINAL JUSTICE PROCESS

Pre-Trial Actions

Police Discretion to Arrest

For most crimes, after the police arrest you, they have the authority to take you to the police station. If you are arrested for a petty crime such as failing to stop completely at a stop sign, or possession of a little marijuana in one of the eleven states that only impose a fine for this crime (see Appendix), the officer is usually instructed simply to write you a ticket. Even if your offense is minor, however, the police always have the power (and almost always the authority) to take you to the station. They normally won't arrest you, of course, unless you anger them. Even if the police don't have the authority in your state to take you to the station for possession of a small amount of marijuana or for speeding or some other minor infraction, they can always charge you with a more serious crime such as reckless driving. Another possible police ploy when you have annoyed them is to charge you with possession of more than one ounce of marijuana even though they know you have less. Because police are not required to carry scales to weigh your marijuana, they can always take you to the station to do the weighing or drug analysis if you give them a hard time. Thus while it's nuts to jeopardize any of your legal rights by trying to get on the good side of the police, it almost always pays to be polite.

Station House Searches

If the police arrest you and escort you down to the jail, you can expect to be catalogued or, in police language, "booked." You have no choice but to surrender all your personal belongings, to submit to fingerprinting, voice printing, and photograph taking in the famous portrait style known as "mug shots." Of course, the police do not subject everyone to all of these procedures. It will depend upon the crime with which you are charged, the attitude of the officers who arrest you, and perhaps on how you look and act. In 1979, the Chicago police were doing vaginal searches of women arrested for minor traffic offenses until some enterprising newspaper reporters exposed the outrageous conduct. Because you are at the mercy of your jailers, it is in your interest to be cooperative. It also pays to be nice to the police because they can often influence whether or not the prosecutor will agree to a good plea bargain. While you do have a constitutional right not to answer any police questions, including your name, address, and occupation (see Chapter 11), you should provide this basic information. After all, most of it can probably be discovered by looking in your wallet, which the police will probably do anyway. Of course, never talk to the police about the crime with which you are charged, give a false name or address, list your occupation as "marijuana cultivator," or otherwise try to be "clever."

Phoning a Lawyer: Your Best Protection

Your best protection against most police abuse is to insist upon permission to telephone your lawyer. Most police departments do not have to allow you to make your phone calls soon after your arrest, but most will. And because there is nothing that you can do if the police conveniently forget to allow you to make a phone call, it often helps to be pleasant as well as insistent. Assuming the police allow you to phone, you will want to call a lawyer who trusts you to pay her later for helping to get you out of jail, or call a friend with cash on hand whom you trust to put up your bail. If you are unlucky enough to be arrested on the weekend, you will probably remain in jail at least until Monday unless you have a lawyer or a friend with money for bail. A lawyer, however, can sometimes find a judge on nighttime duty who will release you. If you don't know a lawyer, your best bet is to call a friend who does or who can be trusted to find one. Thus if you are an established member of the community with a job, a family, and a lawyer, you will probably be able to avoid a single night in jail, while if you are operating on the economic margin, you may cool your heels for a day or two until you can get bail money together or are released on your own recognizance.

Bail

Bail is money that you must give temporarily to the State in order to be released from jail before your trial. If you come to the various court hearings and your trial, the bail money will be returned. On the night of your arrest, the police in most states will set your bail immediately, according to an established bail schedule based on the seriousness of the crime with which you are charged. If you are arrested by the feds, there is no bail until your arraignment.

If you have enough money, you will probably want to pay the entire amount of your bail in order to be released. Some cautious marijuana cultivators entrust money to a friend or lawyer for bail emergencies. In federal court and in some states, you can get out by paying only 10 percent of your bail to the court. The State will give all of your money back to you after your case is concluded. If you do not have enough money to pay the required bail amount at the time of your arrest and can't quickly borrow it, you will probably have to deal with a bail bondsperson unless you qualify for release on your own recognizance.

The way the bail bond business works in the states where you can't post money directly with the court is that you pay 10 percent of your bail to a bondsperson and put up collateral (such as your house, property, or signature of a friend) to secure the remaining 90 percent. The bondsperson then pays the rest of your bail. If you show up in court, the bondsperson gets this money back and pockets the 10 percent you had put up as a fee. Often it comes down to people deciding whether they would prefer a night in jail to paying 10 percent of the total bail amount. By waiting until your bail hearing to post bond, which will be in a day or two, there is a good chance that the judge will reduce or eliminate the bail that the police originally set; thus you can save several hundreds or thousands of dollars which you may need to pay a lawyer. Furthermore, if you rely on a bondsperson to put up your bail, and you then don't show up at trial, the bondsperson will send out "bounty hunters" to find you.

EXAMPLE: Norman pays $400 to sleep at his house instead of at the sheriff's office.

The police arrested Norman for marijuana cultivation on Tuesday evening and set his bail at $5,000. Norman paid $500 cash to a bondsperson and signed a note on his land as collateral for $5,000. The next day at the bail hearing, the judge reduced Norman's bail to $1,000. Thus, if Norman had spent a night in jail, he could have saved at least $400 because the fee to the bondsperson on $1,000 would have been $100. And when the new day dawned, it is always possible that Norman or his friends could have come up with the entire $1,000 to pay the court, thus avoiding any bail bond fee.

Release without Bail (O.R.)

The police also have the authority in certain circumstances to release you immediately without bail if you promise to appear in court. Obviously you should welcome the chance to sign a form promising to appear on a certain date without bail. The police are more likely to release you on your "own recognizance" (O.R.)

by accepting your promise to appear if you are only charged with a misdemeanor and they do not consider you to be dangerous or untrustworthy. If you are charged with a felony, however, the police in most states cannot release you on O.R. Even if the police are uncertain about you, they may still release you without bail to your parents if you are a juvenile or to your lawyer if you are charged with a minor crime. If the police don't release you without bail, a judge still may.

No Releases and No Bail

Under some circumstances, the State also has the power to hold you in jail until after your trial without possibility of bail. If you are charged with a serious crime and the State has reason to believe you might not show up for your trial if you had a choice, don't be surprised if you are denied bail. If you are not released on bail for whatever reason, you should definitely forget about representing yourself. First, you will be unable to do basic investigation or adequate legal research about your case. And second, if you are not released on bail, you are probably in jail for a serious crime for which there is no standard disposition or diversion.

Bail Hearing

Usually a judge will redetermine the amount of your bail within three days of your arrest. This procedure normally occurs at a court hearing known as an arraignment (see the following section). If your lawyer wants to challenge a particularly high bail, the court will usually schedule a separate bail hearing after your arraignment. In federal court and in most states, you have a constitutional right to bail that is not "excessive." Since what is or is not "excessive bail" is commonly difficult to assess, however, judges often have considerable (some would say *excessive*) discretion in setting a bail amount. Whether the judge demands a million dollars bail or releases you on your own recognizance will depend primarily on the likelihood that you will show up at your trial. Also considered will be the seriousness of the crime with which you are charged, the amount of evidence against you, your past criminal record including outstanding traffic warrants, your actions during your arrest, your employment record, your community involvement, your family relations, and your financial ability to pay. Also, some states encourage judges to release people on their own recognizance and have special O.R. programs. The judges are not supposed to set your bail too high to prevent you from paying it, but only high enough to encourage you to appear in court at the proper times. Bringing your family, your employer, or your more respectable friends into court to testify to your willingness to appear in court voluntarily can only help your case. Having a local lawyer who knows what factors are most important to a particular judge and who has the ability to convince a judge to reduce bail can also help. Because the judge has so much discretion in setting your bail, you can usually benefit from all the legal help that you can afford or that the State will provide you.

The Diversion Alternative

As soon as the police release you from jail, your next step is to find out if your state has a program that will allow you to avoid the formal criminal system. Usually, the prosecutor will not talk to you about diversion alternatives in your case until the pretrial conference. These alternatives are commonly called *diversion programs* and are often available for misdemeanor marijuana cases. Although diversion programs vary widely, they share one thing in common—they divert you from the criminal justice system into an educational or rehabilitation system that is quite similar to probation. The major advantage of diversion over probation, however, is that the State usually allows you to avoid a criminal record because you do not have to plead guilty to qualify. Of course, if you are not guilty to start with or if the police have a lousy case, you should not accept the diversion program because you will probably want to seek a more complete vindication.

While diversion programs are usually a good arrangement if you are charged with a crime, occasionally the preconditions for acceptance into a diversion program are more offensive than the penalty for the crime with which you are charged. In one case, for example, a woman who allegedly grew marijuana without her husband's permission would have been required to see a marriage counselor for a year as part of her diversion alternative, presumably to learn the virtue of wifely obedience. Instead she pleaded guilty to possession of marijuana and was placed on probation.

Not everyone, however, can qualify for a diversion program. In many states, the diversion program is an option only for people who have been caught with a small amount of marijuana for the first time. In other cities and states, the diversion programs allow for considerable discretion on the part of judges and prosecutors, so that you can qualify even if you are charged with a more serious drug or marijuana offense.

While the eligibility requirements for diversion programs differ widely among cities and states, you are less likely to be eligible if you have committed a crime classified as a felony or a violent crime, or if you have previously been convicted either of one serious crime or of several misdemeanors. People who don't appear to be receptive to rehabilitation, and in some areas those who are over a certain age or who are addicted to drugs, are also not diverted. Check your local rules.

Diversion programs are not "free rides." By accepting the diversion program you will be exchanging one form of probation for another. You will probably have to attend counseling sessions, remain employed if the diversion program can find you a job, and stay out of trouble. If you fail in the program, criminal charges can be refiled against you and you will again be faced with dealing with the real criminal justice system. If you have qualified for a diversion program in the first place, you are probably the type of person who would not be sent to jail after pleading guilty or being convicted. Oftentimes, therefore, if you fail in the diversionary program and you are convicted for a crime or plead guilty to it, you will end up on probation. If you are convicted and placed on probation, however, you not only have a

criminal record, but you are considerably closer to jail. Why? Unlike the diversion program, if you violate the conditions of your probation, you will probably be jailed. In summary, diversion programs are usually a good idea, but only after you consult a lawyer about the alternatives and about the specifics of your program. A quite readable example of a diversionary law is found in the Georgia statutes:

79A-9917:Conditional discharge for possession as first offense

Whenever any person who has not previously been convicted of any offense under Chapters 79 A-7, known as the Dangerous Drug Act, 79-8, known as the Uniform Narcotic Drug Act, or 79A-9, known as the Georgia Drug Abuse Control act, or of any Statute of the United States or of any State relating to narcotic drugs, marijuana, or stimulant, depressant, or hallucinogenic drugs, pleads guilty to or is found guilty of possession of a narcotic drug, marijuana, or stimulant, depressant or hallucinogenic drug, the court may, without entering a judgment of guilt and with the consent of such person, defer further proceedings and place him on probation upon such reasonable terms and conditions as the court may require, terms, preferably, which require the person to undergo a comprehensive rehabilitation program (including, if necessary, medical treatment), not to exceed three years, designed to acquaint him with the ill effects of drug abuse and to provide him with knowledge of the gains and benefits which can be achieved by being a good member of society. Upon violation of a term or condition, the court may enter an adjudication of guilt and proceed accordingly. Upon fulfillment of the terms and conditions, the court shall discharge such person and dismiss the proceedings against him. Discharge and dismissal under this section shall be without court adjudication of guilt and disqualifications or disabilities imposed by law upon conviction of a crime. Discharge and dismissal under this section may occur only once with respect to any person.

Arraignment

An *arraignment* is the legal word for bringing you before the judge. At your arraignment, the judge will read to you the crimes that the State charges you with committing. At this time you or your lawyer should ask for the "charges" in writing. Most states require that the police arraign you or bring you before a judge without unnecessary delay after your arrest. In many states, without unnecessary delay means within twenty-four hours after arrest, while in other states it means within forty-eight or seventy-two hours. Unfortunately, in most states there are few if any sanctions if the police fail to arraign you within these time limits, even if they purposely delay.

If you do not yet have a lawyer and you are too poor to afford one, the judge will either appoint the public defender or a private lawyer to represent you at this time. If you are not *indigent,* the judge will allow you time to hire your own lawyer. Assuming you do need time to talk with a lawyer, the judge will probably schedule another hearing when you will have to enter a plea of guilty or not guilty. If you already have a lawyer at your arraignment, you may want to enter your plea right then.

The arraignment is also the time that you request a bail reduction or ask to be released on your own recognizance. If you have no lawyer you can ask the judge to allow you to enter a plea of not guilty, and argue for a bail reduction yourself. You should try to convince the judge that you are a stable and reliable member of the community and should emphasize family and other community attachments as well as your inherent honesty and decency. You may well succeed in convincing the judge to be lenient, but even if the judge refuses this request, your lawyer may be able to schedule a second hearing, if it appears necessary. Whatever you do, of course, don't lie to the judge about anything. Liars often get caught and lawyers have more difficulty in helping them avoid jail.

Pleading Not Guilty—It's the Thing to Do

If you are representing yourself at the arraignment, you should always plead not guilty. Because you cannot possibly understand the consequences of pleading guilty until you talk with a lawyer, it is definitely wise not to do so. Pleading not guilty also allows you and your lawyer time to plea bargain and to determine the strength of the State's evidence. If it appears to be in your best interest to do so, you will have plenty of time to change your plea to guilty before your trial. It's worth emphasizing that it is never dishonest to plead not guilty. That is to say, pleading not guilty at this stage is not considered to be lying by the judges.

Make Your Decision About Self-Representation before the Preliminary Hearing

If you are still in jail after the arraignment and bail hearing, chances are good that you are either poor enough to qualify for State appointment of counsel or you are charged with a rather serious crime. Either way, you are not in a position to represent yourself and shouldn't attempt to do so.

If you really want to represent yourself, however, and are determined to do so, you should make that decision *before* your preliminary hearing. A preliminary hearing may be an important way to discover the strengths and weaknesses of the prosecution's case, but it is normally too technical for you to handle yourself competently. Indeed, the preliminary hearing is so important that some lawyers will refuse to represent you if they are unable to represent you at this hearing. Although most lawyers will probably agree to represent you at a later stage, you can seriously harm your legal defense by representing yourself at this hearing. And often you will find that hiring a lawyer late in your case will cost as much as hiring the same lawyer from the beginning. So, before the preliminary hearing is the time for you to decide whether or not you really want to gamble by representing yourself.

Looking at the Police Report

If you do decide to represent yourself, one of your first steps is to read the police report, in which your arresting officer describes his view of the arrest. Getting a copy of this report is not always as simple as it should be, but persistence will bring you success. In most states you can ask at the prosecutor's office or go to the police station and ask your way to the appropriate counter. Tell the person at the office that you are acting as your own lawyer and that you want a copy of the police report describing your arrest. It is important that you explain to the person in charge that you have no lawyer, that you are representing yourself, and that you need a copy of the police report in order to defend yourself. Most prosecutor's offices will give it to you without a problem. Although the police often do not like turning their reports over to mere citizens, they have no legal choice but to give it to you. If your police department does not understand the law—which is not unusual—then you should call the prosecutor's office and explain to someone there that you want your police report. The prosecutor's office will probably tell you to come to them, but if not, you can always wait to explain the situation to the judge at your next hearing. The judge will give you the report and at your request will undoubtedly postpone the rest of the trial process to make up for any lost time. In many areas there is a small charge (often per page) for police reports.

What to Look for in the Police Report

There are many details to check in a police report, including the times of *Miranda* warnings and of arrest, the name of the police officer, and the order of events. You may find that the arresting officer's view of what happened at your arrest coincides pretty closely with your own. Human nature being what it is, however, you are at least as likely to view the facts leading up to your arrest with entirely different glasses. If you do discover a significant discrepancy, you should talk to a lawyer about it. For example, there may have been an illegal search that the police officer is trying to cover up. If the police report rings true, then you will want to ask yourself such questions as whether the police conduct seemed fair and whether any police search was done with a proper warrant. If not, then you should ask a lawyer for her opinion about the legality of what occurred. An experienced criminal defense lawyer can usually give you a fairly accurate estimate of the chances of proving impermissible police conduct to a judge.

Consulting with a Criminal Defense Lawyer, or Two or Three

If you want to be your own lawyer, you should at least consult with an attorney about the technical procedures you face. Always bring the police report with you, if possible. Many prosecutors will be delighted to take advantage of you if you are not sure of how to defend yourself. Not only do you want a lawyer's opinion about the legality of the police conduct, but you need to know whether there is a standard disposition for your type of case and what sorts of plea bargains are possible. For example, in most areas of the country, there are standard ways that the prosecutor's office disposes of first offense marijuana possession cases. If you face a conviction for a second or third offense, there are also fairly predictable ways in which these cases are handled. Consulting a lawyer is also a good opportunity to double-check any information that you learn about diversion programs, including their eligibility requirements.

NOTE: If you have the time and opportunity, it is often wise to speak to several lawyers. Not only is a second or third opinion helpful, but it is also a good way to educate yourself.

Discussing Your Case With the Prosecutor

If you hire a lawyer, it will be her job to discuss your case and the possible terms of its disposition with the prosecutor. If you don't yet have a lawyer, you will want to talk to the prosecutor. Simply call up and tell the prosecutor that you are trying to save the cost of a lawyer and want to ask how he plans to handle your case. First you should make certain that he is still planning to prosecute you. Assuming that he is, now is the appropriate time to suggest an alternative, such as enrollment in a diversion program. If this suggestion isn't acceptable to the prosecutor, ask what the standard disposition is for cases such as yours.

Prosecutors do not have to plea bargain with anyone, so they don't have to plea bargain with you. They are free to refuse you the standard disposition because you have not hired a lawyer or for any other reason. But because prosecutors like to avoid trials, and after you have found out what type of punishment most people receive, they will often agree to a "fair deal."

CAUTION: You must watch what you say when you talk with any prosecutor! Remember that whatever you say—even when you are plea bargaining—can be used as evidence to convict you. Therefore never admit to the prosecutor that you committed a crime or even talk about your crime. Be careful to say that you are charged with marijuana possession or cultivation, not that you actually possessed or cultivated it. If you do say the wrong thing, the prosecutor can repeat to a jury at your trial what you told him while you were trying to get a fair deal without burdening the system with a trial. If you are doubtful as to your ability to keep clear of damaging admissions, get a lawyer. In federal court and in some states, the prosecutor is not allowed to use plea bargaining statements in court, but even then, *you* have to prove that you were actually engaged in plea bargaining.

IMPORTANT: Should the prosecutor refuse to treat your case as being routine and refuse to offer you the standard disposition for cases of that type, you should understand that you have lost the first roll of the dice and that the stakes (your freedom) will get higher if you continue to gamble with the legal system. So if you do decide to continue to represent yourself through the plea bargaining stage, be sure to see a lawyer at the first indication of trouble.

Hiring a Lawyer for Plea Bargaining Only

It may occur to you that you don't want to risk engaging in plea bargaining yourself, but because the charge against you isn't very serious you want to save yourself the expense of hiring a lawyer to do a full-scale trial if possible. In this situation you should consider hiring a lawyer for the limited purpose of talking to the prosecutor to see if the case can be settled on terms that you find acceptable. Such terms might be enrollment in a diversion program, or perhaps a small fine and a suspended sentence. If the prosecutor has a weak case, plea bargaining could result in the charges being dropped altogether. Some lawyers will bill you as little as a couple of hundred dollars for this service. Others may charge you more. Some lawyers will refuse to represent you on this basis because of the time they believe it is necessary for them to spend on legal research to give you good advice. They demand a flat fee, no matter whether they work out a quick deal or go through a lengthy trial. Usually it is best to avoid this type of lawyer if you are considering self-representation or if you want to save money.

REMINDER: No matter on what terms you hire a lawyer, it should always be clear that it's your case and that you are making the crucial decisions.

Accepting a Plea Bargain: Pleading Guilty

Of course, only you can decide whether or not to accept a bargain offered by the prosecutor. Your lawyer should be able to tell you what your chances of winning a jury trial are if you refuse to accept the plea bargain, but pleading guilty is solely your choice. If you are innocent of the charged crime, try to stand up to any pressure to plea bargain. Insist that your lawyer investigate. If you have paid for your lawyer up front, be aware that your interests and your lawyer's interests may differ. Of course, if you hear your accusers lie at your preliminary hearing and the prosecutor offers you a relatively "good deal," such as probation, then it is your choice whether or not to plead guilty to a crime that you did not commit.

Aside from the prosecutor's disposition and your defense lawyer's expertise, the plea bargain will depend upon such factors as the seriousness of the alleged crime, the strength of the State's evidence, the likelihood that the police illegally seized important evidence, your past criminal record, and perhaps political pressure. Even if the State has strong evidence that you grew marijuana, however, you should insist that the prosecutor dismiss some of your charges and promise to recommend a lighter penalty than he would have recommended after your conviction before a jury. You deserve some consideration for pleading guilty and thus giving up your constitutional rights to a jury trial, to confront your accusers, and to remain silent. The judge will almost always agree to a plea bargain acceptable to the prosecutor and to you, but she is not required to do so. If she does not agree to it, you have the right to plead not guilty and start over again. If the judge does accept your guilty plea, she must make certain in open court that your plea is voluntary and that you understand all the consequences of pleading guilty. If the prosecutor has tried to change the bargain or if you have misunderstood the bargain, you must speak up in court. It may be your last chance. If you are forced to rely on a secret bargain, you should realize that you may receive a more severe sentence than you were promised, and be unable to prove the doublecross.

The Preliminary Hearing

A preliminary hearing, which is also known as a "probable cause" hearing in some states, is usually held only for felony crimes. At this hearing, the judge decides if there is probable cause to believe that you have committed the crime or crimes with which you have been charged. Of course, the fact that the State has evidence to show probable cause to believe that you are guilty of a crime does not mean that you are, in fact, guilty, or that the State can prove your guilt beyond a reasonable doubt to a jury. For example, the judge may be able to consider illegal evidence in making the probable cause determination. But if the prosecutor cannot show probable cause to believe that you are guilty of a crime at this hearing, then the judge will dismiss your case and order you released, at least until the police find stronger evidence against you.

Unfortunately, a preliminary hearing is not a constitutional right and some states will have the grand jury make the "probable cause" determination rather than give you a preliminary hearing. Most states, however, will hold a preliminary hearing if you are charged with a felony and if you request (or do not waive) the hearing. Normally, you will want to have a preliminary hearing, but this point is a good one to discuss with a lawyer because under certain circumstances you may want to waive the preliminary hearing.

Discover the State's Case

A preliminary hearing is one of the best ways (and sometimes the *only* way) to learn the details of the State's evidence against you. If you know what evidence the State has against you, you will be better prepared to defend yourself at trial. In many states, unless there is a preliminary hearing, the prosecutor is not required to tell you the names of his witnesses or their expected testimony. Your lawyer has other ways to find out some of the prosecution's case (see the next section) but this discovery often involves trouble and expense.

At a preliminary hearing, the prosecutor must present at least some of the State's witnesses to testify against you. Your lawyer can cross-examine the prosecution witnesses to force them to testify to as many details as possible and may even be able to catch them in a lie. Most importantly, your lawyer has had a chance to observe the witnesses' attitudes or demeanors and later can investigate the witnesses' stories to determine their truth or falsity. Furthermore, once witnesses testify at a preliminary hearing, they cannot change their stories at your trial unless they admit to lying. The burden of proof at the preliminary hearing is on the prosecutor. You don't have to introduce any evidence and rarely is it advisable for you to testify. If you do testify, you give the prosecutor an opportunity to think of ways to cast doubt on your story.

Other Pretrial Discovery Methods

Before your trial, you or your lawyer should learn as much about the prosecutor's case against you as possible. If the State does not give you a preliminary hearing, it is particularly important to discover the State's evidence against you. The prosecutor must tell you about any evidence that creates a reasonable doubt as to your guilt if you do not know about this evidence and you request that he tell you. But the prosecutor does not have to tell you about this favorable material unless you make a *specific* request for it. There is other important information that can be discovered if you know how to ask. Since most prosecutors respond better to other lawyers using their legal lingo, discovery is another reason why you need a lawyer. Other pretrial procedures differ from state to state and are simply more detailed than can be summarized here. For example, although you usually do not have to tell the prosecutor the names of your witnesses (just as the prosecutor does not have to tell you the names of his), there is a major exception to this rule in some states. In these states, the State may force you to identify any witnesses that can provide you with an alibi, and failure to do so may result in serious penalties. The State may also be able to force you to give the prosecutor any pretrial statements— formal or otherwise—made by your defense witnesses concerning any matter about which your witnesses will testify at your trial. In some cases, this rule means that you must divulge practically your whole case.

The Suppression Hearing

In nearly all cases involving searches and seizures, your lawyer should file a motion to suppress illegal evidence. Even if the search and seizure appears to be legal, the filing of an exhaustive suppression motion is important as a bargaining chip in later plea bargain negotiations. If this motion is filed, a judge will schedule a *suppression* hearing before your trial. In most states, a suppression motion *must* be filed *before* trial. A "motion" is a written argument in a particular legal form that tries to set a judge into motion by convincing her to do a certain thing. Thus when your lawyer files a motion to suppress illegal evidence, she wants her legal essay to "move" the judge, emotionally and intellectually, to suppress and exclude certain evidence from your trial because the police came by it as a result of an illegal search and seizure or an illegal interrogation.

In many marijuana and drug cases, the motion to suppress illegal evidence is by far the most important part of your legal ordeal. If your lawyer convinces the judge to suppress the marijuana evidence, the State will probably have to dismiss any charges of possession, cultivation, or sale of the marijuana. Why? Without the marijuana itself, there is usually no case. Since marijuana cases don't involve victims, there is often no way to prove a case without showing that you possessed the illegal substance. In contrast, if a judge suppresses a murder weapon as illegal evidence (which seldom happens), the State can still convict the criminal on the testimony of witnesses and on the basis of other legally seized evidence.

The suppression motion is as complicated as it is important to your future. Unfortunately many lawyers who are adequate on their feet or on the phone border on incompetence when it comes to preparing motions. Still, the chances that a person without legal training can prepare an excellent motion are poor. Only an experienced lawyer in your own state will know the fine points of your state's criminal law.

As long as there is any *possibility* that the police violated your constitutional rights, your lawyer has a duty to bring this matter to the attention of a judge. It is up to the judge to decide whether or not the police acted unlawfully, not up to your lawyer. Furthermore, the suppression hearing, at which some of the police officers involved in the search and seizure must testify, may reveal hidden police misconduct. Therefore, if your lawyer does not want to try to suppress evidence seized in the search that led to your arrest, it's time to get a second opinion.

The Pre-Trial Conference

To avoid the expense and time involved in a trial, the judge, the prosecutor, and your defense lawyer will usually meet together without you to discuss your case prior to a trial. The judge will want to know whether or not the prosecutor and you have agreed to settle the case by a plea bargain. If so, then in court you will change your original "not guilty" plea to a "guilty" plea after the judge, the prosecutor, and your defense lawyer all agree on what crime you will admit to and what sentence the prosecutor will recommend or guarantee. You should realize that there is no way that you can complain later that the prosecutor did not keep his part of a "secret deal" if it is not stated at this time. What is said in court when you change your plea to guilty determines what your sentence will be.

If you or the prosecutor have not agreed to a "plea bargain," then the judge may suggest one. You do not have to accept and probably should make no decision until you and your attorney have had a chance to discuss the offer privately. The pre-trial conference is also used to give your lawyer and the prosecutor a chance to agree on as many facts as possible with the idea of shortening the time it will take to try your case. During this conference the judge may encourage the prosecutor to drop some of the charges against you and to try to convict you only of the crime for which the State has the most evidence.

The Trial

If you are innocent, or if you have refused to accept a plea bargain, or if the prosecutor does not offer you a plea bargain, and if the judge decides at your suppression hearing that the police respected your constitutional rights during their investigation and your arrest, then you face a trial. In most states, you must go through a trial simply to be allowed to appeal the judge's refusal to suppress illegal evidence. The great majority of criminal cases (over 90 percent), however, do not go to trial; but if you do go to trial, you usually have nothing to lose by asserting your constitutional right to a jury trial, although you can choose to be tried by a judge alone. The normal issues in a marijuana trial include your intent, your knowledge, your possession, chemical tests, plant identification testimony, weight, and percentage of THC in the marijuana.

Speedy Trial

Your constitutional right to a speedy trial does not have anything to do with the number of days your trial can take. Instead, your right to a speedy trial sets a limit on the number of days that you must wait between the time you are arrested or accused of a crime, and the time your trial *begins*. In most states, you can ask for a trial within sixty or ninety days after your arrest, but the prosecutor can legally delay your trial for months, the exact length of time depending upon whether you protest the delay, whether the delay hurts your defense, and whether the prosecutor has "good reasons" for the delay. Trying to convince a judge that the prosecutor did not have good reasons for a delay or that a delay hurt your case is extremely difficult, not only because these factors are so vague but primarily because the judge *must* dismiss your case if she decides that the State denied you your constitutional right to a speedy trial.

Even though you can insist on a reasonably quick trial, you may not want to, assuming of course that you are not in jail. Often, the longer your trial is postponed, the better chance your lawyer has to strike a good deal with the prosecutor. (In legal lingo, a postponement of your trial is called a continuance.) Indeed, some defense lawyers believe that one of the most valuable services they can offer a paying client is to continue his case for as long as possible. Continuing a case can be important because there is a general feeling that prosecutors tend to be more flexible about older, less important cases that are being postponed by "smart" lawyers. In addition, continuances give the lawyer more time to prepare for trial or for the probation report. Perhaps most importantly, continuances allow an accused person to prove his potential for rehabilitation by getting a job, going to school, attending a drug education program, or doing whatever a particular judge likes best. Since the law on this issue varies from state to state, and since this issue can be extremely important to you, you will want to check it out with your lawyer.

Public Trial

To ensure fairness, you have a right to a public trial. While it is wonderful that your trial cannot be held secretly, it may not seem so terrific that some state courts have begun to allow trials to be videotaped. Only if admitting the press to your trial or filming it will seriously threaten its fairness is the judge allowed to restrict these activities. You are unlikely to encounter any media attention unless your case is unusual, you are a well-known person, or you live in one of a few states that routinely films trials.

Impartial Jury

Knowledgeably asserting your constitutional right to an impartial jury can be critical to protecting your right to a fair trial. Without an impartial jury to determine your guilt or innocence, your trial cannot be fair.

You do not have a constitutional right to a jury trial if you are only charged with a minor offense for which the maximum sentence possible is six months in prison or less (see the Appendix for the maximum and minimum prison sentences for marijuana crimes). In some states, however, jury trials are available for any offense that could result in a small amount of jail time. The size of juries normally ranges from six people in a few states, on up to the more traditional twelve. If you do qualify for a jury trial, the prosecutor in most states must convince all of the people on the jury of your guilt beyond a reasonable doubt. In some states, however, unanimity is no longer required and the prosecutor need only convince nine of the twelve jurors of your guilt beyond a reasonable doubt.[1]

In most states, you or your lawyer can play an important role in selecting the people for your jury. In other states, the judge is primarily in charge of the selection process. Even in these states, however, there is much that your lawyer can do to be sure that either she or the judge excludes all those people who appear to be prejudiced against you. This process is called challenging (or excluding) a juror for cause. Asking the right questions of the prospective jurors is critically important to demonstrate to the judge that there is a good reason to believe that a particular person cannot be an impartial juror. In legal lingo, this procedure is called *voir dire*. From long experience, your lawyer will undoubtedly know the sorts of questions to ask prospective jurors as well as the "good reasons" that will be sufficient to exclude a person from your jury for cause. If the judge disagrees with your lawyer about a particular person's capacity for fairness, your lawyer can also exclude a certain number of people (from six to thirty) without the judge's permission and without giving a reason. This procedure is called making a peremptory challenge. The prosecutor can do the same thing and will undoubtedly use his challenges to exclude everyone who looks even a little bit "antiestablishment." The idea is that if both you and the prosecutor exclude the people you like least, you will end up with something like a cross section of the community. Unless you are practiced and knowledgeable in the art of jury selection, however, you should not try to make this selection on your own.

Jurors Can Refuse to Convict a "Guilty" Person

Requesting a jury trial is sometimes wise, even if you are guilty of the violation of one or another marijuana law as charged. The reason is that millions of people believe our marijuana laws are so unfair and ridiculous that they will refuse to convict. In a few communities, people are so against marijuana laws that the prosecutor will make extremely favorable plea bargains just to avoid going to trial. When a jury refuses to convict when the evidence strongly points to guilt, it is not simply committing an illegal act. Under our "common law" tradition, every juror not only has the right, but the duty, to nullify the law by refusing to convict for a crime which should not be legally condemned. This doctrine is called "jury nullification." One of the historical reasons why every American has a right to a jury trial in serious matters is that the jury is supposed to protect Americans from unfair laws and unfair prosecutions. Therefore a juror can vote to acquit no matter how overwhelming the evidence if she believes that the "criminal" activity does not justify punishment, or that the prosecution has unfairly singled out a few people to prosecute in a situation—like marijuana use—in which millions of others commit the crime with relative impunity.

Rarely will judges tell the jury, or allow any lawyer to inform it, of its right to refuse to convict a technically guilty person. In fact, judges tell juries that they must follow the law as interpreted by them, and that the jury has only the power to decide the factual matter of guilt or innocence. Judges believe that to tell juries of their right to nullify the law would only encourage their more irresponsible members to act in irresponsible ways. Thus only a nonlegal person representing herself at trial is free to "misbehave" by explicitly telling the jurors about their right to refuse to convict if they believe that conviction would be sufficiently unfair.[2] But since the dangers and difficulties of self-representation almost always outweigh the benefit of telling the jury of this right, you will not want to represent yourself just so you can make this argument. While you may be able to arrange to act as a "cocounsel," it is probably better simply to rely on the fact that lots of Americans already intuitively know that putting someone in jail for smoking a joint or growing a few marijuana plants makes no sense. Furthermore, lawyers can usually find a way to tell the jury about jury nullification without using the forbidden words.

The Prosecutor's Case

The prosecutor must present evidence against you first. You are supposed to have a constitutional right "to be confronted with the witnesses" who accuse you of a crime. Although the State usually respects this right, you should realize that there are many instances (too complicated to explain here) when a witness can testify on the basis of unreliable hearsay evidence. An example of hearsay is "Janice told me that Sally said you did it!" Therefore it makes little sense to try to conduct your own trial. While the rules could be simplified to make self-representation possible, lawyers have created a maze of technical procedures so complicated that you pretty much have to hire a member of their union to pilot you through. For example, unless you have a lawyer, it is doubtful that you can effectively assert your right to cross-examine all the witnesses who testify against you. A lawyer usually tries to show the jury by carefully prepared cross-examination that the prosecution witnesses are forgetful, untrustworthy, or untruthful. While this "Perry Mason-type" questioning may seem simple on the surface, technical rules of court make it very difficult. And remember that many police witnesses have testified many times before and are very adept at staying out of obvious verbal traps.

The Defense Case

Under the Sixth Amendment, you have the right "to have compulsory process for obtaining witnesses in [your] favor." This phrase means that the State must compel anyone whom you think will testify in your favor to come to your trial as a witness. To ensure the presence of friendly witnesses, you must mail or have someone personally deliver subpoenas ordering them to appear at your trial upon threat of imprisonment for wilful disobedience. To avoid upsetting your friendly witnesses, you should tell them in advance about the necessity of formally sending them a subpoena. If your witnesses cannot come to court on a certain date and you can prove they were subpoenaed, your trial may be delayed to allow them to appear as soon as possible.

While you have a constitutional right to remain silent throughout your entire trial, you will usually want to declare your innocence to the jury. If you don't testify to your innocence, the jury is much more likely to convict you, even if your lawyer tries to educate the jurors about your Fifth Amendment right to remain silent. There are many situations, however, when you will be "afraid" to testify. This situation can arise if you have been convicted of earlier crimes, if you have talked to the police before your trial, or if the police have violated your Fourth Amendment right to be free from unreasonable searches and seizures. In many states, the prosecutor can tell the jury about all this information if you testify but not if you remain silent. The prosecutor's reason for introducing extraneous evidence of past crimes is of course to convince the jury that "once a criminal always a criminal," but technically it is allowed to show that you are not to be believed. Similarly, if you were foolish enough to lie to the police before your trial instead of remaining silent, then you cannot tell the truth in court without the prosecutor telling the jury of your earlier story to the police (see Chapter 11). Of course, you can try to explain to the jury why you lied to the police, but this situation is another one in which it may make sense not to take the witness stand at all. Also, even if you have remained silent until your trial, the prosecutor can thoroughly cross-examine you about your alleged crime, your testimony in court, and sometimes about illegally seized evidence. In summary, whether or not you testify is a decision for you and your lawyer to make after careful thought. You may want to remain silent yourself and present your case through favorable witnesses.

Appeals to a Higher Court

If you are convicted of a crime after a trial, you do *not* have a United States constitutional right to appeal to a higher court for a review of the fairness of your trial or the sufficiency of the State's evidence against you. This fact may surprise you, but don't worry, it's practical effect is minimal. All states and the federal courts independently give you a right to have one appeal to a higher court to review the fairness of your conviction. If you cannot afford to pay a lawyer, the State will provide you with one to review the written record (transcript) of your trial and to write a legal argument (brief) that informs the appellate judges of any possible unfairness in your trial. The appellate judges then review the brief and may hear oral argument which is presented by your lawyer. Sometime later—often a year or two after your trial—they will make a decision. In the great majority of cases, the judges will decide that you received a fair trial. If the judges decide that you did not receive a fair trial, the prosecutor can appeal the decision to the state supreme court and sometimes, though rarely, to the U.S. Supreme Court.

You can make a second appeal after an unfavorable appellate court decision only if you do it yourself, or if you can afford to hire a lawyer or can convince one to help you voluntarily, because the State need not pay for your lawyer for a second appeal. Except in a few states like Alaska, you have little chance of having your state supreme court review your case and even less of a chance that the U.S. Supreme Court will review the case. Supreme courts are organized not to make decisions that have to do with fairness or justice but to review only those cases which present important and unusual legal issues or cases that could mean the difference between life and death. Even if a higher court decides that your first trial was unfair, the prosecutor is oftentimes not required to release you. Instead, the prosecutor will probably prepare for your second trial, unless she believes that a jury will not convict you at a fair trial, or if you have already completed most of your sentence.

Even though the chances that a higher court will overturn your conviction are statistically slim, you will want to appeal your case if there was any possible unfairness at your trial and especially if you are doing jail time. Whether or not the prosecutor used illegal evidence to convict you and whether the prosecution introduced sufficient evidence to prove guilt beyond a reasonable doubt are two examples of issues frequently contested on appeal. In some states and in federal court, the judges will often allow you to remain free on bail for the year or two that it takes for a higher court to review your conviction *if* they believe that you have a good reason to appeal, *and* that you will not run away, *and* that you are not dangerous.

The rules relating to appeals are relatively complicated and differ widely from state to state. For example, you often must file a notice of appeal within ten days of the final judgment. And to be allowed to appeal an illegal search and seizure in some states, you must not only make your motion to suppress illegal evidence before trial, but you must object to the evidence again during your trial. In most states, you cannot appeal a judge's decision to deny your motion to suppress illegal evidence if you later plead guilty. Furthermore, in Missouri, Tennessee, and Texas you cannot appeal the judge's denial of your motion to suppress illegal evidence if you testify at your trial about the illegal search.

Sentencing

At some time after your conviction, a judge will sentence you. This procedure will occur at a special hearing in court. The sentence you receive is usually set down in very broad terms in your state's laws. Often the possible range of sentences open to the judge is so large as to give him almost complete discretion. The great difference between the minimum and maximum punishments that the judge can impose in some states is illustrated by the marijuana crimes listed by state in the Appendix. For some crimes, the judge can place you on probation or send you to prison for twenty-five years, depending upon your present crime, your past, and your attitude. In California and several other states such as Arizona, Indiana, and Iowa, there is "determinate" sentencing that narrowly restricts a judge's discretion by setting out specific factors that the judge must consider before choosing one of several definite sentences, such as one, two, or three years in prison.

In most areas of the country, the trend in marijuana cases involving the possession or cultivation of small quantities is toward shorter jail sentences, probation and a small fine, or often diversion from the criminal system altogether. In some states, judges themselves have authority to impose a creative sentence as an alternative to fines and imprisonment, such as free work for the community. Still, it's up to the judge, who will listen to the prosecutor's recommendation and who will consider the seriousness of your activities, your past criminal record, if any, your age, your potential for "rehabilitation and reformation," your employment record, your family situation, and his professional impression of you. Obviously the judge will also be influenced by his own prejudices about the world. A judge who has smoked marijuana (and lots have) is likely to be a good deal more lenient than one who believes that one toke leads to heroin addiction every time. The U.S. Supreme Court has also recently decided that a judge can impose a more severe sentence if you refuse to provide information about the criminal activities of your friends and associates. This rule of law can mean that as long as the State has reason to believe that you have accomplices in crime, you must either inform on your friends or sit in jail for a longer time.[3]

To help your case, there is nothing like acting respectfully in court, dressing well, and showing some sorrow for your illegal behavior. Of course, not following this advice can be a political choice for many people who believe that marijuana laws are stupid and that it's a travesty of both common sense and justice that they were arrested in the first place. Still, a little creative contrition is probably better than free room and board courtesy of the county. Your lawyer will probably be more skilled at persuading judges to show some mercy by discussing the *proper* factors. But if you are sincerely contrite and are good at speaking publicly, you may want to stand up and plead for mercy yourself.

Unfortunately, in many states a judge can sentence you to a long prison term for marijuana possession or cultivation. As noted, this absurdity is rarely done, but there is usually not much you can do about it if it is. Your constitutional right to be free from "cruel and unusual punishment" has not been interpreted to prevent you from going to jail for smoking a joint. That this fact is true, and that most white-collar criminals go free, says a lot about our society.

Juvenile Proceedings

If you are under a certain age (nineteen to fourteen, depending upon your state and your alleged crime), you may be considered a juvenile. Though you have no right to a jury trial or to bail in juvenile proceedings, being under a certain age permits you to avoid adult punishments and adult prisons. In juvenile proceedings, you still have a right to a lawyer and the judge still must find you guilty beyond a reasonable doubt. If the judge finds you guilty, she may place you on probation, send you to a youth camp, a juvenile home, or a youth prison for a few months or until you reach the age of twenty-one, or older in some states depending in large part upon your juvenile officer's report. Therefore it pays to be nice to your juvenile officer. Since juvenile proceedings can result in your imprisonment, and since you do have the right to cross-examine the witnesses against you and to remain silent, you should always find a lawyer familiar with juvenile law, which is a specialty of its own. If you cannot afford a lawyer, you should assert your constitutional right to have a lawyer appointed to represent you. Even if your family can afford a lawyer but refuses to pay for one, the State must provide you with counsel.

NOTE: Many states now have juvenile diversion programs which are open to people who are caught with a little marijuana. These programs are almost always preferable to a formal juvenile court proceeding as they don't result in any record of conviction.

Getting Your Arrest or Conviction Record Destroyed

Some states allow you to get your arrest or conviction record erased from the official records so that you will never be obligated to tell anyone about your criminal past when applying for a job, a professional license, or anything else. Even if you can get your record sealed, however, there is little that you can do to erase your record from the computers of law enforcement agencies around the country. To explain the detailed requirements of all the states for record sealing, which are all different, would require an additional chapter, if not an entire book. Therefore you'll have to consult a local lawyer if you wish to try to get your record sealed. Often, the State will destroy your criminal or arrest record in the following circumstances:

1. You were convicted of a crime as a juvenile and you have not gotten into any criminal trouble for several years after your probation ended.

2. You were convicted of a minor marijuana or other drug offense. Indeed, California, and probably a few other states, will automatically destroy your record of possession of less than one ounce of marijuana two years after any conviction after 1976.

3. In some states, you were found not guilty at your trial, and the judge believed you were innocent.

NOTE: If you are convicted of a felony drug crime as an adult, it is unlikely that the State will ever wipe the slate clean, unless you can convince a governor to give you a pardon.

Suing the Police for Illegal Behavior

If the police treat you in a way which you consider to be seriously unfair, you face a real dilemma. If the police have abused you, they will almost always have arrested you, if for no other reason than to cover their own misconduct. While you should complain about police misbehavior, you should probably talk to a lawyer first to make sure that you complain at the right time. You wouldn't want the prosecutor to refuse to dismiss your case or refuse to offer you a good deal just because you've complained. If you complain too soon, the prosecutor may bring you to trial just to try to show that the police acted properly.

It is important, however, that, at the proper time, you complain either at the police station itself, to the city manager or council, or to a citizen's police review board. After enough valid citizen's complaints, bad police officers can eventually be thrown off the force. For your single complaint, however, not much is likely to happen.

What are your other choices? If you're wealthy enough to hire a lawyer or lucky enough to find a lawyer or an association who can afford to work for justice without your money or on a contingency fee basis, then you can bring a civil lawsuit against the police for violating your constitutional rights. The hard truth is that these lawsuits are very difficult to win even if the police have acted in an unreasonable and outrageous manner. The one time that the police are most likely to lie is when they feel threatened by charges that could, if proven, damage their careers and pocketbooks. And even if you can win the lawsuit, the judicial system will compensate you with a significant amount of money *only* if the police seriously hurt you, seriously damaged your home, or significantly hurt your reputation, not simply because the police violated your constitutional rights. The following two cases demonstrate how difficult it is for citizens who are subjected to illegal police behavior to win their cases.

Needless Strip Searches May Violate Only Your Dignity, Not the Law

Someone accused Diane Shaw of "harassment," a petty offense for which the maximum sentence was fifteen days in jail in the unlikely event she was convicted. On the basis of this complaint, the police mailed a summons to Shaw, but to the wrong address. When she didn't show up to talk to the police, the police issued a warrant for her arrest—for failing to obey a summons that she hadn't received. When Shaw heard about the warrant for her arrest, she immediately went down to the Suffolk County, New York Police Department to clear up the problem. Loraine

Nixon greeted her, then arrested her, hancuffed her, and forced her to strip and bend over to view her private parts. Naturally, there was no evidence of harassment secreted in Shaw's body, but Nixon was only following routine Suffolk County jail house procedure. Shaw sued the county for violation of her civil rights, but the jury did not have a chance to hear her case. All the judges believed that the Suffolk County Police Department conducted their needless, routine strip search in "good faith," and dismissed her case. Suffolk County changed its routine strip search procedure in 1979, but Shaw got nothing.[4]

A Ten Dollar Constitutional Violation

One jury decided that two Charlotte, North Carolina police officers illegally arrested Mrs. Antonia Moyer without probable cause or a warrant during a raid on a small-time gambling operation in August, 1969. Mrs. Moyer, a forty-year-old black taxi driver, apparently found herself on the wrong street at the wrong time. The jury decided that this illegal arrest violated Mrs. Moyer's civil rights under the Civil Rights Act of 1871 (42 U.S.C. §1983) and that the police had falsely imprisoned her. Despite the illegality, the jury gave Mrs. Moyer only ten dollars—five dollars from each police officer. The police appealed the case and the judges of the U.S. Court of Appeals decided that the trial was unfair. The judges said that the police did not have to pay any money, even if the arrest was illegal, so long as they acted in "good faith" and with a "reasonable belief."[5]

Though most of the thousands of lawsuits brought against law enforcement officials for violation of civil rights end up the same way that these two cases did, a few people do win a significant amount of damages. Published cases in which persons were awarded money for an illegal search and seizure are difficult to find. There are a handful of people, however, who are reported to have won a civil rights suit for an illegal arrest. Two examples will suffice.

A Tennessee College Student and a Minnesota College Professor Win

A Tennessee college student won $40,000 after a police officer struck him in the mouth, knocking him to the floor and causing head injuries, and then arrested him. His crime was going to a hospital to visit a friend, and not leaving immediately on the command of the officer.[6]

A Minnesota college professor and his family were awarded $5,500 for their illegal arrests. Undercover police raided a benefit party at their home for a group called "People Against Missiles." The police arrested them for the crimes of having a party ("operating a disorderly house") and setting a basket by the refrigerator asking for donations for beer ("selling liquor without a license"). With legal help from the Minnesota Civil Liberties Union, they won their 42 U.S.C. §1983 law suit.[7] Unfortunately, judges and juries tend to be less sympathetic about the routine violations of the constitutional rights of marijuana users.

Conclusion

HAMLET: Denmark's a prison.
ROSENCRANTZ: Then is the world one.
HAMLET: A goodly one, in which there are many confines, wards, and dungeons, Denmark being one o' the worst.
ROSENCRANTZ: We think not so, my lord.
HAMLET: Why, then, 'tis none to you; for there is nothing either good or bad, but thinking makes it so.

William Shakespeare
THE TRAGEDY OF HAMLET, Act II, Scene 2

These last words are not about the law as it is, but about how it can and should be changed to enhance our individual freedoms. Perhaps you think that enough opinion has been slipped into the first thirteen chapters, and will say "enough already." But why not stick with us for a few more pages while we suggest a rational, humane, and, above all, simple alternative to the repressive drug laws that America now so futilely tries to enforce. We realize, of course, that this simple proposal about a complex problem leaves unanswered more questions than it considers.

Simply put, it is our thesis that America's drug laws are the product of the same sorts of paternalistic attitudes that in the larger political arena have caused so much of the world to be encircled by barbed wire and guarded from watchtowers. We believe that when a government tells its citizens what they can do or think or say or even swallow or smoke, there is something fundamentally wrong that will inevitably lead to resistance and civil disobedience.

Certainly marijuana causes problems, as do tobacco, alcohol, gambling, pornography, and the more dangerous drugs such as Valium and heroin. In America, we have sporadically tried to solve these problems through prohibition, although the traditional European intoxicants and the modern chemical drugs have been more widely accepted than the favorite drugs of minorities (see Chapter 1). But is telling people that they can't use a particular substance really a workable solution? We think not. We Americans are rightly proud of our tradition of individual rights and freedoms. Perhaps this heritage helps explain why we almost always are uncomfortable and do an incompetent job when it comes to punishing those of our neighbors who dare to taste of forbidden fruit.

Laws telling people what they can eat and smoke and how they can and cannot make love stem from an attitude that surrenders to government the power to "know best." In other parts of the world, this approach justifies laws restricting travel, speech, religion, and at some times and in some places, even the right to have a vegetable garden. The publication of this book, for example, would be impossible in large parts of South America, Asia, the Middle East, and the "Commissar knows best" countries of the Soviet Bloc. Understanding this sad reality, those of us who are lucky enough to live in this relatively free country must be particularly sensitive to check for overregulation by our own government. If we don't, we too may wake up one day to find that a permission slip from some governmental agency is necessary before we can drive across town or kneel before our God.

How should drugs be treated? Assuming we could rewrite the drug laws, what would we propose? How would we arrive at a logical solution that protects our individual rights and, at the same time, assures that all citizens are alerted to the very real dangers of drug abuse? We believe that any rational drug policy must have as its basis the legalization of all drugs for use by adults. Legalization of drugs should, of course, include the basic freedom to grow and smoke marijuana. But at the same time that legalization becomes a reality, the State should outlaw all drug advertising, including that for coffee, cigarettes, and liquor, and it should instead require that drug sellers warn their customers of the drugs' dangers. The required warnings should be similar to current cigarette warnings, but preferably in more detail. Naturally, only the federal government could undertake the expense of a reliable drug evaluation and education program, and the Federal Food and Drug Administration is already set up to do this type of important work. Moreover, the State should tax all harmful drugs enough to compensate society for the money it will have to spend to deal with a comprehensive testing program, as well as any economic and health losses caused by the use of the drugs. For example, government health officials estimate that tobacco smoking alone costs the United States twenty to twenty-five billion in health care, absenteeism, and lost wages. One immediate result of this sort of taxation and legalization policy would certainly be substantial increases in the cost of tobacco and alcohol and a reduction in the cost of marijuana and cocaine.

A great benefit of the legalization of all drugs would be that it would help us deal in a rational way with the problems we have with tobacco and alcohol. We now promote a ridiculous double standard under which tobacco and alcohol sellers are welcome in our country clubs and boardrooms and allowed to use slick advertising to entice everyone to drink and smoke, while at the same time users and growers of marijuana are imprisoned. It is our belief that if liquor and cigarette advertising were stopped and these products were taxed enough to pay for their full societal cost, at the same time that other drugs such as marijuana were legalized

and taxed, this country might well be a healthier place. At the very least, our law enforcement costs would drop; and legalization would eliminate millions of criminals, people who never should have been labeled criminals in the first place. Of course, we realize that it will be difficult to assess the societal costs of each drug and to collect the taxes, but that hasn't stopped the IRS yet.

But what about truly dangerous chemicals and poisons? Doesn't the State have a responsibility to protect its citizens from nerve gas or Thalidomide or the herbicide 2,4,5-T? Yes, there are some substances that are so dangerous that they should be carefully regulated. A sophisticated society obviously has some role to play in the "better living through chemistry" game. For example, it should have the responsibility to test poisons and wonder drugs; to warn the public of their dangers; and to prevent the unknowledgeable and involuntary ingestion of dangerous chemicals that can result from such activities as chemical waste disposal and pesticide spraying. In addition, we believe that the government has the right to tax harmful substances to compensate for social and environmental costs; to prohibit activities that endanger others while using drugs, such as driving while intoxicated; to regulate the conflict of interest between doctors and prescription drug companies; and to hold drug and chemical companies financially liable for the harmful side effects of their products.

But what about substances such as the animal tranquilizer PCP and glue that have legitimate uses but are foolishly used by some people—particularly minors—in search of thrills? We believe that legalization of legitimate "thrill" drugs should go far toward eliminating the demand for substances such as airplane glue. For adult members of society, however, we believe that the State should restrict its role to informing its citizens about the dangers of drugs, as well as taxing all harmful drugs to compensate for any societal costs, and then stand back and let people make their own choices. If that choice is to get strung out on speed, so be it.

Let us say loud and clear that when it comes to minors, the State does have a paternalistic role in protecting them from the consequences of their own impetuousness, ignorance, and bravado. Nearly all societies recognize that certain freedoms cannot sensibly be extended to children and we see no need to rewrite this basic wisdom. Should minors unlawfully emulate their drug-using elders, however, we don't believe that they should be subject to criminal sanctions. It is as hypocritical to punish America's teenagers, many of whom are neglected, bored, or frustrated, for falling victim to the omnipresent alcohol and tobacco advertisements as it is to punish them for trying popular illegal drugs that are irrationally classified as "forbidden fruits." So long as adult society subjects its children to an unloving, dishonest, and irrational world, we can expect them to turn to drugs in search of an answer to their troubles.

While we are absolutists about the need for the ultimate legalization of all recreational drugs, we also understand that small steps in the right direction are better than no steps at all. One important first step toward rational drug laws would be legalizing the cultivation of a small number of marijuana plants—say six to twelve—as well as the possession of a pound or two for personal use. A second step would be the legalization of small-scale cultivation and distribution for sale. Not everyone who likes to smoke marijuana likes to garden. It makes sense for the State to forbid the corporate cultivation and mass marketing of marijuana to avoid its glorification by the alcohol or tobacco conglomerates.

When it comes to cocaine, opium, heroin, and other illegal drugs such as the psychedelics, the argument for legalization is basically the same as that for marijuana. Peruvian peasants have chewed coca leaves (cocaine) for centuries; American and Mexican Indians have used peyote and psilocybin mushrooms far longer than tribal remembrance; and the people of China, as well as much of the rest of the world, have traditionally relied on opium products as pain killers. None of these societies fell apart because they allowed their citizens to choose for themselves when, how, and if to use a particular drug. Again, we believe that we would be far better off if the State were less paternalistic and punitive; and instead concentrated on convincing its citizens that the use of a particular drug may be hazardous to health, addictive, psychologically damaging, or whatever.

Many governments down through history, including those in at least half of today's world, justify totalitarianism by asserting that their laws are good for their citizens. Thus, the State tells its citizens where to work, where to live, where to travel, and what to think. America does essentially the same for selected "dangerous drugs." We can reach our potential as a truly free, democratic society only when we stop imprisoning our neighbors who choose to eat, drink, and smoke unpopular substances. Perhaps if the pressures and stresses of everyday life weren't so intense, we wouldn't be tempted by the various mood elevators and mind-altering drugs, but for most of us a glass of wine or a toke on a joint provides a welcome relief from the boredom of eternity. And even the persistently self-destructive among us who abuse drugs deserve our understanding and support—not our prisons.

Appendix

ASSORTED MARIJUANA CRIMES AND THEIR PUNISHMENTS—STATE-BY-STATE

A Note of Caution

The following appendix of marijuana penalties, listed by state, applies to only a few of the most popular drug crimes, and is intended only to give you a taste of the absurdity of these laws. Because the states cannot even agree on a standard weight measurement, you may be interested in knowing that 1 ounce (oz.) = 28.35 grams (gm.); 16 oz. = 1 pound (lb.) = 453.59 gm.; and 2.2 lb. = 1 kilogram = 1000 gm.

Because your state legislature in its wisdom may change the law at any moment, and because the appendix does not list every marijuana crime, you should not rely solely on this chart if you are ever charged with a crime. For example, this appendix does not list the different state penalties for an adult who sells marijuana to a minor. Suffice it to say that in most states if you are over eighteen, nineteen, twenty, or twenty-one and you are caught selling marijuana to a friend of yours who is a few months or years younger than you are (usually under eighteen), you are in big trouble. In many states, the minimum penalty is around four years, while the maximum is life imprisonment.

In most states the penalty for sale of marijuana on a first offense increases from 50 percent to 300 percent for a second or a third offense. And, in many states, there is separate crime for possession of marijuana with the intent to sell, though its punishment is usually similar to the penalty for actual sale.

If you are into other drugs, such as cocaine, psilocybin, or opium, the penalties for possession in most states approximate the penalty for several pounds of marijuana. Furthermore, in most states, hashish penalties are more severe than those for marijuana.

Of course, young persons under a certain age, depending upon the state, are subject to the completely different penalties of the juvenile law.

And lastly, depending upon your state or city, you may be eligible for a diversion program, probation or conditional discharge if you commit a drug crime, particularly if it's your first offense (see Chapter 13).

Special note: As a general rule, a *felony* is a crime for which the maximum sentence is more than one year in prison; a *misdemeanor* is an offense for which you may be imprisoned only in the county jail for one year or less; and an *infraction* can be punished only by fine.

Amount	Possession—First Offense	Possession—Second Offense	Cultivation—First Offense	Sale—First Offense
FEDERAL LAW				
UNITED STATES 21 U.S.C. §841				
Any amount	0–1 yr. & $5,000	0–2 yr. & $10,000	0–5 yr. & $15,000	0–5 yr. & $15,000
STATE LAWS				
ALABAMA §20-2-70; §20-2-80				
Up to 2.2 lb. "for personal use"	0–1 yr. & $1,000	2–15 yr. & $25,000	2–15 yr. & $25,000	2–15 yr. & $25,000
Up to 2.2 lb. *not* "for personal use"	2–15 yr. & $25,000	2–30 yr. & $50,000	2–15 yr. & $25,000	2–15 yr. & $25,000
2.2 lb.–2,000 lb.	3–15 yr. & $25,000	3–30 yr. & $50,000	3–15 yr. & $25,000	3–15 yr. & $25,000
2,000 lb.–10,000 lb.	5–15 yr. & $50,000	5–30 yr. & $100,000	5–15 yr. & $50,000	5–15 yr. & $50,000
More than 10,000 lb.	15 yr. & $200,000	15–30 yr. & $400,000	15 yr. & $200,000	15 yr. & $200,000
ALASKA §17.12.110				
Any amount for personal use within the home	IT'S LEGAL	IT'S LEGAL	IT'S LEGAL	N.A.
Any amount "not in a public place" for personal use	$0–$100	$0–$100	$0–$100	N.A.
Up to 1 oz. in a public place	$0–$100	$0–$100	$0–$100	N.A.

Amount	Possession–First Offense	Possession–Second Offense	Cultivation–First Offense	Sale–First Offense
Smoking marijuana in public	$0–$1,000	$0–$1,000	N.A.	N.A.
More than 1 oz. in public for peronal use	$0–$1,000	$0–$1,000	$0–$1,000	N.A.
Any amount for personal use in a motor vehicle or airplane or by a person under 18	$0–$1,000	$0–$1,000	$0–$1,000	N.A.
More than 1 oz. *not* for personal use	0–25 yr. & $20,000	0 yr.–life & $25,000	0–25 yr. & $20,000	0–25 yr. & $20,000
ARIZONA §36-1002.05				
Any amount not for sale	1½ yr. & $0–$150,000	1½–3 yr. & $0–$150,000	1½ yr. & $0–$150,000	7 yr. & $0–$150,000
Any amount for sale	4 yr. & $0–$150,000	4–8 yr. & $0–$150,000	4 yr. & $0–$150,000	7 yr. & $0–$150,000
ARKANSAS §§82-2617; §41-901				
Up to 1 oz. for personal use	0–1 yr. & $1,000	0–5 yr. & $10,000	2–10 yr. & $10,000	2–10 yr. & $10,000
More than 1 oz.— presumed to be not for personal use	2–10 yr. & $10,000	2–10 yr. & $10,000	2–10 yr. & $10,000	2–10 yr. & $10,000
CALIFORNIA—Health & Safety Code §11357-§11360				
Up to 1 oz.	$0–$100	$0–$100	16 mo., 2, or 3 yr.	2, 3, or 4 yr.
More than 1 oz.	0–6 mo. & $500	0–6 mo. & $500	16 mo., 2, or 3 yr.	2, 3, or 4 yr.

Amount	Possession–First Offense	Possession–Second Offense	Cultivation–First Offense	Sale–First Offense
COLORADO §12-22-412				
Up to 1 oz. not in public	$0–$100	$0–$100	1–14 yr. & $1,000	1–14 yr. & $1,000
Up to 1 oz. in public	0–15 days & $100	0–15 days & $100	1–14 yr. & $1,000	1–14 yr. & $1,000
More than 1 oz.	0–1 yr. & $500	probation–2 yr. & $500–$1,000	1–14 yr. & $1,000	1–14 yr. & $1,000
CONNECTICUT §19-480				
Up to 4 oz.	0–1 yr. & $1,000	0–5 yr. & $3,000	0–7 yr. & $1,000	0–7 yr. & $1,000
4 oz.–2.2 lb.	0–5 yr. & $2,000	0–10 yr. & $5,000	0–7 yr. & $1,000	0–7 yr. & $1,000
More than 2.2 lb.	0–5 yr. & $2,000	0–10 yr. & $5,000	5–20 yr.	5–20 yr.
DELAWARE 16 §4751				
Any amount	0–2 yr. & $500	0–7 yr. & $500	0–10 yr. & $1,000–$10,000	0–10 yr. & $1,000–$10,000
FLORIDA §893.13				
Up to 20 gm.	0–1 yr. & $1,000	0–1 yr. & $1,000	0–5 yr. & $5,000	0–5 yr. & $5,000
20 gm.–100 lb.	0–5 yr. & $5,000	0–5 yr. & $5,000	0–5 yr. & $5,000	0–5 yr. & $5,000
100–2,000 lb.	3–30 yr. & $25,000	3–30 yr. & $25,000	3–30 yr. & $25,000	3–30 yr. & $25,000
2,000–10,000 lb.	5–30 yr. & $50,000	5–30 yr. & $50,000	5–30 yr. & $50,000	5–30 yr. & $50,000

Amount	Possession– First Offense	Possession– Second Offense	Cultivation– First Offense	Sale– First Offense
More than 10,000 lb.	15–30 yr. & $200,000	15–30 yr. & $200,000	15–30 yr. & $200,000	15–30 yr. & $200,000
GEORGIA §79A-811; §79A-9917				
Up to 1 oz.	0–1 yr. & $1,000	1–10 yr.	1–10 yr.	1–10 yr.
1 oz.–100 lb.	1–10 yr.	1–10 yr.	1–10 yr.	1–10 yr.
100–2,000 lb.	5–10 yr. & $25,000	5–10 yr. & $25,000	5–10 yr. & $25,000	5–10 yr. & $25,000
2,000–10,000 lb.	7–10 yr. & $50,000	7–10 yr. & $50,000	7–10 yr. & $50,000	7–10 yr. & $50,000
More than 10,000 lb.	15 yr. & $200,000	15 yr. & $200,000	15 yr. & $200,000	15 yr. & $200,000
HAWAII §712-1247; §706-640				
Up to 1 oz.	0–30 days & $500	0–30 days & $500	0–30 days & $500	0–1 yr. & $1,000
1–2 oz.	0–1 yr. & $1,000	0–1 yr. & $1,000	0–1 yr. & $1,000	0–1 yr. & $1,000
2 oz.–2.2 lb.	0–1 yr. & $1,000	0–1 yr. & $1,000	0–1 yr. & $1,000	0–5 yr. & $5,000
More than 2.2 lb.	0–5 yr. & $5,000	0–5 yr. & $5,000	0–5 yr. & $5,000	0–5 yr. & $5,000
IDAHO §37-2732				
Up to 3 oz.	0–1 yr. & $1,000	0–2 yr. & $2,000	0–5 yr. & $15,000	0–5 yr. & $15,000
More than 3 oz.	0–5 yr. & $10,000	0–10 yr. & $20,000	0–5 yr. & $15,000	0–5 yr. & $15,000

Amount	Possession—First Offense	Possession—Second Offense	Cultivation—First Offense	Sale—First Offense
ILLINOIS 56½§8704-§8705; 38§1005-8-1; 9-1				
Less than 2.5 gm.	0–30 days & $500	0–30 days & $500	0–6 mo. & $500	0–6 mo. & $500
2.5–10 gm.	0–6 mo. & $500	0–6 mo. & $500	0–1 yr. & $1,000	0–1 yr. & $1,000
10–30 gm.	0–1 yr. & $1,000	1–3 yr. & $10,000	1–3 yr. & $10,000	1–3 yr. & $10,000
30–500 gm.	1–3 yr. & $10,000	2–5 yr. & $10,000	2–5 yr. & $10,000	2–5 yr. & $10,000
More than 500 gm.	2–5 yr. & $10,000	2–5 yr. & $10,000	3–7 yr. & $10,000	3–7 yr. & $10,000
INDIANA §35-48-4-10				
Up to 30 gm.	0–1 yr. & $5,000	0–2 yr. & $10,000	0–1 yr. & $5,000	0–1 yr. & $5,000
More than 30 gm.	0–2 yr. & $10,000	0–2 yr. & $10,000	0–2 yr. & $10,000	0–2 yr. & $10,000
IOWA §204.401				
Any amount	0–6 mo. & $1,000	0–18 mo. & $3,000	0–5 yr. & $1,000	0–5 yr. & $1,000
KANSAS §65-4127b; §21-4501				
Any amount	0–1 yr. & $2,500	1–10 yr. & $5,000	0–1 yr. & $2,500	1–10 yr. & $5,000

Amount	Possession—First Offense	Possession—Second Offense	Cultivation—First Offense	Sale—First Offense
KENTUCKY §218A.990				
Any amount	0–90 days & $250	0–90 days & $250	0–1 yr. & $500	0–1 yr. & $500
LOUISIANA §40:967				
Up to 100 lb.	0–6 mo. & $500	0–5 yr. & $2,000	0–10 yr. & $15,000	0–10 yr. & $15,000
100–2,000 lb.	5–10 yr. & $25,000	5–10 yr. & $25,000	5–10 yr. & $25,000	5–10 yr. & $25,000
2,000–10,000 lb.	10–15 yr. & $50,000	10–15 yr. & $50,000	10–15 yr. & $50,000	10–15 yr. & $50,000
More than 10,000 lb.	15–20 yr. & $200,000	15–20 yr. & $200,000	15–20 yr. & $200,000	15–20 yr. & $200,000
MAINE 17-A §§1103; 22 §2283;				
Any amount for personal use	$0–$200	$0–$200	$0–$200	N.A.
Up to 1½ oz.	$0–$200	$0–$200	$0–$200	0–1 yr. & $1,000
1½ oz.–2 lb. (presumed to be for sale)	0–1yr. & $1,000	0–1 yr. & $1,000	0–1 yr. & $1,000	0–1 yr. & $1,000
2–1,000 lb. (presumed to be for sale)	0–5 yr. & $2,500	0–5 yr. & $2,500	0–5 yr. & $2,500	0–5 yr. & $2,500
More than 1,000 lb. (presumed to be for sale)	0–10 yr. & $10,000	0–10 yr. & $10,000	0–10 yr. & $10,000	0–10 yr. & $10,000

Amount	Possession–First Offense	Possession–Second Offense	Cultivation–First Offense	Sale–First Offense
MARYLAND 27 §286				
Any amount for personal use	0–1 yr. & $1,000	0–2 yr. & $2,000	0–1 yr. & $1,000	0–5 yr. & $15,000
Any other amount	0–5 yr. & $15,000	0–10 yr. & $30,000	0–5 yr. & $15,000	0–5 yr. & $15,000
More than 100 lb. imported into the state	0–25 yr. & $50,000	0–50 yr. & $100,000	N.A.	0–25 yr. & $50,000
MASSACHUSETTS 94C §32				
Any amount	Probation	0–6 mo. & $500	0–2 yr. & $5,000	0–2 yr. & $5,000
MICHIGAN §333.7403				
Any amount	0–1 yr. & $1,000	0–2 yr. & $2,000	0–4 yr. & $2,000	0–4 yr. & $2,000
Use of marijuana	0–90 days & $100	0–180 days & $200	N.A.	N.A.
MINNESOTA §152.15				
Up to 1½ oz. not in vehicle (except trunk)	$0–$100 & drug education program	(Within 2 yr. of first offense) 0–90 days & $500	0–5 yr. & $15,000	0–5 yr. & $15,000
More than 1½ oz.	0–3 yr. & $3,000	0–6 yr. & $6,000	0–5 yr. & $15,000	0–5 yr. & $15,000

Amount	Possession–First Offense	Possession–Second Offense	Cultivation–First Offense	Sale–First Offense
MISSISSIPPI §41-29-139				
Up to 1 oz. not in vehicle	$100–$250	(Within 2 yr. of first offense) 5–60 days & $250 and drug education program	0–10 yr. & $15,000	0–20 yr. & $30,000
1 gm.–1 oz. in vehicle (except trunk)	0–90 days & $500	0–180 days & $1,000	0–10 yr. & $15,000	0–20 yr. & $30,000
1 oz.–2.2 lb.	0–3 yr. & $3,000	0–6 yr. & $6,000	0–10 yr. & $15,000	0–20 yr. & $30,000
More than 2.2 lb.	3 yr. & $10,000	6 yr. & $20,000	0–10 yr. & $15,000	3–20 yr. & $30,000
MISSSOURI §195.200				
Up to 35 gm.	0–1 yr. & $1,000	0–5 yr. & $1,000	0–5 yr. & $1,000	5 yr.–life
More than 35 gm.	0–5 yr. & $1,000	0–5 yr. & $1,000	0–5 yr. & $1,000	5 yr.–life
MONTANA §45-9-101				
Up to 60 gm.	0–1 yr. & $1,000	0–3 yr. & $1,000	1 yr.–life	1 yr.–life
More than 60 gm.	0–5 yr.	0–5 yr.	1 yr.–life	1 yr.–life

Amount	Possession—First Offense	Possession—Second Offense	Cultivation—First Offense	Sale—First Offense
NEBRASKA §28-416				
Up to 1 oz.	$100 & possibly drug education program	O–5 days & $200	0–5 yr. & $10,000	0–5 yr. & $10,000
1 oz.–1 lb.	0–7 days & $500	0–7 days & $500	0–5 yr. & $10,000	0–5 yr. & $10,000
More than 1 lb.	0–5 yr. & $10,000	0–5 yr. & $10,000	0–5 yr. & $10,000	0–5 yr. & $10,000
NEVADA §453.336				
Up to 1 oz. by a person *under 21*	0–6 yr. & $2,000	1–6 yr. & $5,000	1 yr.–life & $20,000	1 yr.–life & $20,000
Any other amount for all ages	Probation–6 yr. & $5,000	1–10 yr. & $10,000	5 yr.–life & $20,000	5 yr.–life & $20,000
NEW HAMPSHIRE §318-B:26				
Up to 1 lb.	0–1 yr. & $1,000	0–7 yr. & $2,000	0–15 yr. & $2,000	0–15 yr. & $2,000
More than 1 lb.	0–7 yr. & $2,000	0–15 yr. & $2,000	0–15 yr. & $2,000	0–15 yr. & $2,000

Amount	Possession—First Offense	Possession—Second Offense	Cultivation—First Offense	Sale—First Offense
NEW JERSEY §24:21-19				
Up to 25 gm.	0-6 mo. & $500 & 2 yr. driver license suspension	0-6 mo. & $500 & 2 yr. driver license suspension	0-5 yr. & $15,000	0-5 yr. & $15,000
More than 25 gm.	0-5 yr. & $15,000	0-5 yr. & $15,000	0-5 yr. & $15,000	0-5 yr. & $15,000
NEW MEXICO §30-31-23				
Up to 1 oz.	0-15 days & $50-$100	0-1 yr. & $100-$1,000	9 yr. & $0-$10,000	18 mo. & $0-$5,000
1-8 oz.	0-1 yr. & $100-$1,000	0-1 yr. & $100-$1,000	9 yr. & $0-$10,000	18 mo. & $0-$5,000
8 oz.-100 lb.	Conditional discharge or 5 yr. & $5,000	1-5 yr. & $0-$5,000	9 yr. & $0-$10,000	18 mo. & $0-$5,000
More than 100 lb.	3 yr. & $0-$5,000	9 yr. & $0-$10,000	9 yr. & $0-$10,000	3 yr. & $0-$5,000
NEW YORK Penal Law §221; Public Health Law §3382				
Up to 25 gm. in private	$0-$100	$0-$200	0-1 yr. & $1,000	0-1 yr. & $1,000
25 gm.-2 oz. or up to 2 oz. in public	0-3 mo. & $500	0-3 mo. & $500	0-1 yr. & $1,000	0-4 yr.
2-4 oz.	0-1 yr. & $1,000	0-1 yr. & $1,000	0-1 yr. & $1,000	0-4 yr.
4-8 oz.	0-1 yr. & $1,000	0-1 yr. & $1,000	0-1 yr. & $1,000	0-7 yr.
8 oz.-1 lb.	0-4 yr.	0-4 yr.	0-4 yr.	0-7 yr.
1-10 lb.	0-7 yr.	0-7 yr.	0-7 yrs.	0-15 yr.
More than 10 lb.	0-15 yr.	0-15 yr.	0-15 yr.	0-15 yr.

Amount	Possession–First Offense	Possession–Second Offense	Cultivation–First Offense	Sale–First Offense
NORTH CAROLINA §90-95				
Up to 1 oz.	$0–$100	0–6 mo. & $500	0–5 yr. & $5,000	0–5 yr. & $5,000
More than 1 oz.	0–5 yr. & $5,000	0–10 yr. & $10,000	0–5 yr. & $5,000	0–5 yr. & $5,000
NORTH DAKOTA §19-03.1-23				
Up to ½ oz. not in vehicle	0–30 days & $500	0–60 days & $1,000	0–10 yr. & $10,000	0–10 yr. & $10,000
½–1 oz. or up to ½ oz. in vehicle	0–1 yr. & $1,000	0–2 yr. & $2,000	0–10 yr. & $10,000	0–10 yr. & $10,000
More than 1 oz.	0–5 yr. & $5,000	0–5 yr. & $5,000	0–10 yr. & $10,000	0–10 yr. & $10,000
OHIO §2925.03				
Up to 100 gm.	0–$100	0–$100	6 mo.–5 yr. & $2,500	6 mo.–5 yr. & $2,500
10u–200 gm.	0–30 days & $250	0–30 days & $250	6 mo.–5 yr. & $2,500	6 mo.–5 yr. & $2,500
200–600 gm.	6 mo.–5 yr. & $2,500	1–10 yr. & $5,000	1–10 yr. & $5,000	1–10 yr. & $5,000
More than 600 gm.	1–10 yr. & $5,000	2–15 yr. & $7,500	2–15 yr. & $7,500	2–15 yr. & $7,500
OKLAHOMA 63 §2-401				
Any amount	0–1 yr.	2–10 yr.	2–10 yr. & $5,000	2–10 yr. & $5,000

Amount	Possession—First Offense	Possession—Second Offense	Cultivation—First Offense	Sale—First Offense
OREGON §475.992				
Up to 1 oz.	$0–$100	$0–$100	0–10 yr. & $2,500	0–10 yr. & $2,500
More than 1 oz.	Probation–10 yr. & $2,500	0–10 yr. & $2,500	0–10 yr. & $2,500	0–10 yr. & $2,500
PENNSYLVANIA 35 §780-113				
Up to 30 gm.	0–30 days & $500	0–30 days & $500	0–5 yr. & $15,000	0–5 yr. & $15,000
More than 30 gm.	0–1 yr. & $5,000	0–3 yr. & $25,000	0–5 yr. & $15,000	0–5 yr. & $15,000
RHODE ISLAND §21-28-4.01				
Any amount	0–1 yr. & $500	0–2 yr. & $1,000	0–30 yr. & $50,000	0–30 yr. & $50,000
SOUTH CAROLINA §44-53-370				
Up to 1 oz.	0–3 mo. & $100	0–6 mo. & $200	0–5 yr. & $5,000	0–5 yr. & $5,000
More than 1 oz.	0–6 mo. & $1,000	0–1 yr. & $2,000	0–5 yr. & $5,000	0–5 yr. & $5,000
SOUTH DAKOTA §22-42-6				
Up to 1 oz.	0–30 days & $100	0–30 days & $100	0–30 days & $100	0–1 yr. & $1,000
1–8 oz.	0–1 yr. & $1,000	0–1 yr. & $1,000	0–1 yr. & $1,000	0–2 yr. & $2,000

Amount	Possession—First Offense	Possession—Second Offense	Cultivation—First Offense	Sale—First Offense
8 oz.–1 lb.	0–1 yr. & $1,000	0–1 yr. & $1,000	0–1 yr. & $1,000	0–5 yr. & $5,000
More than 1 lb.	0–2 yr. & $2,000	0–2 yr. & $2,000	0–2 yr. & $2,000	0–5 yr. & $5,000
TENNESSEE §52-1432				
Up to ½ oz.	0–1 yr. & $1,000	1–2 yr.	1–5 yr. & $3,000	0–1 yr. & $1,000
More than ½ oz.	0–1 yr. & $1,000	1–2 yr.	1–5 yr. & $3,000	1–5 yr. & $3,000
TEXAS Art. 4476-15 §4.05				
Up to 2 oz.	0–180 days & $1,000	30–180 days & $1,000	0–180 days & $1,000	Conditional discharge or 2–10 yr. & $5,000
2–4 oz.	0–1 yr. & $2,000	90 days–1 yr. & $2,000	0–1 yr. & $2,000	Conditional discharge or 2–10 yr. & $5,000
More than 4 oz.	Conditional discharge or 2–10 yr. & $5,000	2–20 yr. & $10,000	Conditional discharge or 2–10 yr. & $5,000	Conditional discharge or 2–10 yr. & $5,000
UTAH §58-37-8				
Any amount	0–6 mo. & $299	0–1 yr. & $1,000	0–5 yr. & $5,000	0–5 yr. & $5,000

VERMONT Title 18 §4224				
Up to ½ oz.	0–6 mo. & $500	0–2 yr. & $2,000	0–5 yr. & $5,000	0–5 yr. & $5,000
½–2 oz.	0–3 yr. & $3,000	0–3 yr. & $3,000	0–5 yr. & $5,000	0–5 yr. & $5,000
More than 2 oz.	0–5 yr. & $5,000	0–5 yr. & $5,000	0–5 yr. & $5,000	0–5 yr. & $5,000
VIRGINIA §18.2-248.1				
Up to ½ oz.	0–30 days & $500	0–1 yr. & $1,000	0–30 days & $500	0–1 yr. & $1,000
½ oz.–5 lb.	0–30 days & $500	0–1 yr. & $1,000	0–30 days & $500 (Personal use only)	0–10 yr. & $1,000
More than 5 lb.	0–30 days & $500	0–1 yr. & $1,000	0–30 days & $500 (Not for personal use) 5–30 yr.	5–30 yr.
WASHINGTON §69.50.401; §9.92.030				
Up to 40 gm.	0–90 days & $250	0–90 days & $250	0–5 yr. & $10,000	0–5 yr. & $10,000
More than 40 gm.	0–5 yr. & $10,000	0–10 yr. & $10,000	0–5 yr. & $10,000	0–5 yr. & $10,000
WEST VIRGINIA §60A-4-401				
Up to 15 gm.	Conditional discharge	90 days–6 mo. & $1,000	1–5 yr. & $15,000	1–5 yr. & $15,000
More than 15 gm.	90 days–6 mo. & $1,000	90 days–1 yr. & $2,000	1–5 yr. & $15,000	1–5 yr. & $15,000

Amount	Possession—First Offense	Possession—Second Offense	Cultivation—First Offense	Sale—First Offense
WISCONSIN §161.41				
Any amount	0–30 days & $500	0–30 days & $500	0–5 yr. & $15,000	0–5 yr. & $15,000
WYOMING §35-7-1031				
Any amount	0–6 mo. & $1,000	0–1 yr. & $2,000	0–6 mo. & $1,000	0–10 yr. & $10,000

QUASI-STATE LAWS

Amount	Possession—First Offense	Possession—Second Offense	Cultivation—First Offense	Sale—First Offense
AMERICAN SAMOA 21 §2251				
Any amount	0–1 yr. & $500	0–2 yr. & $1,000	0–20 yr. & $20,000	0–20 yr. & $20,000
DISTRICT OF COLUMBIA §33-401				
Any amount	0–1 yr. & $100–$1,000	0–10 yr. & $500–$5,000	0–1 yr. & $100–$1,000	0–1 yr. & $100–$1,000
GUAM §626.10				
Any amount	0–3 mo. & $500	0–6 mo. & $1,000	0–5 yr. & $5,000	0–5 yr. & $5,000
PUERTO RICO §24-2401				
Any amount	1–5 yr. & $5,000	2–10 yr. & $10,000	5–20 yr. & $20,000	5–20 yr. & $20,000

Amount	Possession—First Offense	Possession—Second Offense	Cultivation—First Offense	Sale—First Offense
TRUST TERRITORY OF MICRONESIA 63§291				
Up to 1 oz.	$0-$50	$0-$50	0-5 yr. & $5,000	0-5 yr. & $5,000
1 oz.–2.2 lb.	0-3 mo. & $500	0-3 mo. & $500	0-5 yr. & $5,000	0-5 yr. & $5,000
More than 2.2 lb.	0-1 yr. & $1,000	0-1 yr. & $1,000	0-5 yr. & $5,000	0-5 yr. & $5,000
VIRGIN ISLANDS 19 §604				
Any amount	0-1 yr. & $5,000	0-2 yr. & $10,000	0-5 yr. & $15,000	0-5 yr. & $15,000

A GUIDE TO THE REFERENCES USED IN THIS BOOK

As you have probably noticed, this book provides citations primarily for its case histories and quotations, and not for every legal proposition.

Here is an example of a footnote referring to a court case: United States Supreme Court: United States v. Nixon, 418 U.S. 683, 687 (1974). The citation first gives the name of the court that decided the case and then the people in the case. The people in the case are separated by a v., which stands for versus. When a crime is prosecuted, the case is normally brought on behalf of the "People," the "State," or the "United States." The first number listed is the volume number of a specific set of books, which is abbreviated such as U.S., F.2d, A.2d, P., or Cal. App. 3d. In the order listed, these abbreviations stand for United States Reports; Federal Reporter, second edition; Atlantic Reporter, second edition; Pacific Reporter; and California Appellate Reports, third edition. The number that follows is the page on which the case begins in that particular volume, and any other numbers refer to the specific pages on which the quotation or anecdote appears. Finally, the citation gives the year in which the court decided the case, which is usually between one and five years after the "crime" took place. For the United States Court of Appeals, the citation will specify which of the twelve circuit courts made the decision. The Second Circuit (2d Cir.), for instance, encompasses the New York area, the Fifth Circuit (5th Cir.), the South, and the Ninth Circuit (9th Cir), the Far West.

For any reader who wants to learn about marijuana and drug decriminalization, I recommend for your enlightenment and reading pleasure *Licit and Illicit Drugs* (Boston: Little, Brown & Co., 1972) by Edward Brecher and the Editors of Consumer Reports; *Marijuana Reconsidered* (Cambridge, Mass.: Harvard University Press, 1977) by Lester Grinspoon, a Harvard medical professor; and *Marijuana—The New Prohibition* (New York: World Publishing, 1970) by John Kaplan, a Stanford law professor. For any reader who wants another critical view of the police and courts, I recommend *Criminal Violence, Criminal Justice* (New York: Random House, 1978) by Charles E. Silberman. And for any reader who is determined to learn more about the law of criminal procedure, I highly recommend *Search and Seizure: A Treatise on the Fourth Amendment* (St. Paul: West Publishing, 1978), a three-volume, two thousand page exposition by Wayne R. LaFave, a University of Illinois law professor.

NOTES

Introduction

[1] National Organization for the Reform of Marijuana Laws, *Marijuana: The Facts,* (January 1979); National Institute on Drug Abuse, *Marijuana Research Findings:* 1980, pp 7-8 (Washington, D.C.: U.S. Government, 1980).

Chapter 1

[1] John Allen Krout, *The Origins of Prohibition,* pp. 3-4 (New York: Russell & Russell, 1925).

[2] Edward M. Brecher, *Licit and Illicit Drugs,* p. 403 (Boston: Little, Brown, 1972).

[3] Paul E. Isaac, *Prohibition and Politics: Turbulent Decades in Tennessee 1885-1920,* pp. 8-16 (Knoxville: The University of Tennessee Press, 1965).

[4] Isaac, p. 8.

[5] Henry Lee, *How Dry We Were: Prohibition Revisited,* preface (Englewood Cliffs: Prentice Hall, 1963).

[6] Brecher, pp. 42-45.

[7] Brecher, pp. 197-198.

[8] Lester Grinspoon & James B. Bakalar, *Cocaine: A Drug and Its Social Evolution,* p. 22 (New York: Basic Books, 1976).

[9] Jerome E. Brooks, *The Mighty Leaf: Tobacco Through the Centuries,* p. 274 (Boston: Little, Brown, 1952).

[10] Brooks, p. 258.

[11] Brecher, p. 339.

[12] Brecher, pp. 49-50.

[13] Lee, p. 58.

[14] Brecher, p. 410.

[15] Lee, pp. 156-157.

[16] Lee, p. 153.

[17] Richard J. Bonnie & Charles H. Whitebread II, *The Marijuana Conviction: A History of Marijuana Prohibition in the United States,* pp. 42-47 (Charlottesville: University Press of Virginia, 1974).

[18] Grinspoon and Bakalar, p. 258.

[19] Bonnie and Whitebread, pp. 118-126.

[20] Brecher, pp. 419-420.

[21] *Newsweek,* p. 114 (December 3, 1979).

[22] United States Court of Appeals: Davis v. Davis, 601 F. 2d 153 (4th Cir. 1979).

[23] Missouri Supreme Court: State v. Mitchell, 563 S.W. 2d 18 (1978); National Organization for the Reform of Marijuana Laws, *News Digest,* (July 1979).

[24] National Organization for the Reform of Marijuana Laws, *In the Courts,* (July 1979).

[25] United States District Court of Louisiana: Louisiana Affiliation of the National Organization for the Reform of Marijuana Laws v. Guste, 380 F. Supp. 404 (1974).

[26] United States Supreme Court: Griswold v. Connecticut, 381 U.S. 479, 485-486 (1965); Eisenstadt v. Baird, 405 U.S. 438, 453 (1972); Stanley v. Georgia, 394 U.S. 557, 565-566 (1964).

[27] California Supreme Court: People v. Woody, 61 Cal. 2d 716, 727-728 (1964).

[28] Florida Supreme Court: Town v. State ex. rel. Reno, 377 So. 2d 648 (1979).

[29] Alaska Supreme Court: Ravin v. State, 537 P. 2d 494 (1975).

[30] Alaska Supreme Court: Ravin v. State, 537 P. 2d 494, 506 (1975).

[31] Hawaii Supreme Court: State v. Katner, 493 P. 2d 306, 317 (1973).

[32] Michigan Supreme Court: People v. Sinclair, 194 N.W. 2d 878, 896 (1972).

[33] Michigan Supreme Court: People v. Sinclair, 194 N.W. 2d 878, 881 (1972).

[34] Washington Supreme Court: State v. Smith, 610 P. 2d 869 (1980).

Chapter 2

[1] For the early history of the Fourth Amendment, I have relied heavily upon Jacob W. Landynski, *Search and Seizure and the Supreme Court: A Study in Constitutional Interpretation* (Baltimore: Johns Hopkins Press, 1966).

[2] Landynski, p. 23.

[3] Landynski, p. 28.

[4] Landynski, p. 25.

[5] Landynski, p. 36.

[6] Landynski, p. 39.

[7] United States Supreme Court: Federal Trade Commission v. American Tobacco Company, 264 U.S. 298, 305–306 (1924).

[8] United States Supreme Court: Olmstead v. United States, 277 U.S. 438, 478 (1928).

[9] United States Supreme Court: United States v. Rabinowitz, 339 U.S. 56, 69 (1950); (Landynski, p. 269).

[10] United States Supreme Court: Harris v. United States, 331 U.S. 145, 157 (1947); (Landynski, p. 269).

[11] United States Supreme Court: Mapp v. Ohio, 367 U.S. 643 (1961).

[12] United States Supreme Court: Barron v. The Mayor and City Council of Baltimore, 32 U.S. 242 (1833).

[13] United States Supreme Court: Fiske v. Kansas, 274 U.S. 380 (1927) (freedom of speech); Near v. Minnesota, 283 U.S. 697 (1931) (freedom of the press): Cantwell v. Connecticut, 310 U.S. 296 (1940) (freedom of religion).

[14] United States Supreme Court: Boyd v. United States, 116 U.S. 616 (1886).

[15] United States Supreme Court: Weeks v. United States, 232 U.S. 383, 393–394 (1914).

[16] United States Supreme Court: Silverthorne Lumber Company v. United States, 251 U.S. 385, 392 (1920).

[17] United States Supreme Court: United States v. Havens, 446 U.S. 620 (1980); United States v. Payner, 100 S. Ct. 2439 (1980).

[18] United States Court of Appeals: United States v. Williams, 622 F. 2d 830, 846–47 (5th Cir. 1980).

[19] United States Supreme Court: Bivens v. Six Unknown Federal Narcotics Agents, 403 U.S. 388, 413–25 (1971); United States v. Janis, 428 U.S. 433 (1976).

[20] Landynski, pp. 116, 124.

[21] United States Supreme Court: United States v. Mendenhall, 446 U.S. 545, 561–66 (1980).

[22] For the early history of the Fifth Amendment, I have relied heavily upon Leonard W. Levy, *Origins of the Fifth Amendment* (New York: Oxford University Press, 1968).

[23] Levy, pp. 3, 96.

[24] Levy, p. 231.

[25] Levy, pp. 406–409.

[26] United States Supreme Court: Brown v. Mississippi, 297 U.S. 278 (1936).

[27] United States Supreme Court: Malloy v. Hogan, 378 U.S. 1 (1964).

[28] United States Supreme Court: Miranda v. Arizona, 384 U.S. 436 (1966).

[29] United States Supreme Court: Brown v. Walker, 161 U.S. 591, 631, 632, 637 (1896).

[30] United States Supreme Court: Kastigar v. United States, 406 U.S. 441 (1972).

Chapter 3

[1] Washington Supreme Court: State v. Manley, 530 P. 2d 306 (1975).

[2] Pennsylvania Superior Court: Commonwealth v. Hernley, 263 A. 2d 904 (1970).

[3] United States District Court of Hawaii: United States v. Kim, 415 F. Supp. 1252, 1257 (1976).

[4] California Court of Appeal: People v. Arno, 90 Cal. App. 3d 505, 524 (1979).

[5] California Supreme Court: Dillon v. Superior Court of Santa Barbara County, 7 Cal. 3d 305 (1972).

[6] California Court of Appeal: People v. Vermouth, 42 Cal. App. 3d 353 (1974).

[7] United States District Court of the District of Columbia: United States v. McMillon, 350 F. Supp. 593 (1972).

[8] Oregon Court of Appeals: State v. Corbett, 516 P. 2d 487 (1973).

[9] California Supreme Court: People v. Bradley, 1 Cal. 3d 80, 91–92, (1969).

[10] California Court of Appeal: Dean v. Superior Court of Nevada County, 35 Cal. App. 3d 112, 114 (1973).

[11] New Hampshire Supreme Court: State v. Hanson, 313 A. 2d 730, 731 (1973).

[12] Pennsylvania Superior Court: Commonwealth v. Janek, 363 A. 2d 1299, 1300 (1976).

[13] California Court of Appeal: Phelan v. Superior Court of Mariposa County, 90 Cal. App. 3d 1005, 1011–12 (1979).

[14] United States Court of Appeals: United States v. Allen, 633 F. 2d 1282 (9th Cir. 1980).

[15] Hawaii Supreme Court: State v. Stachler, 570 P. 2d 1323, 1325 (1977).

[16] California Court of Appeal: Dean v. Superior Court of Nevada County, 35 Cal. App. 3d 112 (1973).

[17] California Court of Appeal: People v. Superior Court of Los Angeles County (Stroud), 37 Cal. App. 3d 836, 838 (1974).

[18] Mississippi Supreme Court: Wolf v. State, 281 So. 2d 445 (1973).

[19] California Court of Appeal: People v. Cohn, 30 Cal. App. 3d 738 (1973).

[20] California Court of Appeal: People v. Sneed, 32 Cal. App. 3d 535 (1973).

[21] Florida Court of Appeal: Huffer v. State, 344 So. 2d 1332, 1333 (1977).

Chapter 4

[1] United States Supreme Court: Hampton v. United States, 425 U.S. 484, 498 (1976).

[2] United States Supreme Court: Sherman v. United States, 356 U.S. 369, 376 (1958).

[3] North Carolina Supreme Court: State v. Stanley, 215 S.E. 2d 589, 597, 598 (1975).

[4] Georgia Court of Appeals: Brooks v. State, 189 S.E. 2d 448 (1972).

[5] Wyoming Supreme Court: Janski v. State, 538 P. 2d 271 (1975).

[6] Missouri Court of Appeal: State v. Hyde, 532 S.W. 2d 212 (1975).

[7] Wisconsin Supreme Court: Hawthorne v. State, 168 N.W. 2d 85 (1969).

[8] Michigan Court of Appeals: People v. Perry, 254 N.W. 2d 810 (1977).

[9] United States Court of Appeals: United States v. Ewbank, 483 F. 2d 1149 (9th Cir. 1973).

[10] For the remainder of this chapter, I have relied upon James Carr, *The Law of Electronic Surveillance* (New York: C. Boardman, 1977); Clifford Fishman, *Wiretapping and Eavesdropping* (Rochester, N.Y.: Lawyers Cooperative Publishing, 1978); National Lawyers Guild, *Raising and Litigating Electronic Surveillance Claims in Criminal Cases* (San Francisco: Lake Law Books, 1977).

[11] Ohio Court of Appeals: State v. Day, 362 N.E. 2d 1253, 1958 (1976).

[12] "Report on Wiretapping", 16 *Criminal Law Bulletin,* 50, 51 (Jan.–Feb. 1980).

[13] United States Court of Appeals: United States v. Bynum, 485 F. 2d 490 (2nd Cir. 1973); United States v. Manfredi, 488 F. 2d 588 (2nd Cir. 1973).

[14] United States Supreme Court: Smith v. Maryland, 442 U.S. 735 (1979).

[15] United States Supreme Court: United States v. Dalia, 441 U.S. 238 (1979).

Chapter 5

[1] Yale Kamisar, Wayne LaFave, and Jerold Israel, *Modern Criminal Procedure*, p. 266 (St. Paul: West Publishing Co., 1974).

[2] Dean Heller, "A Conflict of Laws: The Drug Possession Offense and the Fourth Amendment," 26 *Oklahoma Law Review*, 317, 332 (1973)

[3] United States Supreme Court: Draper v. United States, 358 U.S. 307, 313, 324 (1959).

[4] New Jersey Court of Appeals: State v. Blaurock, 363 A. 2d 909, 911 (1976).

[5] Maine Supreme Court: State v. Willey, 363 A. 2d 739, 742 (1976).

[6] United States Court of Appeals: United States v. Pond, 523 F. 2d 210 (2nd Cir. 1975).

[7] Colorado Supreme Court: People v. Leahy, 484 P. 2d 778, 781 (1970).

[8] United States Court of Appeals: Rutherford v. Cupp, 508 F. 2d 122 (9th Cir. 1974).

[9] Wayne LaFave, *2 Search & Seizure: A Treatise on the Fourth Amendment*, p. 116 (St. Paul: West Publishing Co., 1978).

[10] California Court of Appeal: People v. Thompson, 89 Cal. App. 3d 425 (1979).

[11] California Court of Appeal: People v. Rand, 23 Cal. App. 3d 579 (1972).

Chapter 6

[1] Oregon Court of Appeals: State v. Hinsvark, 471 P. 2d 859, 860 (1970).

[2] United States District Court of Pennsylvania: Santos v. Bayley, 400 F. Supp. 784 (1975).

[3] Delaware Supreme Court: State v. DeKoenigswarter, 177 A. 2d 344, 345 (1962).

[4] Florida Court of Appeal: Mack v. State, 298 So. 2d 509, 510-11 (1974).

[5] New Mexico Supreme Court: State v. Bidegain, 541 P. 2d 971, 973 (1975).

[6] United States Court of Appeals: United States v. Turbyfill, 525 F. 2d 57, 58 (8th Cir. 1975).

Chapter 7

[1] United States Court of Appeals: Thomas v. Parett, 524 F. 2d 779, 784 (8th Cir. 1975).

[2] New York Court of Appeals: People v. Clements, 339 N.E. 2d 170, 178, 180 (1975).

[3] United States Court of Appeals: United States v. McLaughlin, 525 F. 2d 517 (9th Cir. 1975).

[4] California Supreme Court: People v. Block, 6 Cal. 3d 239, 242 (1971).

[5] California Supreme Court: People v. Superior Court of San Bernardino County, 10 Cal. 3d 645, 650 (1974).

[6] United States Supreme Court: Gouled v. United States, 255 U.S. 298 (1921).

[7] United States Court of Appeals: United States v. Flores, 540 F. 2d 432, 434-36 (9th Cir. 1976).

[8] United States Supreme Court: Payton v. New York, 445 U.S. 573 (1980).

[9] United States Court of Appeals: United States v. Baratta, 397 F. 2d 215, 223 (2nd Cir. 1968).

[10] United States Court of Appeals: United States v. Carter, 522 F. 2d 666, 674-75 (D.C. Cir. 1975).

[11] United States Court of Appeals: United States v. Marshall, 488 F. 2d 1169, 1171 (9th Cir. 1973).

[12] United States Court of Appeals: United States v. Mason, 523 F. 2d 1122, 1131 (D.C. Cir. 1975).

Chapter 8

[1] United States Supreme Court: Arkansas v. Sanders, 442 U.S. 753 (1979).

[2] Arizona Court of Appeals: State v. Cantor, 479 P. 2d 432, 433 (1971).

[3] Florida Supreme Court: State v. Nittolo, 317 So. 2d 748, 749 (1975).

[4] California Supreme Court: People v. Superior Court of Yolo County (Kiefer), 3 Cal. 3d 807, 818 (1970).

[5] Florida Court of Appeal: Mattson v. State, 328 So. 2d 246, 247 (1976).

[6] Arizona Supreme Court: State v. Goldberg, 540 P. 2d 674, 677 (1975).

[7] California Supreme Court: Wimberly v. Superior Court of San Bernardino, 16 Cal. 3d 557 (1976); New Jersey Superior Court: State v. Murray, 376 A. 2d 1255 (1977).

[8] California Court of Appeal: People v. Superior Court of Los Angeles County (Karpel), 63 Cal. App. 3d 990 (1976).

[9] United States Supreme Court: South Dakota v. Opperman, 428 U.S. 364, 369 (1976).

[10] Arizona Supreme Court: State v. Mahoney, 475 P. 2d 479, 480–481 (1970).

[11] United States Supreme Court: Rakas v. Illinois, 439 U.S. 128 (1978); Rawlings v. Kentucky, 100 S. Ct. 2556 (1980).

Chapter 9

[1] California Court of Appeal: People v. Atmore, 13 Cal. App. 3d 244 (1970).

[2] United States Supreme Court: Gustafson v. Florida, 414 U.S. 260, 267–268 (1973).

[3] United States Court of Appeals: United States v. Mehciz, 437 F. 2d 145, 150 (9th Cir. 1971).

[4] Note, "Effect of Mapp v. Ohio on Police Search and Seizure Practices in Narcotics Cases," 4 Columbia Journal of Law and Social Problems, pp. 87–104 (1968).

[5] United States Supreme Court: Hill v. California, 401 U.S. 797 (1971).

[6] United States Court of Appeals: United States v. Honigman, 633 F. 2d 1336, 1338 (9th Cir. 1980).

[7] United States Supreme Court: Rochin v. California, 342 U.S. 165, 172 (1952).

[8] Texas Court of Criminal Appeals: Hernandez v. State, 548 S.W. 2d 904, 905 (1977).

[9] New York Supreme Court, Appellate Division: People v. Haskins, 369 N.Y.S. 2d 869 (1975).

Chapter 10

[1] United States District Court of Michigan: United States v. Chamblis, 425 F. Supp. 1330, 1333 (1977).

[2] United States District Court of New York: United States v. Westerbann-Martinez, 435 F. Supp. 690, 697 (1977).

[3] United States District Court of Michigan: United States v. Allen, 421 F. Supp. 1372, 1375 (1976).

[4] United States Court of Appeals: United States v. Smith, 574 F. 2d 882, 884 (6th Cir. 1978).

[5] United States District Court of New York: United States v. Flores, 462 F. Supp. 702, 704 (1978).

[6] United States Supreme Court: United States v. Mendenhall, 446 U.S. 545 (1980).

[7] United States District Court of Michigan: United States v. Van Lewis, 409 F. Supp. 535, 540 (1976).

[8] United States District Court of Michigan: United States v. Chamblis, 425 F. Supp. 1330, 1334 (1977).

[9] United States Court of Appeals: United States v. Asbury, 586 F. 2d 973, 976 (2nd Cir. 1978).

[10] United States Court of Appeals: United States v. Ivey, 546 F. 2d 139, 142 (5th Cir. 1977).

[11] United States Court of Appeals: United States v. Nelson, 593 F. 2d 543 (3rd Cir. 1979).

[12] United States Court of Appeals: United States v. Driscoll, 632 F. 2d 737 (9th Cir. 1980).

[13] United States District Court of Texas: United States v. May May, 470 F. Supp. 384, 389 (1979).

[14] United States Court of Appeals: United States v. Sarmiento-Rozo, 592 F. 2d 1318, 1319 (5th Cir. 1979).

[15] United States Court of Appeals: United States v. Whitaker, 592 F. 2d 826, 828 (5th Cir. 1979).

[16] United States Court of Appeals: United States v. Whitmire, 595 F. 2d 1303, 1319 (5th Cir. 1979).

[17] United States Court of Appeals: United States v. Piner, 608 F. 2d 358 (9th Cir. 1979).

[18] United States Court of Appeals: Morales v. United States, 406 F. 2d 1298, 1300 (9th Cir. 1969).

[19] United States Court of Appeals: Huguez v. United States, 406 F. 2d 366, 372-73 (9th Cir. 1968).

[20] United States Court of Appeals: United States v. Martinez, 481 F. 2d 214, 217 (5th Cir. 1973).

[21] William Petrocelli, *Low Profile: How to Avoid the Privacy Invaders,* pp. 188-189 (New York: McGraw Hill Book, Co., 1981).

[22] United States District Court of New York: United States v. Fisher, 377 F. Supp. 1298, 1300 (1974).

[23] United States Supreme Court: United States v. Miller, 425 U.S. 435 (1976).

[24] United States Code: 22 U.S.C. §881.

[25] United States Court of Appeals: United States v. One 1974 Jeep, 536 F. 2d 1285 (9th Cir. 1976).

[26] United States Court of Appeals: United States v. One (1) 43 Foot Sailing Vessel "Winds Will," 538 F. 2d 694 (5th Cir. 1976).

[27] United States District Court of California: United States v. One 1967 Cessna Aircraft, 454 F. Supp. 1352 (1978).

Chapter 11

[1] United States Supreme Court: Miranda v. Arizona, 384 U.S. 436 (1966).

[2] California Court of Appeal: People v. Jones, 96 Cal. App. 3d 820, 827 (1979).

[3] United States Court of Appeals: United States v. Jackson, 544 F. 2d 407, 409 (9th Cir. 1976).

[4] United States Code: 18 U.S.C. §1001.

[5] United States Supreme Court: Harris v. New York, 401 U.S. 222 (1971).

[6] United States Supreme Court: Jenkins v. Anderson, 100 S. Ct. 2124 (1980).

[7] United States Supreme Court: Oregon v. Hass, 420 U.S. 714, 725 (1975).

[8] Louisiana Supreme Court: State v. Cotton, 341 So. 2d 355 (1976).

[9] Pennsylvania Supreme Court: Commonwealth v. Jones, 322 A. 2d 119, 126 (1974).

[10] United States Supreme Court: Beecher v. Alabama, 389 U.S. 35, 36 (1967).

[11] Florida Supreme Court: Grant v. State, 171 So. 2d 361, 362 (1965).

[12] United States Supreme Court: United States v. Henry, 100 S. Ct. 2183 (1980).

Chapter 12

[1] In this chapter, I have relied heavily upon Judge Marvin E. Frankel and Gary P. Naftalis, *The Grand Jury: An Institution on Trial* (New York: Hill & Wang, 1977).

[2] Florida Supreme Court: Town v. State ex. rel. Reno, 377 So. 2d 648 (1979).

[3] United States Court of Appeals: Matter of Wellins, 627 F. 2d 969 (9th Cir. 1980).

[4] United States Supreme Court: United States v. Calandra, 414 U.S. 338 (1974).

Chapter 13

[1] United States Supreme Court: Williams v. Florida, 399 U.S. 78 (1970); Johnson v. Louisiana, 406 U.S. 356 (1972).

[2] Judge Frank Kaufman, "The Right of Self-Representation and the Power of Jury Nullification," 28 *Case Western Reserve Law Review,* pp. 269–288 (1978).

[3] United States Supreme Court: Roberts v. United States, 100 S. Ct. 1358 (1980).

[4] United States Court of Appeals: Sala v. County of Suffolk, 604 F. 2d 207 (2nd Cir. 1979).

[5] United States Court of Appeals: Hill v. Rowland, 474 F. 2d 1374 (4th Cir. 1973).

[6] United States District Court of Tennessee: Gaston v. Gibson, 328 F. Supp. 3 (1969).

[7] United States District Court of Minnesota: Lykken v. Vavreck, 366 F. Supp. 585 (1973).

Index

ABOUT THE AUTHOR

Richard Jay Moller received a Bachelor of Arts degree from Trinity College, Hartford and a Doctor of Laws degree from the University of California, Berkeley. During law school, Richard worked for the United States Environmental Protection Agency, the Environmental Defense Fund, the Natural Resources Defense Council, the California State Public Defenders Office, and the California Supreme Court. Presently, Richard works as a staff attorney for the United States Court of Appeals for the Ninth Circuit in San Francisco. (This book does not represent the views of either court.)

Prior to law school, Richard (then known as Jay) lived in the hills of the Humboldt County in northern California, where the marijuana crop is said to be worth more than the redwood lumber harvest. Though Jay wrote this book to share his legal knowledge with his former neighbors and friends, he feels compelled to add that he personally recommends against the use of all drugs. Having given up his last intoxicant several years ago, he would like to report that he feels much better than when he was ingesting alcohol, cocaine, coffee, hashish, LSD, marijuana, meat, opium, peyote, psilocybin, speed and tobacco.

Jay also wants to say that he now believes that loving others as yourself, not drug-taking, is the way to happiness.